Rewriting Resistance
Caste and Gender in Indian Literature

Edited by

Md Rakibul Islam
Aligarh Muslim University Centre at Jangipur Murshidabad,
West Bengal, India

and

Md Jakir Hossain
Chitta Mahato Memorial College, Purulia, West Bengal, India

Series in Literary Studies

Copyright © 2022 by the authors.

All rights reserved. No part of this publication may be reproduced, stored in a retrieval system, or transmitted in any form or by any means, electronic, mechanical, photocopying, recording, or otherwise, without the prior permission of Vernon Art and Science Inc.

www.vernonpress.com

In the Americas:	*In the rest of the world:*
Vernon Press	Vernon Press
1000 N West Street, Suite 1200	C/Sancti Espiritu 17,
Wilmington, Delaware, 19801	Malaga, 29006
United States	Spain

Series in Literary Studies

Library of Congress Control Number: 2021950201

ISBN: 978-1-64889-461-9

Also available: 978-1-64889-349-0 [Hardback]; 978-1-64889-414-5 [PDF, E-Book]

Product and company names mentioned in this work are the trademarks of their respective owners. While every care has been taken in preparing this work, neither the authors nor Vernon Art and Science Inc. may be held responsible for any loss or damage caused or alleged to be caused directly or indirectly by the information contained in it.

Cover design by Vernon Press. Cover's pattern designed by visnezh / Freepik.

Every effort has been made to trace all copyright holders, but if any have been inadvertently overlooked the publisher will be pleased to include any necessary credits in any subsequent reprint or edition.

Table of Contents

Foreword by *Nazia Hasan*	vii
Preface	ix
Acknowledgements	xi
Note on Editors	xiii
Note on Contributors	xv
Caste and Gender: An Introduction	xix

PART I Gender and Resistance — 1

Chapter 1 — **Power Politics and Reclaiming Identity: A Study of the Transgender in Arundhati Roy's** *The Ministry of Utmost Happiness* — 3
Safiul Islam
Aliah University, West Bengal, India

Chapter 2 — **Redefining Women, Reconstructing Space in Attia Hosain's** *Sunlight on a Broken Column* — 13
Afsha Naaz
GGS Indraprastha University, Delhi, India

Chapter 3 — **Women in Premchand's Stories Are Types, Not Individuals: A Contemporary Study of Select Short Stories of Munshi Premchand** — 23
Shreya Ghosh
Holy Cross College, Tripura, India

Chapter 4 — *The God of Small Things*: **Revisiting the Bible of the Indian Feminist Movement** — 33
Mohosin Mandal
Aligarh Muslim University, Uttar Pradesh, India

Chapter 5 — **Bodies that Matter: Interrogating the Discourses around the 'Body' in Samina Ali's** *Madras on Rainy Days* — 41
Hasina Wahida
Aliah University, West Bengal, india

Chapter 6	**Body on the Market: A Marxist–Feminist Study of the Novel *Masooma* by Ismat Chughtai**	51
	Md Mizanur Rahaman Samuktala Sidhu Kanhu College, West Bengal, India	
Chapter 7	**Searching for Self and Autonomy, Breaking Claustrophobic Domesticity: A Critical Analysis of Kavery Nambisan's *Mango-Coloured Fish***	61
	Tanbir Shahnawaz Rishi Bankim Chandra College, West Bengal, India	
Chapter 8	**Technocracy versus Theocracy: A Critical Study of *Sultana's Dream***	73
	Abdul Mabood Chandigarh University, Panjab, India	

PART II Caste-Gender Intersectionality and Resistance 81

Chapter 9	**Individual and Agency in Derozio's "The Fakeer of Jungheera"**	83
	Siddhartha Chakraborti Aligarh Muslim University, Uttar Pradesh, India	
Chapter 10	**Understanding Dalit Feminist Perspective through Bama's *Karukku***	91
	Fouzia Usmani Aligarh Muslim University, Uttar Pradesh, India	
Chapter 11	**Reinterpreting to Retrieve Lost Women's Voices: Gendered Subalternities in Mahasweta Devi's "Bayen" and Raja Rao's "Javni"**	101
	Kusumika Sarkar Aligarh Muslim University, Uttar Pradesh, India	

PART III Caste and Resistance   109

Chapter 12   **Casteism and Colonial Discourse: A Projection of Marginality in Bama's *Karukku***   111
Abdus Sattar
Galsi Mahavidyalaya, Purba Bardhaman, West Bengal, India

Chapter 13   ***Bhimayana* as a Biographical Stance on Resistance**   119
Anisha Ghosh
University of Kalyani, West Bengal, India

Chapter 14   **Orthodoxy in Rituals Creating the Burden of Tradition and Existential Crisis: A Critical Reading of U. R. Anantha Murthy's *Samskara***   129
Ismail Sarkar
University of Kalyani, West Bengal, India

Chapter 15   ***Bhimayana*: A Graphic Projection of History and Plight of Dalits in India**   139
Eeshan Ali
Dukhulal Nibaran Chandra College

Motahar Hossain
Aliah University, West Bengal, India

Imtiaj Alam
Aliah University, West Bengal, India

Further Readings   147

Index   149

Foreword
by *Nazia Hasan*

I wish something laudatory could be written about caste and gender. There are massive changes but sometimes many turn out to be deceptive. It may be denying a seat to a female state representative in an international meeting to the everyday humiliation that a substantial number of persons go through across our glorified nation for they lost in the gender or caste lottery.

Casteism and gender bias have been issues too ancient and too contemporary, too obvious, too ignored or too unkown, too apologized, too shielded, too resisted. Both issues are at times declared as residue of our revered and repressed past; but the ongoing stories are outrageous and capable of gripping one with fear or pity! The contemporary situation has seen new lows. They are simply glaring, staggering and hit hard upon the peace of mind.

Casteism is no longer only in the traditional sense of the nimno varga, or the lowest caste, it is anybody who is out of the mainstream populace. Gender bias appears as another kind of casteism. The tyranny of the majority comes back to reinforce the malaise in different colours and garbs every now and then. The mythology of the 'Other' keeps going strong and traumatising all who fall below the fabricated line.

Only an Edenesque society may be pure and purged of casteism and gender bias. Yet let's always remember that the persistence does not justify it to be natural. It is a cultivated and harvested practice.

How did we reach this state where we trample upon or let others crush civil rights and humanitarian solutions to secure the comfort and glory of some persons? Our constitutional and human rights are going through another phase of impoverished and undignified compromise. If this soul-destroying belligerence and malice are not addressed urgently, we will annihilate ourselves to a society where everybody becomes irrelevant in some way. The mistakes of the so-called scared past need to be addressed by rising against hidden and revealed lies, cultivated ignorance, manufactured starvation and diseases (did I mean pandemics?), ignited chaos. The enforced silence has been reigning for too long.

Recent analysis of Indian textbooks and other media proves that for 16 pages of writing about the majority or upper castes, only one page gives space to the Dalits and less than half to women, not even a paragraph to other genders! Mass graves are filled out even today, for if someone is dropped out of a text- it is more than not recognising the very presence or existence. It gets a replica in all those denied or denigrated rights, opportunities and benefits! For this kind of a situation with a history, 're-memory' is the act prescribed by the wise and the astute; in order to get out of the abridged or fabricated, or submerged histories. It involves recollecting and reassembling of facts and details to get strength at a time when 'the battle between remembering and forgetting is more than a device of the narrative' (Morrison, T). The collective amnesia has already caused such massive losses and victims. It's time the marginalised caste people, women and other genders become the subject of our discussions and writings.

The silences, the submerged experiences, the distorted or evasive parts of our social life and history have a tremendous potential for not only better narratives but also contain opportunity for critical thinking and problem-solving. It has already given voice to new art forms like Dalit genre, women's literature, queer literature and the genre of the marginalised. They are shedding light on the human capacity to wreak and bear inhuman treatment; etching new paths of going through life, but the categories still carry the flag of difference and othering. Our general, every day thinking and writings need to embrace these areas.

We need to ascertain for our times that humanity as equality is the supreme thing to do; not only exploring the space, going for vanity projects or building up empires of industries to manufacture more products and more consumers. We need to pay heed to the chaos around us, the breaking up and pushing downs going within.

I hope this book is not only informative or instructive but also uplifting and encouraging towards dialogues, by inviting compassion and ethical, humane thinking. I wish the editors and the contributors the strength to make a bright change!

Nazia Hasan
Professor
Aligarh Muslim University

Preface

Some recent phenomena that shook the very chord of our consciousness primarily help us developing the volume *Rewriting Resistance: Caste and Gender in Indian Literature*. An incident in the United States where a black man named George Floyd was brutally tortured to death by a white policeman in custody on 25 May 2020 shocked the world. It led to demonstrations and protests from millions spreading across the country and abroad. In India, a Facebook post of a Professor of History at Jadavpur University over holding an examination during the pandemic (Covid-19) created a great uproar as she was being trolled with nasty comments for her tribal status. This same incident points to how the notion of caste is still deeply ingrained in our society. In a more recent case, four upper-caste men allegedly gang-raped a 19-year-old Dalit woman in the Hathras district of Uttar Pradesh on 14 September 2020, and she finally died that quivered the entire nation. Many such cases are occurring daily all over India, and we hardly bother to pay attention or raise our voices against such issues. It is born out of the hegemonic oppression of a particular section of our society operating at a level where other things fail to show the result.

Resistance through writing is one such tool that can bring a lot of change for the people of the deprived section if used effectively. Like any other art form, literature engages in a pivotal role divulging an individual's resistance against the hegemony through their writing. So, there has been a conscious effort on the part of the writers from different sections of our society as they bring forth issues to the world through their pen. Literary scholars, over the years, have keenly paid attention to the subject of caste, class, and gender; it witnessed a massive surge through the publication and translation of regional literature in India and Indian literature in English. As it functions in society as a continuing symbolic criticism of values, literature exposes and transforms experiences through various genres. It consists of all the aspects of life. It helps us to bring out the problems of class division and caste discrimination existing in our society from the very past, but that has always remained in the state of constant flux or fluidity. Writers like M. R. Anand, Raja Rao, U. R. Ananthamurthy, Urmila Pawar, Subramanian Shankar, Rohinton Mistry, Arvind Adiga, Meena Kandasamy, and Manu Joseph express their deep concern on the issues through various genres and try to create a world which would be free from any discrimination. The other writers such as Arundhati Roy, Shashi Deshpande, Kiran Desai, Mahasweta Devi, Shobha De, Manju Kapur, Amrita Pritam, Jhumpa Lahiri, Mahesh Dattani, Nayantara Saghal, Anita Desai, as the list goes long, come forward to fight against any institutionalized gender prejudice and speak up in a constructive way exposing gender inequality in society, government and non-governmental offices, educational institutions, and in the political sphere, etc. They draw accurate pictures of our society portraying the subjugation and objectification of the female body.

The primary aim of this volume is to re-visit literary texts in terms of what it reveals about the resistance registered through the sufferings of human beings in the hand of fellow human beings in the Indian scholarly writings, which will surely be an impetus effort to write about the issues.

Editors

Acknowledgements

Editing a collection of research articles on 'caste' and 'gender' would have been an excruciating process as it had not have been possible without the contributors' help, sincerity, and commitment. The chapters have been collected from different contributors belonging to different parts of India. Despite the ongoing crisis due to the COVID-19, almost all the contributors have kept their promises and submitted their manuscripts within the given time. So, we are immensely grateful to all the contributors and express our sincere thanks to the anonymous reviewers for their insightful inputs and valuable comments, which have helped us to revise the given chapters and bring the volume together.

We have given a proper shape and an acceptable form to our edited volume with the help of our mentor Professor Nazia Hasan (at Women's College, Aligarh Muslim University, UP, India). We are also very thankful to all our colleagues for their constant encouragement and supports. We further thank our friends (too many to list here, but you know who you are!) for providing support during the preparation of the book. We must end by thanking the *Vernon Press*, America, for the constant support, cooperation, and agreement to publish this work.

Note on Editors

Md Rakibul Islam is working as an Assistant Professor of English for the last five years at the Murshidabad Centre of Aligarh Muslim University, India. He has published several papers in various national and international journals and in edited books. He has already edited a book entitled *Diaspora Poetics in South Asian English Writings* published from Cambridge Scholars Publishing, England, and recently got published his research paper entitled "Kim and Kip in the Mirror of Mimicry: A Postcolonial Study" in *The Groves: Working Papers on English Studies*, from Spain. He is presently working as one of the reviewers for *The Criterion: An International Journal in English*.

Md Jakir Hossain is working as an Assistant Professor of English for the last four years at Chitta Mahato Memorial College (affiliated to Sidho-Kanho-Birsha University), Purulia, India. He has published several research papers in various National and International journals. He has also served as the college coordinator IQAC for three years and currently serves as the Teacher-in-Charge of the College.

Note on Contributors

Safiul Islam, an alumnus of Aligarh Muslim University, is an Assistant Professor of English at Aliah University, Kolkata. He has been in the teaching profession since 2012. Earlier, he has served as an Assistant Professor of Language in IMS Engineering College, Ghaziabad, UP, for about three years. He has also served as an Assistant Professor of English at Muralidhar Girls' College for one year. His Doctoral Thesis is on the fictional and non-fictional works of Arundhati Roy. He has published research articles in several international journals. His areas of interest include Indian English Literature, Australian Literature, Modern Linguistics, and English Language Teaching.

Afsha Naaz is currently working as an Assistant Professor of English at Fairfield Institute of Management and Technology, affiliated with GGS Indraprastha University, Delhi. She has completed her Master in English from Miranda House College, the University of Delhi in 2019, and worked with the British council. She writes about city, culture, and compassion on 'Purani Dilli Walo Ki Baatein' (The Story of Old Delhi people). Her poetry has been published in various anthologies, while her research interest lies in the hermeneutics of place and understanding cities in the text.

Shreya Ghosh obtained her Ph.D. from the University of Tripura. She is currently employed as an Assistant Professor of English at Holy Cross College, Tripura, where she has been teaching English for the last two years.

Mohosin Mandal completed his Ph.D. from Aligarh Muslim University, Uttar Pradesh, India, and working as an independent researcher. He has published several papers in national/international journals and in edited books.

Hasina Wahida is an Assistant Professor of English at Aliah University, Kolkata, since April 2016. Earlier she had been Assistant Professor at Dewan Abdul Gani College, Harirampur in Dakshin Dinajpur district of West Bengal for one year. She has been in the teaching profession since 2012 and has served as a guest faculty in colleges and universities. Presently she is pursuing her Ph.D. in American Literature from The University of Burdwan. She has published articles in many journals and has published papers in International Conferences and Seminars. Her areas of interest include post-1950s British literature, American Literature, and Indian English Literature, particularly on the Partition, ethnicity, and identity literature.

Md Mizanur Rahaman is an Assistant Professor in the Department of English of Samuktala Sidhu Kanhu College, Alipurduar. He has been teaching English

Literature at the undergraduate level. His research area includes Postmodern Subjectivity, Postcolonial Studies, Psychoanalysis, and Film Studies.

Tanbir Shahnawaz is working as an Assistant Professor in the Department of English at Rishi Bankim Chandra College (affiliated to West Bengal State University), West Bengal, India. He completed his B. A. from Malda College (affiliated to University of North Bengal) in English in 2006 and M. A. from the University of Gour Banga in 2011. Presently, he is pursuing his Ph.D. from Raiganj University, West Bengal. His research areas are Travel Literature and Indian culture. He has published five research papers in Peer-Reviewed Journals, presented twenty papers from different areas of literature in various national/international seminars/conferences, and participated in multiple Workshops.

Abdul Mabood is working as an Assistant Professor of English in the Department of UILAH, Chandigarh University, Punjab, India. He earned his doctoral degree on Wole Soyinka, the Nigerian Nobel laureate. His interests lie in Post-Colonial Studies, Gender Issues, Human Rights activities, communication skills, public speaking, etc. He has published several articles in online and print journals and presented many papers in national and international seminars/conferences. Currently, along with teaching, he is working with some organizations to uplift the underprivileged people in society.

Siddhartha Chakraborti works as an Assistant Professor in the Department of English at Aligarh Muslim University, Uttar Pradesh, India. He has been an active researcher, with many publications and papers in postcolonialism, education studies, translation studies, digital humanities, Renaissance, and Victorian literature. His Ph.D. is in the area of how postcolonialism has impacted the idea of Imagination. He has been a UGC SAP fellow in JNU. He was involved in a UKIERI tri-nation project to evolve a syllabus for computer gaming across cultures, in association with Bangor University, Wales, and West Virginia University, USA. He also has extensive teaching experience at the undergraduate level in JNU and Delhi University, besides NMIMS, Mumbai, where he has taught literary theory, popular culture, and more traditional literature-oriented subjects, including Victoria, Restoration, and Romantic literature. He has done his undergraduate from Presidency College, Kolkata, and has been the university topper in his graduation from JNU. He has also had extensive seminar and conference experience, both in terms of organization and presentation. He is a life member of the Indian Association for Commonwealth Literature and Language Studies (IACLALS) and the Indian Association for the Study of Australia (IASA).

Note on Contributors

Fouzia Usmani is presently working as an Assistant Professor in English at Aligarh Muslim University, Aligarh. She has been teaching English literature as well as Communicative English at the undergraduate level. Her research area is postmodern poetry. Her Area of interest also includes Gender Studies, Post-Modern Poetry, Afro-American fiction, and Indian English fiction.

Kusumika Sarkar is an assistant professor in the Department of English, Women's College, Aligarh Muslim University (AMU). She has done her Ph.D. in Afro-American Literature from AMU. She is guiding research on the Liberation War of Bangladesh, focusing on gender, on Travel narratives, on the representation of Bengal in English Fiction, amongst others. She has seven publications in journals, book chapters, and proceedings besides participating in over 25 conferences, workshops, and short-term courses. She has also created content for EPG Pathshala. She is the TCI of Women's College NCC, 3 UP Battalion, and believes in empowering women from the margins. Recently she has been awarded a GIAN project.

Abdus Sattar is an assistant professor in English at Galsi Mahavidyalaya, the University of Burdwan. He has completed his Ph.D. from Aligarh Muslim University on Ted Hughes. His research area focuses on Eco-criticism, Psychoanalysis, Feminism, Humanism, and Postcolonialism. He has already edited a book entitled *Debilitation of Ethics, Values, and Identity in the Postmodern Indian English Literature*. His articles got published in various reputed national/international journals and edited books. He has attended many international and national seminars and conferences.

Anisha Ghosh is a Post-Graduate in English from The University of Burdwan, now an independent researcher. She has been teaching English Literature at Haringhata Mahavidyalaya, University of Kalyani. Besides being an author of many creative and critical writings in Bengali, she has contributed articles in various national and international journals and contributed chapters in various books. Her area of interest includes – Indian Writing in English, feminism, and religious texts consisting of the narratives of the folk deities of rural Bengal.

Ismail Sarkar is a Lecturer, Department of English, under State Aided College Teacher (SACT, Category-I), in Murshidabad Adarsha Mahavidyalaya, Islampur, Murshidabad, WB. He has completed his Master's in English from Aliah University, Kolkata. He participated in a two-days' Workshop on Translation Studies on "Revisiting Nineteenth Century Bengal through Primary Texts" organized by Domkal Girls College in collaboration with The Centre for Comparative Literature, Bhasa Bhavan. Visva Bharat and translated "Banglar Pathok Porano broto." He has recently presented a paper entitled "The Ministry of Utmost Happiness: A portrayal of Dalit and Tribal in Postcolonial India" to an international seminar on "Literature, Culture, and Society: Interrelation and

Search for Identity" organized by Berhamopore Girls College in collaboration with Kalyani University and MAKAIAS. His areas of interest are Dalit Literature, Postcolonial Studies, and Translation Studies.

Eeshan Ali is an Assistant Professor at DNC College of the University of Kalyani, India. He is the author of *A Companion to 50 Indian English Authors* and the editor of *Problematics of Gender Discourse: Perspectives on Masculinism and Feminism, Values and Identity in Post-Modern Indian English Literature,* and *Studies in Mahesh Dattani's Bravely Fought the Queen,* among others. He has also authored numerous articles in various journals. His co-authors *Motahar Hossain* did his M. A. from Aliah University, while *Imtiaj Alam* also completed his M. A., M. Ed. from Aliah University, West Bengal, India. Now both Hossain and Alam are working as independent researchers.

Caste and Gender: An Introduction

I

The word caste, which is etymologically derived from the Portuguese word *casta*, standing for "race, lineage, tribe or breed" (qtd. in Kumar 2020: n. p.), is a widely used term both in the English and Indian languages. In essence, we don't find an exact translated word for the caste, but we have the word 'jati' as its most appropriate form. Moreover, casteism - a "prejudice or discrimination on the grounds of caste" ("Casteism" *Lexico Dictionaries*: web) – is primarily drawn on social, political, and religious factors which may engender a social prejudice where one community/group exclusively segregates or excludes another community/group, thus producing a social hierarchy of upper and lower castes. The upper-caste people impose their hegemonic ideologies on the minds of the lower-caste people as they make them believe that they are inferior and unsocial and are born only to serve them. Such a particular community or group creates social stratification for social, political, economic, and religious gains. So, the hierarchy and divisions are not inborn; instead, they are artificial predispositions that rank people on a scale of ritual purity where "each caste [enjoys] differential access to religious privilege and civil rights" (Hardgrave, Jr. 1968: 1065). The caste system still prevails primarily in India and some other parts of South Asia.

The scholars and philosophers from the West widely define and vividly explore the term 'caste' and its socio-political dimension in their writings. G. D. Berreman delineated the caste system as a "system of birth-ascribed stratification, of socio-cultural pluralism, and of hierarchical interaction" (Berreman 1960: 70). In his book *Homo Hierarchicus: The Caste System and Its Implications* (1966), L. Dumont (a French anthropologist) depicted religious 'purity' and 'pollution' as the essential basis of caste and casteism, which is being actively practised in some parts of India as the upper-caste would not allow the lower-caste people to collect water from the same well or ponds. M. Weber, a German sociologist, defined caste as a "status community having a specific style of life" (qtd. in Gandhi, 1980: 1). The view postulated by Weber was later supported and followed by A. Beteille, a professor at the University of Delhi. Beteille lengthened its definition further as "a status community characterized by endogamy, hereditary membership, occupation, ritual status and a specific style of life" (Beteille 1965: 46). After Weber and Beteille, G. S. Ghurye from the University of Bombay postulated how men created such social hierarchy for men as a "segmental division of society" (qtd. in Gandhi, 1980: 1). The philosopher J. Fowler, the head of Religious Studies at the University of Wales-Newport, held a similar view like Beteille and Weber; he considered caste as an occupational instead of geographical segregation, and also believed that it is impossible to draw the timeline of its existence in her book *Hinduism: Beliefs and Practices* (2014). Broadly, "the caste unit [is] regarded as a normally endogamous, commensally exclusive, and characterized by a hereditary craft or occupation" (Hardgrave, Jr. 1968: 1065).

R. Inden, a famous Indologist, defined caste as a fluid entity referring to endogamous varna (colour), which signifies endogamous 'jatis' in his book *Imagined India* (1990). 'Caste,' for Andre Beteille, is not an appropriate illustration of the word 'jati' in English. Instead, he chose the phrase 'ethnic group' for 'jatis' (not caste) in his essay "Varna and Jati" (1996). From the field of comparative religion, Professor A. Sharma saw 'jatis' and 'caste' as synonymous entities and elaborated this in his book *Classical Hindu Thought: An Introduction* (2000). The word varna "seems to have been employed in contrasting the Arya and the *dasa*, referring to their fair and dark colours respectively" (qtd. in Roy 1979: 297). In India, varna is mainly categorised into four main classes—Brahmins, Kshatriyas, Vaishyas, and Shudras—found in the ancient Indian texts. Other categories of people, such as the 'tribals' and the untouchables/Dalits, known as jatis, do not come under these four orbits. So, varna is something static and very limited in the number that has persistently prevailed in Indian society, while we find thousands of jatis/caste in India. Therefore, caste/jati appears to be the more complex and diverse terms as compared to varna, but it is impossible to separate one from the other as both are closely connected: "It was seen as a closed stratification system in which the various castes (jatis), each symbolically related to the other within the framework of varna, formed an organic whole" (Hardgrave, Jr. 1968: 1065). So,

> Our understanding about caste in Indian society is that changes within the caste hierarchy cannot be properly appreciated without situating all castes and sub-castes in the overall ideological umbrella of Hindu religion. Every caste and sub-caste and Hindu religion of every variety are integrally interlinked and interrelated. (Bhambhri 1999: 2619)

While class stratification based on the varnas is less implemented, the divisions based on caste are numerous. "In a class system it is the family or person who is the bearer of status; in the caste system it is the caste. The caste system emphasizes group status and morality; the individual without a caste is a meaningless social entity" (Cox 1944: 141–142). Unlike class, "…a man's caste, however, does tend to decide his rank. In other words, his class is his rank, while his caste has a rank to be determined" (Cox 1944: 142). The caste division has increased in number as new groups like "forest dwellers" have been included in the emerging hierarchy. Chandrasekhar writes:

> Whereas the caste system, at its inception, recognized only four or possibly five divisions, based on the essential fourfold or fivefold functions in a primitive rural economy, today the system has divided and subdivided itself to such a profuse and alarming extent that about 3,000 castes have been enumerated in modern India; and new castes are in the process of formation even today! (Chandrasekhar 1946: 151)

Due to its discursivity and fluidity, a signifier's caste does not guarantee the 'signified' or a conclusive meaning, as its meaning alters or changes and eventually does not provide any ultimate truth or conclusion. The theory of such social stratification based on caste and casteism is comparable to S. Hall's theory of 'race' as a 'floating signifier' and Chandler's theory of the 'empty signifier.' Here, 'caste', like 'race' and 'ethnicity', works as 'a floating signifier' referring to "the disability of all finite thought" (Mauss 1987: 63) because its value and meaning keep changing from time to time. J. Derrida too aims to diminish any hierarchy, does not stop reversal, rather destabilising "both hierarchies, leaving them in a condition of undecidability" (Abrams 2012: 58). So, it is impossible to orient a permanent meaning of any signified given by the signifier for their arbitrary relationship. Henceforth, 'caste' is not natural rather an artificial postulation created by some people in our society for their own benefits but damaging the social symmetry.

II

According to ideological or religious factors, the caste system in India — as we mentioned earlier — has mainly four hierarchically ranked classes based on the varnas: Brahmins, Kshatriyas, Vaishyas, and Shudras: "Throughout the ages, all societies have divided their people into various groups on the grounds of particular traits and talents, equipment and opportunity, character and culture" (Chandrasekhar 1946: 151). L. Dumont, who quoted from Manu's *Manusmriti*, an ancient Sanskrit text translated by Sir W. Jones into English in 1776, justified the religious factor behind casteism and denied any socio-economic or historical aspect. The Brahmins—priests and scholars—are placed highest in the social hierarchy and are considered superior to other groups.

> The Brahmin class is essentially defined by its supposed priority (as the class created first by the creator god), by knowledge of the Veda, and by the monopoly this class holds on the operation of sacrifice. These traits

justify the social position of the class vis-à-vis others: they are predominant because they are prior, and they claim to stand outside of the power relations that govern social life for others because of their superior knowledge and sole possession of the ultimate "weapons," sacrificial techniques. (Smith 1994: 48)

The Brahmins who mainly occupied the social, economic, and educational spheres slowly lost their flexibility and became very rigid. Here, endogamy played a significant role: the women of the Brahmin caste could not marry men from the Panchama (the fifth) and vice versa. Next comes the Kshatriyas—originating from the Sanskrit word 'kshatra'—which means government, power, and dominion. They consisted of kings, rulers, and soldiers strengthened by their physique and martial knowledge. They reigned on the lands or kingdoms and were often linked with the Brahmins. In ancient times, the Kshatriyas would govern kingdoms and execute their work according to the Holy Scriptures with the aid of the Brahmins. So, they were dependent on the Brahmins, but the Brahmins were not reliant on them as they were self-sufficient. The third group, or the Vaishyas, were known as merchants and worked as tradespeople who controlled commerce, but the Brahmins denied them high social status. Due to such exclusion and discrimination, they resent the Brahmins. Lastly, the Shudras (such as barbers, blacksmiths, and cobblers) were composed of servants, labourers, and the peasant class and were considered unskilled beings and treated as slaves thought to be born to serve the other three varnas mentioned above. So, they were denied their rights and privileges and prohibited from reciting the Vedas and entering temples. They started supporting the Vaishyas in the anti-Brahminical movement because of such mistreatment. The fights or conflicts between the Brahmins and the Kshatriyas over their status were not as important as both groups often combined to exploit the Vaishyas and the Shudras.

> Hinduism lends weighty support to the hierarchy of caste by declaring that a man's caste is the exact index of his soul's behaviour and piety in previous births. If born a Brahman, the so-called "pinnacle of perfection," "lord of creation," his soul has been scrupulous in its observances and ceremonials during countless earlier lives. But if he is born a lowly Sudra, he has not fulfilled his caste dharma, while if he is born a despised Outcaste, that is convincing proof of the foulness of his deeds in previous incarnations. (Corwin 1977: 650)

The fifth group besides these four is known as the *Panchama* or 'Harijan community.' The non-existent fifth varna exists below the other four varnas and includes the untouchables/Dalits. According to Hindu texts, there was never any fifth group except the four varnas. Still, the "Shudras" is the fourth group who belongs to the last rank in the Hindu caste system and was born to serve the upper classes, while the untouchables/Dalits are defined as outcasts who cannot serve them. They, like the Shudras, were disallowed from entering temples, and the freedom given to them was even more menial compared to what even the Shudras were permitted. They were only allowed to perform dirty work like cleaning and skinning dead animals and were also forbidden from walking through the streets used by the upper-caste people. The social hierarchy ignited a distance between the Brahmins and the others, and it was further increased because of the ritual status of the Brahmins. "The son of the *Brahmin* priest became a priest, and the son of a *Panchama* sweeper became a sweeper; the hallmark of caste became birth and heredity" (Chandrasekhar 1946: 154). Furthermore, "[I]deally the high-caste person is paternalistic and authoritarian, while the low-caste person responds with deferential, submissive, subservient behaviour." (Berreman 1960: 124)

As far as caste-based discrimination in India is concerned, the Dalits are the most affected community among the minority communities in India. The upper-caste people have tortured them with physical and psychological violence from the very past. The violence works as an obstacle to their development. The upper-caste people silence the voices on the "margin" by restraining them from accessing social services and systematically denying them all social, political, economic, and educational rights. The upper-caste defines them as uncivilised, impure, worthless, and untouchable and denies them access to water, prevents from moving around areas inhabited by them. They cannot cross the dividing line drawn by the upper-caste people. Such ongoing and unique caste-based discrimination and maltreatment still prevails in our modern-day society. It goes on profusely unchecked despite the growth of civilisation: "Discriminatory and cruel, inhuman, and degrading treatment of over 165 million people in India has been justified on the basis of caste" ("Human Rights Watch" 2007: 2). And oppressed castes who are least concerned with the Hindu ritual system still search for equality. The upper caste of "*dwijas*" (twice-born) still refer to themselves as "brahmins" or "thakurs", "while the oppressed castes may be using Hindu symbols for 'mobilization for power'; otherwise, as newly 'emergent communities in India' the oppressed are fighting for equality in society" (Bhambhri 1999: 2619). The lower castes, particularly the Dalits, are "banding together to protest against violence and violations of their rights and to support each other in demanding respect, dignity, and justice" ("Caste and Gender Justice...." 2019: 6). Anand Teltumbde and Gopal Guru with Shiraz Sidhva define such mistreatment and negligence as "India's hidden apartheid" (Pandita 2005: n.p.). They ask to break the chain of segregation drawn along the lines of caste and agree for the substantial improvements in their positions:

> Despite the fact that in India, the Scheduled Castes and Scheduled Tribes Prevention of Atrocities Act specifically bar violence against Dalits [and] prohibit 'untouchability' and violence against Dalits in the public and private spheres, both Acts lack implementation. ("Caste and Gender Justice...." 2019: 6)

On the other hand, S. Kaufman, K. Reilly, and A. Bodino believe that there is no practice of apartheid in India as the underclass or lower classes (untouchables and tribal people) are getting equal benefits and enjoying power positions from affirmative programmes.

Scholars such as Berreman, Marrit, and Dirks focus on the social factors and historical circumstances behind the origin of caste system. In her book *Caste, Society and Politics in India from the Eighteenth Century to the Modern Age* (1999), S. Bayly, a former editor of the Royal Anthropological Institute and Professor at the Cambridge University Division of Social Anthropology, who is interested in the South Asian caste system, expands her discussion on the caste system by saying that it is predominantly and deeply rooted in socio-economic and political factors. In the Pre-Vedic period, the fair-skinned Aryans from Central Asia started invading and entering India from its north-eastern side. According to Sir E. Blunt, a researcher of caste and social structure of Hinduism, the Aryans did not have any caste system among them but had a hierarchy prevalent in their society that divided it into different group/sects that "formed sacrifices; the chieftains and soldiers, who fought in battle; and the rest, who, although normally nomadic, sometimes ploughed the fields and raised food" (Chandrasekhar 1946: 152). Blunt believed that the caste system was brought to India by the fair-skinned Aryans who slowly eliminated India's "dark-skinned" original inhabitants from different social, political, and economic status, creating an endogamous tendency. E. C. M. Senart, a French scholar, believed that the Aryans met new people and their alien culture and had no similarities. They settled in the Gangetic Valley, where many Hindu kingdoms already prevailed and flourished. Due to the entry of outsiders, the people started increasing in numbers and demanded more shelter, food, and sustenance. So, the Aryans did not confine themselves to India's northern part and slowly explored other parts of India to track their food and new habitats. They gradually controlled everything all over India and started influencing the original inhabitants leading to the clash of civilisations: "The Hindu caste system is an outcome of the contact and conflict between the alien light-skinned Indo-Aryans and the Dravidians, the original and older inhabitants of India" (Chandrasekhar 1946: 152). So, the caste system in India is an "outcome of the clash of cultures" (Chandrasekhar 1946: 152). Besides, the Aryans believed themselves to be pure and superior compared to the indigenous Indians. So, they developed xenophobic attitudes and hatred towards the

Indian natives, whom they believed to be inferior in thought and uncivilised as compared to them. They created a boundary between the conquered and conquerors, separating them from the other Indians. Despite such differences, they had to live side by side under the canopy of the same socio-political and geographical influences, thus failing to keep them away from each other and, therefore, somewhere breaking the myth of ethnic and racial purity.

There is another view behind the origin of the Hindu caste system that is neither based on cultural antagonism nor colour code but instead based on professional or vocational dissimilarities: "Thus *birth* and *occupation* became the twin basic principles on which the caste system in Hindu society rested and revolved" (Chandrasekhar 1946: 151). During the later Vedic period, the "agriculture developed and subsequently surplus increased. Social differentiation increased, and the tribes started breaking up. Settled agriculture indicated a more efficient mode of production resulting in higher surplus" (Bhowmik 1992: 1246). In this period, the division of labour based on exploitation became very complex, creating a social hierarchy. During the period, "monarchy developed, trade and crafts increased and the practice of untouchability also came into being.... It was now possible for groups of people who were not directly connected with production to appropriate the surplus because of their ritual status or control over the means of production." (Bhowmik 1992: 1246)

III

In India, the position and status of women have not always been the same. Their status always remains in a state of constant flux or fluidity due to the evolving nature of society. Sometimes, they are treated like goddesses and sometimes as slaves, which is still the case in some parts of India. They are put in a state of constant ups and downs; sometimes, they have been suppressed and sometimes given freedom, but indeed their space and rights have been curbed mainly by our patriarchal society. G. C. Spivak, in her essay, "Can the Subaltern Speak?" (1994), says that most Indian women do not have a voice because of being thoroughly controlled by the patriarchal society. The subalterns can rarely speak and hardly hear, having no identity of their own as their autonomy is snatched away. They are defined and identified by their men; a woman is what a man is not. To know their status in detail, we have to go for a scholarly exploration down the ages.

In the Vedic period, the status and position of women, as compared to women of other ages, were somewhat better. We find evidence from the Rig Veda on the adoration of women: "The Rig Veda had rendered the highest social status to the qualified woman of those days" (Shanmathi and Shenbagavalli 2018: 199). In the early Vedic period, women had been honoured and worshipped as a mother goddess. They were adorned and treated as "Ardhangini" (wife/better half) and received regard from their parents and in-laws. The Aryans regarded them as critical productive members of their society. They had the right to participate in religious ceremonies and their study to acquire 'absolute knowledge.' Men acknowledged their positions, particularly in religious traditions like recitation and writing of mantras, and honoured them as saints. They were given the right to sacrifice with their husbands. The girls had the right to participate in education, which was considered an essential requisite for marriage. Besides, men gave them an exclusive right to choose their bridegrooms, which was known as 'Swayamvara,' which consists of the Sanskrit word 'swayam' (self) and 'vara' (groom). We hardly find any evidence of the dowry system, divorce, child marriage, sati, and purdah in the Vedic period. Women maintained their virtue, morality, and fidelity, and widows were allowed remarriage under specific conditions. Monogamy was a general practice of the society, but bigamy was also somewhat prevalent but was limited to the higher class people. The married daughters and widows were also allowed to have their right to their father's property. Though women were expected to have sons instead of daughters since sons perform last rites and carry forward the family lineage, a man was considered incomplete without a woman in that for balancing a perfect society.

In the Age of the Upanishads, an upper-caste man would marry a lower-caste woman according to 'anuloma system of marriage.' In the Age of the Sutras, men gave women a strong position in the household and society; they had good knowledge of spiritual subjects and were allowed to participate in social and cultural activities such as singing and dancing. Marriage was not a mere contract instead considered as a holy bond or religious sacrament. It took place only if the bride was of a mature age. Child marriage and sati were also prohibited. According to the "Dharma-Sutras", a girl was given the right to choose her husband if her parents did not get her married on time. As per the "Dharma-Sutras", the most popular one out of the eight marriage forms was the Arsha marriage- a marriage between a girl and a sage. The most negative side of marriage was the lowering of marriageable age that encouraged child marriage, affected the girls' education, and expanded the path of its practice to later generations. In this period, "endogamy as a practice was still not prevalent. The higher castes could marry women from other castes." (Bhowmik 1992: 1246)

The *Manusmriti*, or *Laws of Manu*, a Sanskrit text that the British Philologist Sir William Jones later translated, provides us mixed interpretations about women. On the one hand, it asks for the honour and adoration of women by men, but on the other hand, it defines women as weak and emotional: "Where women are revered, there the gods rejoice; but where they are not, no sacred rite bears any fruit" (Olivelle 2005: 111). It depicts them as fragile, bringing sorrow to families if not protected from evil proclivity and prohibits them from education. Manu considers widow remarriage a sin, while a husband can be devoid of morality and virtue. According to Manu, "[A]s a girl, she should obey and seek the protection of her father, as a young woman her husband, and as a widow her son; and that a woman should always worship her husband as a god" (Olivelle 2005: 98). Conclusively, a wife must serve, please, and obey her husband without any question.

In the post-Vedic period, the status and position of women were deteriorated more and more in society and family. Patriarchal society snatched away women's liberty and treated them as commodities in the later Vedic period. Patriarchal society started preferring sons over daughters and believing that sons could protect them and earn them money and carry forward family responsibilities. Evil practices such as child marriage, sati, divorce, dowry, and polygamy were prohibited or rarely found in the Vedic period but later started rising in gigantic leaps. Girls were denied the right to education and property by men; they were given some property only in brotherless families, while widows were discriminated. Society did not allow girls to choose their partners independently, while the age of marriage was reduced, generating the mass practice of child marriage. The Sanskrit texts *Kumarsambhava* by Kalidasa and *Mrichchhakatikam* by Sudraka provide us with the practice of sati that was considered as a process of purity and innocence. The life of women like that of the Shudras became very pathetic, and they had to face infinite troubles if they refused patriarchal norms and instructions.

Despite such a destructive side of society, the post-Vedic texts such as the *Ramayana* and the *Mahabharata* visualised an ideal and perfect society through different revered women characters such as Sita, Draupadi, and Tara: "For both men and women in Hindu society, the ideal woman has been traditionally personified by Sita portrayed in the *Ramayan* as the quintessence of wifely devotion" (Chakravarti 1983: 70). The *Mahabharata* confirms that women guided and cooperated with men on different issues such as social and religious questions.

The arrival of the Muslim rulers in the eighth century is considered the beginning of Indian medieval history. The early and later Medieval Period lasted from the sixth to the thirteenth centuries and from the thirteenth to the sixteenth centuries, respectively, but the latter started with the Mughal Empire in 1526. The Medieval Age, also known as the patriarchal era, created more problems for women as the status of women began deteriorating. They were treated as objects of sexual gratification and barred from enjoying an equal social position to men in society. Though the Mughals brought innumerable changes to the country's economic condition, the status of women deteriorated in society. The Muslim women, especially those of high classes, were not allowed to move out of their homes. So, *purdah* (home confinement) became a prevalent practice amongst Muslims. In the Mughal period, the birth of a son was celebrated as a special occasion, but that of a daughter was considered to be ominous. The purdah continued in the Medieval Period. Jauhar, Jowhar, or Juhar (the custom of self-immolation introduced by the Rajput community) was very prominent. In the process, women immolated themselves to save their chastity and to save themselves from enslavement by the invading forces. The Mughals and their courtiers kidnapped young girls for their sexual gratification. Such fear forced parents to get their daughters married at a very early age. Thus, child marriage started growing rapidly and became a widespread practice. The giving away of money besides different ornaments by the wealthy or upper-class people during weddings expanded the dowry system. Common people followed the social convention, but the poor people were not able to give dowry. So, they started considering the girl child to be a burden and a curse to the family, which led to female infanticide.

The women's status saw significant changes with British colonizers' arrival and their continuous efforts and collaborations with Indian social and educational reformers such as R. R. M. Roy, I. C. Vidyasagar, S. D. Saraswati, and others. They forced the British government to pass different acts and provisions for their advancement and upliftment in society. The unrelenting campaigns by vociferous campaigners such as R. M. Roy and W. Carey led to the prohibition of sati, practiced in different ages in India. Lord W. Bentinck, the then Governor-General of India, passed *The Bengal Sati Regulation XVII, 1829* to make the practice an illegal and punishable offense in all of British India. Later, *The Sati (Prevention) Act, 1987* was enacted by the Government of Rajasthan that later became *The Commission of Sati (Prevention) Rules, 1988* by the Parliament of India. Female infanticide also became prohibited with the enactment of the *Female Infanticide Act, 1829*. The widows' lives were miserable till Ishwar Chandra Vidyasagar, with other educationists, fought for their upliftment and forced the British government to curb such practices with the *Hindu Widow Remarriage Act, 1856*.

Post-independence India expanded their position and status in Indian society. *The Constitution of India*, the supreme law of India, enshrines the rights of women before the law. There are several articles, such as 14, 15, and 16. Article 14, known as an article for equality before the law, states and guarantees that "[t]he State shall not deny to any person equality before the law or the equal protection of the laws within the territory of India" (*The Constitution of India*, 2019: 25). Article 15 states, "Prohibition of discrimination on the grounds of religion, race, caste, sex or place of birth" (*The Constitution of India* 2019: 04). Article 16 states, "Equality of opportunity in matters of public employment"

(*The Constitution of India* 2019: 04). Despite Article 21 (A) of the Indian Constitution on the Right to Education, many women are debarred from getting primary education due to patriarchal norms. There is the perception that girls' education is a waste of money and time. Though the literacy rate has increased, the female literary rate is still low as compared to men: as per the *Literacy Rate Census of India* (2011), female literacy was around 65.5 percent (approx.) and male literacy was 82.1 percent (approx.). Despite *The Equal Remuneration Act* (1976), women of same educational qualifications like men are denied economic equality do not get equal wages. So, today, "the relationship between men and women in the society is similar to the relations between proletariat and bourgeoisie" (qtd. in Choudhary n. d.: 182). Despite *The Female Infanticide Prevention Act* (1870), the girl child is still being killed by parents, and it is rampant in Haryana and Rajasthan but prevailing in the other parts of India. The female infant mortality rate is higher in India than males, as per the World Bank's Gender Statistics (2012). Such discrimination prevalent for generations has been mostly affecting the females and hampering their social, economic, political, and mental development. Despite *The Prohibition of Child Marriage Act* (2006), child marriage is still deeply ingrained in our society as it continues in several parts of rural India. *The Dowry Prohibition Act* (1961) prohibits giving and taking dowry, still the bridegroom's family sometimes demands dowry, or the bride's family gives it in the fear that their daughter may suffer and be tortured. In some parts of India, women are allowed only to eat food left by men leading to malnutrition.

Despite the constitutional preservation and differnent legislative provisions, policies, special laws, and acts, women are still being oppressed and suppressed by men, directly or in another way. In India, the patriarchal society most of the time treat women rudely and discriminate against them from birth to death making them to suffer in forms of female infanticide and old-age negligence. Here, women dedicate their lives for the welfare and well-being of their families, but their status is constantly being changed. They face domestic violence causing honour killing and marital rape which are increasing day by day at an alarming rate. So, a claustrophobic male-dominated shadow still hangs over them, which considers them inferior in thoughts, passive in nature, and worthy of housekeeping only. In the patriarchal society, the inheritance generally passes from the father to son and the society prefers sons to daughters because people falesley belive that sons will be more helpful in carrying forward the family lineage. Morover, sons only, as it believes, can become the caretakers of parents in their old ages. In reality, things are occurring in reverse as daughters are more supportive and helpful to their parents, emotionally and mentally. So, laws preserved in books need to be executed more effectively to ensure women's safety and right to equality.

Despite different obstacles and hindrances from different sections of society, women have started touching almost all professions in twentieth- and twenty-first-century India. They participate in politics, science, arts, and other social activities. They are raising their voices in large numbers and fighting for their rights for the last few decades as they have achieved a lot compared to women of pre-independence India. They have conquered and excelled in every sphere like literature, media, management, civil services, space, politics, aviation, technology, medical science, cinema, and others. Mrs. V. L. Pandit became the president of the United Nations General Assembly in 1953, while we cannot forget the names of Anita Desai and Arundhati Roy from literature; Anjum Chopra and Saina Nehwal from sports; and Rekha and Shabana Azmi from cinema. I. Gandhi, the first woman prime minister of India, and P. D. S. Patil, the first woman president of India, should also be remembered.

IV

Despite the end of colonial regime and absolute freedom, the lower-caste people, especially the Dalits, are still being suppressed and tortured by a neocolonial man-made mechanism stemming from internal culture and politics. This has become a substance of rigorous social discussion in our contemporary time and if they are women Dalits and Adivasis (tribals), they remain at the significant receiving end of injustice. Dalit women go through double oppression; first, they become victims for being a Dalit in the upper-caste people's hands and then by their own community people. They are mistreated everywhere by everyone from home to police stations to courts. They have been targeted and tortured by pulling out their nails and hairs; they are also hit, beaten, raped, and paraded naked by male-dominated society for centuries. "Minority Rights Group International reported a study finding that 70% of cases of atrocities against Dalit women were committed as Dalit women tried to assert their rights and challenge caste and gender norms" ("Dalit Women Fight!" 2015: 4). So, if they raise their voice or dare to challenge violence, rape, and discrimination, they have to bear the brunt of retaliation: "Violence, exploitation, and exclusion are used to keep Dalit women in a position of subordination and to maintain the patriarchal grip on power throughout Indian society" (Sarkar 2016: 320). They are excluded from significant spheres of society like proper education and are being forced to work household chores. "According to the National Commission for Scheduled Castes and Scheduled Tribes 2000, approximately 75% of the Dalit girls drop out of primary school despite the strict laws of the Government of India, which hold reservations for Dalit children" (Mahey 2003: 151). Despite being elected via elections; they are not permitted to participate in socio-political activities. South African Professor R. Manjoo from the University of Cape Town, who is also a co-convenor of the Human Rights Program in the Law Faculty, highlights that "[t]he reality of Dalit women and girls is one of exclusion and marginalization.... They are often victims of civil, political, economic, social, and cultural rights violations, including sexual abuse and violence. They are often displaced; pushed into forced and/or bonded labour, prostitution and trafficking" (qtd. in "Dalit Women Fight!" 2015: 3). Besides, "they will continue to be key targets for traffickers. Tackling trafficking means tackling caste and gender discrimination head-on and ensuring that Dalit girls and women have access to exercising their rights" ("Caste and Gender Justice...." 2019: 6).

> Intersectional caste and gender discrimination leaves Dalit women and girls as some of the furthest behind when it comes to achieving the UN Global Goals and therefore this type of discrimination needs special focused attention. Dalit women are leading the way by standing up for their rights, they need global solidarity and justice to catalyze their access to rights and dignity. In this publication we highlight some of the key challenges faced by Dalit women and girls in relation to the specific UN Global Goals and targets and offer advice on what you can do to stand in solidarity with these women and be a catalyst of change. ("Caste and Gender Justice...." 2019: 3)

Though traditional caste-based discrimination no longer exists, its remnants still prevail in different forms. Recently, nasty comments were directed at Dr. M. Murmu (an associate professor of History at Jadavpur University) for her remarks over holding examinations during the pandemic on Facebook. "All I had said was that life is long and that it did not matter if exams were not held for one year in view of COVID-19" (Ghosh 2020: n. p.). The opinion created a great uproar and she was very severely trolled and ridiculed for her tribal status on social media. A student said, "she better not comments on the matter considering that she had been benefitted from 'quota' (reservation)" (Ghosh 2020: n. p.). The incident points to how casteism is ingrained in our society. Later, Dr. Murmu, in an interview with *The Hindu* said that

> [In] West Bengal, the intensity of symbolic violence of casteism has overshadowed physical violence. Because of their grudging inclusion in professional and academic spaces, Adivasis and Dalits face silent social exclusion. Since the present atmosphere breeds politics of hate, an overt articulation of caste-based discrimination has become rampant. (Ghosh 2020: n. p.)

In another recent case, four upper-caste men allegedly gang-raped and inflicted gruesome physical assault on a 19-year-old Dalit girl in Hathras district of Uttar Pradesh, India. The same incident led her to death that shook the entire nation. Instead of supporting the victim and her family, the upper-caste people conspicuously remained silent and shifted the blame onto the victim. So, this is the level of shamelessness of the upper-caste people rallying in support of the perpetrators. Thousands of such cases are occurring daily in our society worldwide, and we hardly bother to pay attention or raise our voices against such cases. We can earn the trust of the dispossessed, or vulnerable people when we have genuine empathy for them. This will surely boost the confidence of the people of vulnerable or deprived section.

The upper-caste community has failed to stop the Dalits from occupying a vital position in society. The list is long, but the first name that comes to our mind is B. R. Ambedkar, a social reformer and father of the Indian Constitution. The others are S. Murli, a journalist; M. Prasad, a former chairman of Union Public Service Commission; and economist Narendra Jadhav, etc. The Dalit women writers such as Bama, Babytai Kamblwe, Joopaka Subhadram, Sujatha Gidla, Gogu Shyamala, and C. S. Rani, many more to count, have brought the issue of caste identity to forefront and challenged the intersectional forms of oppression faced by them. The names which come from the film industry are Dhanush, Chirag Paswan, and Shailendra, etc. The list of renowned social activists is very long such as G. P. Walangkar, A. Teltumbde, N. S. Tanwar, and I. Sekaran, etc. The names listed in politics are Ramnath Kovind, the present president of India; Jagjivan Ram, the former deputy prime minister of India; and Kanshi Ram, the founder of the Bahujan Samaj Party besides Ram Vilas Paswan, Sushil Kumar Shinde, D. Sanjivayya, Ram Sundar Das, Jagannath Pahadia, Mayawati, J. R. Majhi, K. R. Narayanan, D. Raja, and A. Raja, and so on. In sports, mainly in cricket, we find the names such as Vinod Kambli, Karsan Ghavri, Eknath Solkar, etc.

V

Resistance, if used effectively, as a social tool can bring tremendous change for the deprived sections. To break the myths of casteism, the Indian literary writers come forward and take the responsibility on their shoulders, raising their voices against such discrimination. They engage themselves in scholarly activities to highlight the issues they feel are necessary to end discrimination by any possible means. They dream of a pretty natural community with no discrimination based on caste, class, and gender. They are successful in identifying the problems faced by people daily. They feel that caste-based discrimination is a "hidden apartheid" (qtd. in Narula 2008: 273). P. K. Nayar aptly says that "any politics of race, gender, caste or class demands a way of speaking, a method of representation, and a method of narrative organization to make meaning for the reader" (Nayar 2013: n. p.). It operates at a level where other things fail to show a result. It is born out of hegemonic oppression of a particular class, section, or society. It is the result of atrocities unleashed by the mighty. We need to learn to speak up for others when they are in distress. Subjugated victims often opt for various routes to register their protest against the mighty or influential. Writing is one such weapon to show resistance against dominance. Like any other art, literature plays a pivotal role in divulging an individual's resistance against hegemony. It has been observed that literature from the oppressed or marginalised sections has primarily been a saga of cruel treatment meted out by the upper-caste people. There has been a conscious effort on the writers' writing from the margin to bring forth the issues that matter to them and that the world needs to know through their pens. In a recent development in West Bengal, the Dalit Sahitya Academy has been established with the help of young and talented Dalit writers for the proper blooming of Dalit literature. It is because there is a conscious attempt to continue the process of writing about the dispossessed sections of the society with more zeal and vigour. This effort will undoubtedly give impetus to writers about things that have been neglected for years.

Over the last several years, scholarly attention to the subject of caste, class, and gender has increased almost as dramatically as the recent surge in the publication and translation of regional works of literature in India. Literature, being one of the modes of communication, reflects life and gives us aesthetic pleasure talking about casteism, class conflict, and gender inequalities, etc. These issues have been present since time immemorial. So, literature, as an art, not only gives us pleasure but also elevates and transforms our experiences. It further works as an essential weapon of society, rectifying our values for a better society. It consists of all the aspects of life, and it is a tool that helps us bring out the problems of class division and caste discrimination that exist in a society. Many authors express their love for the nation, gender, and caste through their writings. Some writers write with a social cause in mind. They come forward to reform their society courageously and criticise the current irrational practices of uncivilised people. The authors reveal how necessary it is to abolish evil practices such as class differences, caste systems, and gender discrimination through various literary genres.

The brunt of double bondage (caste and gender) can be found in our Indian literary texts such as M. R. Anand's *Untouchable* (1935) and *Coolie* (1936). Anand's first novel, *Untouchable*, is based on an actual incident faced by his aunt treated as an outcast by a Muslim woman when having her meal. The book, which is set in the north Indian town of Bulandshahr, revolves around a sweeper named Bakha, the son of Lakha. Bakha, though an intelligent boy, is mistreated and marginalised as an untouchable who cleans latrines. Here,

Anand appeals for the end of untouchability because of its unjust and inhumane nature.

In *Coolie*, Anand further endeavours to break the myth of social stratification through a highly exploited Munoo's character. Raja Rao's *Kanthapura* (1938) criticises the traditional caste system of India where the dominant caste, such as the Brahmins, govern the village of Kanthapura while the low castes are called *pariahs* and are exiled and ostracised by the upper-caste people but embraced by the character Moorthy. Moorthy demands to change the existing orthodox social structure for a better society as both the castes meet, interact, and unite during festivals like Bakhtin's *carnival*.

In his essay "The Annihilation of Caste" (1936), B. R. Ambedkar, though he was not a literary writer, portrayed an accurate picture of Indian Hindu society and criticised the caste system of the Hindu religion. He found the Hindu religious texts as misogynistic for spreading hatred and suppressing women's interests. Ambedkar believed that inter-caste marriage could not only defeat casteism but "the real method of breaking up the Caste System was … to destroy the religious notions upon which caste is founded" (Fitzgerald 2003: 124). Later, the novel that created a buzz amongst the people was U. R. Ananthamurthy's *Samskara*, published in 1965. The book develops around the life of Naranappa, an anti-Brahminical Brahmin, who openly drinks alcohol besides eating non-vegetarian food and revolts against his Brahmin community and people by defying their orthodox beliefs and lifestyles.

Arvind Adiga's *The White Tiger* (2008), his debut novel and a Booker prize-winning fiction, unveils problems in our Indian society by targeting the Hindu religion and its caste system, besides poverty and corruption prevalent in our Indian society. The novel reflects the reality and shows us the systematic marginality—social, political, and economic—caused by one community to another community. Balram Halwai, the novel's narrator, defines India by saying: "India is two countries in one: an India of Light and an India of Darkness" (Adiga 2008: 14). It reveals the class dichotomy between the rich and the poor. The rich landlord lives in a well-furnished mansion with ponds and temples, whereas the poor live in squalor with "families of pigs … sniffling through the sewage…. Besides, the prime of place at the entrance of the house is the water buffalo." (Missal 2015: n. p.)

The novel *Serious Men* (2010) by Manu Joseph is about the differences between Dalits and Brahmins in India. Meena Kandasamy's *The Gypsy Goddess* (2014) "explored caste, poverty, and violence in southern India" (Taneja 2017: n. p.) and talked about the plight of the Dalit community and its labourers who are forced to work in inhuman conditions. They are oppressed and tortured by the heartless upper-caste landlords. The novel's story takes place in a village called Kilvenmani of Tanjore district in Tamil Nadu, where the Dalit people, including women and children, raise their voices for their human rights, and wages are burnt to death. *When I Hit You: Or, A Portrait of the Writer as a Young Wife* (2017), the second novel by Kandasamy portrays true domestic violence where a newly-wed woman is isolated from society and brutally tortured by her husband.

> When she moves with him to an unfamiliar city, an assault on her tongue, mind and body begins. The language barrier ensures that in public she can only speak words of wifely domesticity, shopping for vegetables or cleaning products. Her husband manipulates her into the surrender of her email accounts, the suspension of her Facebook page; he polices her mobile phone. Beatings and rapes follow, with everyday middle-class implements weaponised: the hose of the washing machine, the power cord for her laptop. Shame, pride and a society in which everyone from parents to police expects a woman to put up and shut up force the realization that only she can save herself. (Taneja 2017: n. p.)

Arundhati Roy is well known for raising her voice for the human cause and received the Booker Prize (1997) for her masterpiece *The God of Small Things* (1997), which deals with misogyny, social discrimination, and prejudice against women through the character of Ammu. She got divorced and started a love affair with Velutha and was further mistreated by a police officer. The upper-caste people consider themselves pure and pious while defining the Paravan caste as untouchable, living in subhuman conditions, and doing menial jobs. They cannot even touch the people of the higher castes. Moreover, Vellya Paapen, a lower-caste fellow, feels grateful to the upper-caste people for willing to kill his son. The caste system, which is thought to create a balance in society, actually misbalances the community. Due to such casteism, the upper-caste members can marry from the same caste, while inter-caste marriage is prohibited. Contemporary works like Urmila Pawar's *The Weave of My Life: A Dalit Woman's Memoir* (2008), Subramanian Shankar's *Ghost in the Tamarind: A Novel* (2017), and Rohinton Mistry's *A Fine Balance* (1995) genuinely reflect the caste and casteism that prevail in India.

Other female writers are at par with their male counterparts and have widely and explicitly discussed the plight of Indian women, such as Toru Dutt, Shashi Deshpande, Anita Desai, A. Roy, Kiran Desai, Mahasweta Devi, Shobha De, Manju Kapur, Amrita Pritam, Jhumpa Lahiri, and Nayantara Sahgal. The feminist writers have come forward to combat institutionalised gender prejudice and speak up for a productive society, exposing the gender inequality prevalent in our community, government, non-governmental sectors, educational institutions, political spheres, and so on. They raise their voices against the biased principles of society. When our male-dominated society constrains women's liberty, they, along with some male writers, come forward for their human rights. They indeed condemn all kinds of exploitation through their writings. Toru Dutt explicitly depicts the sufferings, subjugation, and objectification of the female body in her collection *A Sheaf Gleaned in French Fields* (1876).

Roots and Shadows (1983), the first novel by Shashi Deshpande, raises a voice against traditional oppression and defies the tradition as a means of social destruction. The story develops around the life of an educated woman named Indu, who fights against her womanhood and reveals her frustration against the superstitions and beliefs prevailing in our society. She fights to set herself free from the clutches of men and seeks independence from our male-dominated society's socio-political and cultural oppressions. She, throughout the novel, quests for her identity, debunking male hegemony over females. Her next book *Dark Holds No Terror* (1990) exposes how women perform traditional jobs to appease and please their husbands.

Cry, the Peacock (1963), the first novel by Anita Desai, deals with Indian women's suppression. Here, Maya wants to enjoy her life to the lees and feels excessive love for her father. She says, "no one, no one else, loves me as my father does" (Desai 1980: 46). She has a carefree life and demands equal attention from her aged husband, Gautama, a prosperous lawyer like her father. Still, he fails to fulfill her demands, for both are opposite to each other, which slowly leads to her becoming neurotic.

In Kiran Desai's *The Inheritance of Loss* (2006), "men are associated with the West's characteristics while women are associated with the typical features of the East" (Choudhary n.d.: 181).

> Nimi, the judge's wife represents marginalized, subjugated young women from the Third World. Her role as a minor subaltern character in the novel goes in harmony with her social status as in terms of class and gender. Both Sai and Nimi live a life that is controlled by the judge. Nimi is mostly seen in association with her husband, and is reduced to mere property of Jemubhai, the judge. (Choudhary n. d.: 181)

Mahasweta Devi (1926–2016), who works for the upliftment of the tribal people in India, is conferred with the Sahitya Akademi Award and the Jnapith Award. Her notable works are *The Queen of Jhansi* (2000) and *Mother of 1084* (1998), which reveal the struggles of women against the odds of patriarchal society. *The Queen of Jhansi* is the recreation of the life of Rani Lakshmi Bai. *Mother of 1084* (1998) is the story of a strong mother, Sujata, fighting against the odds of society when her son, Brati, a vibrant Bengali youth, is killed by the

State for his ideology. She tries to justify and defend her son's ideology throughout the novel.

In the last decade of the 20th Century, women novelists enrich Indian English writings focusing on almost all sections of Indian women, such as M. Kapur and J. Lahiri. M. Kapur has presented how the male-dominated society of India creates problems for women, basically highlighting the issues of the joint family. Kapur's novel, *Difficult Daughters* (1998) explores the contrastive nature of her women characters. Virmati, the protagonist, appears to be a traditional woman with a traditional outlook. She faces many problems, while her cousin Shakuntala with a modern perspective, is different from her. Here, Kapur brings forth the conventional idea of marriage and shows us the characters' different attitudes. Shakuntala, as an educated and independent woman, defies marriage, especially the traditional concept of marriage. Shakuntala suggests that Virmati comes out from such conventional thinking and asks her to live like a free bird. According to Shakuntala, "times are changing and women are moving out of the house, so why not you?" (qtd. in Patil 2016: 65). The female voice is the reaction for Kapur raising her voice for freedom in thinking and education. She raises her voice for the independent identity of women who should come out from the domestic barrier. "However, the novelist highlights her ideas of women and their relationship with others, women's sexuality, love, infatuation, jealousy, marriage, gender roles, self-discovery and various other problems" (Patil 2016: 65). As Virmati puts it, "Study means developing the mind for the benefit of the family [because] a girl lives for others, not for herself" (qtd. in Patil 2016: 65). "Thus, Kapur has studied the problems of Virmati as a socialist feminist for her situation and struggle for identity and self-expression." (Patil 2016: 66)

Jhumpa Lahiri's *Interpreter of Maladies* (1999), a short-story collection, reveals the miserable life of a woman named Bibi Haldar in "The Treatment of Bibi Haldar", who is ostracised and marginalised by a conservative society. Lahiri, through the story, criticises the notion of femininity prevailing in India. In "A Temporary Matter", Shoba and Shukumar live as aliens creating distance in their marriage.

> Patriarchy is an imbalanced, fear-based, warlike and truly insane system that completely lack and fears the feminine. A patriarchy is on top, obsessed with control and completely inhumane to everything below. What it fears, it wants to control; what it cannot control, it wants to terrorize and destroy. (Means 2011: 515)

In *Interpreter of Maladies* (1999), we find Mr. Kapasi's feeling for Mrs Das. In "Sexy", we see the affair between Miranda, a white woman, and Dev, a married

Indian man, and the abandonment of Laxim's cousin by her husband for another woman.

> These stories highlight the elided female diasporic subject and invest food practices-the things characters eat and the ways they eat them, as well as how characters relate to the preparation of food-with significance that speaks to conditions of migration and diaspora. The women in these stories, wives of Indian academics, all utilize foodways to construct their own unique racialized subjectivity and to engender agency. (Williams 2007: 70)

In *The Namesake* (2003), we see characters like Moushumi, Graham, and Gogol. It depicts the psychological dilemma faced by Moushumi, who gets married to Gogol but regrets the marriage. We also find that an extramarital affair happens between Moushumi and Dimitri, an old acquaintance.

Many more like G. Deshpande, C. Narendran, and S. Namjoshi primarily talk about the man-woman relationship. Tara Patel's *Single Woman* (1991) reveals the harsh reality and trauma of separation. The Indian English novelists also describe about the concept of "New Woman" who struggles to survive in a male-dominated society and quests for their new individuality. The voice of the "New Woman" and her quest for identity are the main themes of their writings that also debunk the conventional thought process. Ruth Prawar Jhabvala's *To Whom She Will* (1955), Santha Rama Rau's *Remember the House* (1956), and Kamala Markandaya's *Two Virgins* (1973) are good examples of those women who struggle and suffer inequalities. The writers of the late twentieth century, particularly Indian women writers, reveal the exact picture of Indian society and how it treats women. Shobha De's *Socialite Evenings* (1989) talks about the high-class lives and their exotic sex in the financial capital of Mumbai. Rama Mehta's *Inside the Haveli* (1977), Nayantara Sahgal's *Rich Like Us* (1986), and Githa Hariharan's *The Thousand Faces of Night* (1992) talk about traditional issues like Indian culture and its education system. The other women writers further write on urban middle-class contemporary Indian society. Meena Alexander's *Nampally House* (1991), Chitra Banerjee Divakaruni's *The Mistress of Spices* (1997), Rani Dharker's *The Virgin Syndrome* (1997), and Anuradha Mawah-Roy's *Idol Love* (1999) are remarkable examples, while Manju Kapur's *Difficult Daughters* (1998) talks about women's struggles. The writings which quest for self-discovery include Bharti Mukherjee's *Jasmine* (1989), Ameen Meer's *Bombay Talkie* (1994), and Bharti Kirchner's *Shiva Dancing* (1998).

VI

Part I: Gender and Resistance deals with the oppression of women by men from other or their own community people. Men see and treat women as commodities, but they sometimes fight back to reclaim their lost or fading identity, (re)creating their own space and breaking the male-dominated claustrophobic domesticity.

Chapter 1, titled "Power Politics and Reclaiming Identity: A Study of the Transgender in Arundhati Roy's *The Ministry of Utmost Happiness*," deals with the life of transgender people being deliberately marginalised and oppressed. Pushed to the fringe in every walk of life by the powerful, the transgender people fight back to get their rights. This chapter aims to delve into the lives of transgender people—their place and their untiring effort to establish their identity in society. They insist on raising a voice against the humiliation and slurs and urge for the need to live a life with human dignity. It further deals with the sad plight, physical twinge, mental trauma, dreams, ambitions, and aspirations of the Indian transgender community.

Chapter 2, titled "Redefining Women, Reconstructing Space in Attia Hosain's *Sunlight on a Broken Column*," attempts to investigate the lives of Muslim women, deconstructing the diversity among Muslim women and their agency in the private and public space. A woman has to perform different roles from being a social mother to the matriarch of the house and then administrating the family business and voicing her opinions in front of the decisions of the male members of the house.

Chapter 3, titled "Women in Premchand's Stories Are Types, Not Individuals: A Contemporary Study of Select Short Stories of Munshi Premchand," deals with the lives of the oppressed and the marginalised sections of society. Munshi Premchand's awareness of the plight of women is a widely known fact. Although his portrayal of women is grossly termed as conservative in most cases, in the long run, he has proven himself to be ahead of his times in being critically observant of the women's agonies faced in a patriarchal society. Women in all their possible roles find special treatment at the hands of Premchand. However, humanity has considerably evolved over the ages, the agony of the poor, the oppressed, and the weak. This chapter attempts to study the dusty or troubled reality of pre-independent India with special emphasis on women as they were depicted in the short stories of Premchand. It is interesting to see how the author creates characters as types rather than individuals that remain etched in readers' minds.

Chapter 4, titled "*The God of Small Things*: Revisiting the Bible of Indian Feminist Movement," does not leave any issues untouched which Indian women suffer in their lives, be it marriage, motherhood, divorce, female education, domestic violence, or discrimination inside the home. Roy's female character challenges the old patriarchal system and exposes the unholy nexus among the institutions. The novel is by one of those rare writers who venture to talk about inter-caste love and the sexuality of mothers, as Indian myths, scripters, and social values established the sexless image of a mother who will devout her life in the service of husband and taking care of children. If women refuse to be a part of this power structure, the whole system will collapse like a castle of cards.

Chapter 5, titled "Bodies that Matter: Interrogating the Discourses around the 'Body' in Samina Ali's *Madras on Rainy Days*," portrays the centrality of the "body" as the locus of relationships in the heteronormative social structure and has baffled readers and critics alike. Many writers have tried to scrutinise the cultural implications surrounding the "body" and have endeavoured to reflect upon the possibilities beyond the socially registered heteronormative framework. This chapter aims to look into the myriad possibilities and presences surrounding the "body" and therefore project the problematics regarding the various concerns of the "identity of the body" through Samina Ali's novel *Madras on Rainy Days*.

Chapter 6, titled "Body on the Market: A Marxist-Feminist Study of the Novel *Masooma* by Ismat Chughtai," examines the mechanism of the commodification of the female body and its various ramifications. It also considers the corrosive consequence of this capitalist reification in the forms of identity crisis and the inhuman experiences of the protagonist. In the matrix of the "endogamous ties" of the patriarchy, a colonial discourse is established, endowing the men (sometimes the women too) privilege and power to exploit, subjugate, and commodify the women's bodies. *Masooma*, a scathing critique of society and its people, mainly untangles the dishonesty and two-facades of middle-class gentility. It depicts the predicament and transformation of the main protagonist from a shy pretty Muslim girl to Nilofar, often treated as an exchangeable commodity by men.

Chapter 7, titled "Searching for Self and Autonomy, Breaking Claustrophobic Domesticity: A Critical Analysis of Kavery Nambisan's *Mango-Coloured Fish*," talks about a discriminatory practice woman have been facing immemorial. They have been usually subjugated and dominated in history throughout the ages and all countries. *Mango-coloured Fish* talks about the protagonist of the novel named Shari, who goes or flees to her brother's house just before two weeks of her marriage ceremony with a person whom she does not like properly. She is in a kind of moral dilemma about the choice as she loves another man. So she does not want to sacrifice herself to choose her parent's will and thus suffer all her life. She wants to break away from claustrophobic domesticity and violence and live her life according to her will. The journey is an extended trip into the nook and crannies of herself. It is a novel about exquisite self-discovery and focuses on insight into others and oneself.

Chapter 8, titled "Technocracy versus Theocracy: A Critical Study of *Sultana's Dream*," intends to deal with Rokeya's creative ambition. In this novella, *Sultana's Dream*, which is both science fiction and a feminist utopia, the author emphasises running the world peacefully. We do not need masculine power but the use of the human brain. She strongly advocates the use of harmless science and technology in everyday life.

Part II: Caste-Gender Intersectionality and Resistance deals with the interconnectedness of caste and gender and their discrimination highlighted in popular Indian literary texts. The framework is created to understand the multiple texts and marginalisation of certain groups of women, especially Dalits. The findings show interesting gender-caste intersections and the reasons behind the Dalit uprising.

Chapter 9, titled "Individual and Agency in Derozio's "The Fakeer of Jungheera"" deals with Henry Derozio's long narrative poem "The Fakeer of Jungheera", which has often been read as an indictment of the practice of Sati and as an example of Derozio's own modest attempt in raising public opinion against the horrific practice. This chapter proposes to read the poem to extract the degree of agency afforded to the woman protagonist Nuleeni and her assertion of self, life, and love in the face of bigotry and religious oppositions. In what may very well be the first recorded instance of inter-religious love in Indian English, this chapter, through close reading, hope to find and uncover the timeless tropes that continue to inform narratives of purity, community, and honour that colour imaginations of "ghar wapsi" (back to home) and "love jihad" (or Romeo Jihad) prevalent today.

Chapter 10, titled "Understanding Dalit Feminist Perspective through Bama's *Karukku*," is about Bama Faustina Soosairaj's *Karukku*, which is not only a significant contribution to Dalit literature but also recognised globally for considerable energy and universality at its core. The socio-political conditions of Dalit Christians, who embraced Christianity just to come out of their subaltern position within the Hindu religion, form the backdrop of Bama's literary ventures on the whole. After their conversion, Dalit Christians lost the privileges they were entitled to as Hindu Dalits. Their status as low-caste people remains unchanged even within Christianity. In her works, Bama unfolds how caste and gender intersect to exercise power at all levels. Dalit feminists address three different modes in which Dalit women are oppressed: firstly, as a Dalit by the upper-caste community; secondly as low-paid workers exploited by the upper-caste landowners; and thirdly as women subjugated by the men of their community.

Chapter 11, titled "Reinterpreting to Retrieve Lost Women's Voices: Gendered Subalternities in Mahasweta Devi's "Bayen" and Raja Rao's "Javni"", extracts the lost voices of the women protagonists. In "Bayen", the protagonist is presented as a demon or witch, whereas in "Javni", the protagonist is shown to be simple-minded or a fool. While Bayen eventually is recognised by the state as a hero, Javni is elevated to be a saint or even a goddess. However, what is not presented clearly or rather is left in between the lines waiting for rediscovery and retrieval are the stories of two Dalit women doubly oppressed due to their gender and caste. This chapter will unravel how the two women, despite all odds, assert their identities and free will to generate a life free of humiliation even though the rewards and recognitions awarded to them at the end of the short stories missed their mark entirely.

Part III: Caste and Resistance projects how upper-caste people have been marginalising the lower-caste people for a very long time till now. This section further portrays how orthodoxy in rituals creates the burden of traditional and existential crises. Here, the condition of the lower caste, the Dalit, is projected along with their history and plight. Though they fail and fall but fight back against such social chauvinism.

Chapter 12, titled "Casteism and Colonial Discourse: A Projection of Marginality in Bama's *Karukku*," depicts how upper-caste force Dalits to accept their inferior status because they are imperfect and born to serve them. This hegemonic ideology has been naturally implanted in the psyche of the Dalits. Bama's *Karukku* delineates the problems of casteism and projects the marginality confronted by the Dalits. The chapter will highlight how the Dalits are discriminated against and marginalised in society and the means of getting rid of the curse of casteism.

Chapter 13, titled "*Bhimayana* as a Biographical Stance on Resistance," is based on caste discrimination and its resistance by lower-caste. The chapter mainly signifies such social discrimination and Ambedkar's endeavour to stop it. His endeavour is anchored to the colossus of caste, though often, he is only blandly credited with designing the Indian Constitution. Ambedkar was born in a Mahar family that was considered to be an "untouchable" caste. Despite being a highly educated Dalit, he was the victim of the Indian caste system since childhood. Also, he witnessed numerous experiences of humiliation and the denial of fundamental human rights. He has described various accounts of such disrespectful and humiliating behaviour in his diary published under the name of *Waiting for a Visa* (1993). It enables the readers to situate the importance of Ambedkar within the Dalit movement in India along with the significance of its narrative style regarding Gond Art.

Chapter 14, titled "Orthodoxy in Rituals Creating the Burden of Tradition and Existential Crisis: A Critical Reading of U. R. Anatha Murthy's *Samskara*", develops through the main event of the death of a non-Brahminical Brahmin Naranappa and his subsequent ritualistic death rite. The novel has questioned the traditional ways of Brahminhood in the Hindu religion. Hypocrisy, dilemma, gluttony, and a pseudo-ascetic life of the people of Agrahara in Durvasapura have been vehemently criticised here in a symbolic way. All Agrahara and their guru, "the Crest Jewel of Vedic-Learning", Praneshacharya, are very conscious about the traditional rituals found in the "Law Books" but unknowingly are blindly guided by the orthodoxies, which destroy their minds and the Agrahara as well. Due to this, they cannot live a free life as a tradition to them becomes a burden, and they begin to suffer from existential and identity crises.

Chapter 15, titled "*Bhimanaya*: A Graphic Projection of History and Plight of Dalits in India," depicts the plights and sufferings of the Dalits. They are not just pushed backward from a social point of view but are also tortured by the upper-caste people. This graphic novel is a voice of the voiceless people who are never heard in their land. They have been socially, politically, and economically subjugated and exploited in every age. The novel is a beautiful amalgamation of the past and present lives of Dalits.

The book primarily investigates all those social issues, mechanisms, and methods used by sociopaths to internally colonise the Dalits (men and women) in particular and women in general. So, the main objective is to revisit Indian scholarly literary texts in terms of what it reveals about the resistance registered through the sufferings of human beings by the hand of fellow human beings.

Bibliography

Abrams, M. H., and G. G. Harpham. *A Glossary of Literary Terms*. Delhi: Wardsworth Publication, 2012. 58.

Adiga, A. *The White Tiger*. New Delhi: Harper Collins, 2008. 14.

Alexander, M. *Nampally Road: A Novel*. San Francisco: Mercury House, 1991.

Ali, S. *Madras on Rainy Days*. New York: Picador, 2004.

Ambedkar, B. "The Annihilation of Caste." n. p.: Amazon Digital Services LLC - Kdp Print Us, 2018.

Anand, M. R. *Untouchable: A Novel* (1935). Harmondsworth: Penguin Books, 1940.

———. Coolie (1936). New Delhi: Penguin Books: 1993.

Bama, F. *Karukku*. 2nd Edition. Translated by Lakshmi Holmstrom. Oxford: Oxford University Press, 2012.

Bayly, S. *Caste, Society, and Politics in India from the Eighteenth Century to the Modern Age*. New York: Cambridge University Press, 1999.

Berreman, G. D. "Caste in India and the United States." *American Journal of Sociology* 66, no. 2 (September 1960): 70, 124.

Beteille, A. *Caste, Class, and Power: Changing Patterns of Stratification in a Tanjore Village*. Berkeley and Los Angeles: University of California Press, 1965. 46.

———. "Varna and Jati." *Sociological Bulletin* 45, no. 1 (March 1996).

Bhambhri, C. P. "Dialectics of Caste and Casteism." *Economic and Political Weekly* 34, no. 36 (September 4–10, 1999): 2619.

Bhowmik, S. K. "Caste and Class in India." *Economic and Political Weekly* 27, no. 24/25 (June 13–20, 1992): 1246.

Butler, J. *Gender Trouble: Feminism and the Subversion of Identity*. New York: Routledge, 2015. 89.

"Caste and Gender Justice: Delivering on the UN Global for Dalit Women and Girls." *International Dalit Solidarity Network: Working Globally Against Caste Discrimination*, 2019. 3 and 6. Accessed 11 January 2020. https://idsn.org/wp-content/uploads/2019/06/Caste-and-Gender-Justice-Low-Res.pdf

"Casteism." *Lexico Dictionaries*. Web. Accessed 07 December 2021. https://www.lexico.com/definition/casteism

Chakravarti, U. "The Development of the Sita Myth: A Case Study of Women in Myth and Literature." *SamyaShakti: A Journal of Women Studies* 1, no. 1 (1983): 70.

Chandrasekhar, S. "Caste, Class, and Color in India." *The Scientific Monthly* 62, no. 2 (February 1946): 151-152 & 154.

Choudhary, N. "Gender Issues among Class Relations: Revisiting Kiran Desai's *The Inheritance of Loss*." *International Conference on Arts, Culture, Literature, Languages, Gender Studies/ Sexuality, Humanities and Philosophy for Sustainable Societal Development* 2: 181-182.

Chughtai, I. *Masooma*, translated by Tahira Naqvi. Delhi: Speaking Tiger, 2018.

Corwin, L. A. "Caste, Class and the Love-Marriage: Social Change in India." *Journal of Marriage and Family* 39, no. 4 (November 1977): 650.

Cox, O. C. "Class and Caste: A Definition and a Distinction." *The Journal of Negro Education* 13, no. 2 (Spring 1944): 141-142.

"Dalit Women Fight!" *International Dalit Solidarity Network: Working Globally Against Caste Discrimination*, 2015. 3-4. Accessed 11 January 2020. https://idsn.org/wp-content/uploads/pdfs/Dalit Women Fight.pdf

Derozio, H. L. V. "The Fakeer of Jungheera". *Songs of the Stormy Petrel: Complete Works of Henry Louis Vivian Derozio*, edited by Dr Abirlal Mukhopadhyay et al. Calcutta: Progressive Publishers, 2001.

Desai, A. *Cry, The Peacock*. Delhi: Orient Paperbacks, 1980. 46.

Desai, K. *The Inheritance of Loss*. New Delhi: Penguin Random House India Private Limited, 2015.

Dé, S. *Socialite Evenings*. New Delhi: Penguin Books Limited, 2014.

Deshpande, S. *Roots and Shadows*. New Delhi Disha Books, 1992.

———. *Dark Holds No Terrors: A Novel*. New Delhi: Penguin Books Limited, 2000.

Debi, M. *The Queen of Jhansi*. Translated by Sagaree Sengupta and Mandira Sengupta. Kolkata: Seagull Books, 2009.

———. *Mother of 1084*. Translated by Samik Bandyopadhyay and Samik Banerjee. Kolkata: Seagull Books, 1997.

———. "Bayen". Translated by Mahua Bhattacharya. In *Separate Journeys: Short Stories by Contemporary Indian Women*, edited by Geeta Dharmarajan and Mary Ellis Gibson, 1–14. South Carolina: University of South Carolina Press, 2004.

Dharker, R. *The Virgin Syndrome*. New Delhi: Penguin Books India, 1997.

Divakaruni, C. B. *The Mistress of Spices: A Novel*. New York: Knopf Doubleday Publishing Group, 2009.

Dutt, T. *A Sheaf Gleaned in French Fields*. Bhowanipur, Calcutta: B.M. Bose, at the Saptahik Sambad Press, 1876.

Dumont, L. *Homo Hierarchicus: The Caste System and Its Implications* Chicago: University of Chicago Press, 1974.

Female Infanticide Prevention Act, 1870. Wikipedia. Acessed 9 December 2021. https://en.wikipedia.org/wiki/Female Infanticide Prevention Act, 1870#cite note-1

Fitzgerald, T. *The Ideology of Religious Studies*. Oxford: Oxford University Press, 2003. 124.

Fowler, J. *Hinduism Beliefs and Practices*. Chicago: Sussex Academic Press, 2014.

Gandhi, R. S. "From Caste to Class in Indian Society." *Humboldt Journal of Social Relations* 7, no. 2 (Spring/Summer 1980): 1.

Ghosh, B. "Jadavpur University Professor Trolled over Tribal Status." *The Hindu*. September 05, 2020. n. p. Accessed 21 October 2020. https://www.thehindu.com/news/national/other-states/jadavpur-university-professor-trolled-over-tribal-status/article32529928.ece

Handbook on the Prohibition of Child Marriage Act, 2006. India: Ministry of Women and Child Development, 2009.

Hardgrave, Jr., R. L. "Caste: Fission and Fusion." *Economic and Political Weekly* 3, no. 26/28, Special Number (July 1968): 1065.

Hariharan, G. *The Thousand Faces of Night*. New Delhi: Penguin Random House India Private Limited, 2000.

Hindu Widows Remarriage Act, 1856. *Wikiwand*. Accessed 9 December 2021. https://www.wikiwand.com/en/Hindu_Widows%27_Remarriage_Act,_1856

Hosain, A. *Sunlight on a Broken Column*. New Delhi: Penguin Books India, 1992.

Hossain, R. S. *Sultana's Dream* and "Padmarag." New Delhi: Penguin Books, 2005.

Human Rights Watch. "Hidden Apartheid: Caste Discrimination against India's 'Untouchables.'" *Centre for Human Rights and Global Justice* 19, no. 3 (c) (February 2007): 2.

Jhabvala, R. P. *To Whom She Will: A Novel*. London: G. Allen and Unwin, 1955.

Joseph, M. *Serious Men*. New Delhi: HarperCollins Publishers India, 2013.

Inden, R. *Imagined India*. Oxford: Blackwell Publishers, 1990.

Kandasamy, M. *The Gypsy Goddess*. New Delhi: HarperCollins Publishers India, 2016.

———. *When I Hit You: Or, A Portrait of the Writer as a Young Wife*. United Kingdom: Europa Editions, 2020.

Kalidasa. *Kumarasambhava*. Edited and translated by Chintaman Ramchandra Devadhar. New Delhi: Motilal Banarsidass Publications, 1985.

Kapur, M. *Difficult Daughters*. London: Faber & Faber Limited, 1999.

Kasturi, M. "Law and Crime in India: British Policy and the Female Infanticide Act of 1870." *Indian Journal of Gender Studies* Vol. 1, 2 (July-December 1994):169-194.

Kirchner, B. *Shiva Dancing*. New York: Plume, 1999.

Kumar, A. "The Caste in Tech Witch-Hunt Explained." 31 October 2020. n. p. Accessed 22 June 2020. https://medium.com/@concernedkumar/the-caste-in-tech-witch-hunt-explained-7d2f28e06762

Lahiri, J. *Interpreter of Maladies*. New York: Houghton Mifflin Harcourt, 2000.

———. *The Namesake*. New York: Mariner Books, 2004.

Mahey, S. "The Status of Dalit Women in India's Caste Based System." *Culture + the State: Alternative Interventions*, 151. Edited by Gabrielle Eva Marie Zezulka-Mailloux, James Gifford. Edmonton: CRC Humanities Studio, University of Alberta, 2003.

Manu. *Manusmriti*. Translated by George Buhler. Oxford: Clarendon Press, 1886.

Markandaya, K. *Two Virgins*. New Delhi: Penguin Group, 2010.

Mauss, M. *Introduction to the Work of Claude Levi-Strauss*. Translated by Felicity Bekar. London: Routledge & Kegan Paul Ltd., 1987. 63.

Means, R. "Patriarchy: The Ultimate Conspiracy, Matriarchy, the Ultimate Solution; History-or-His-story." *Griffith Law Review* 20, no. 3 (2011): 515.

Meer, A. *Bombay talkie*. London: High Risk Books, 1994.

Mehta, R. *Inside The Haveli*. New Delhi: Penguin Random House India Private Limited, 2018.

Missal, S. "Arvind Adiga's "*The White Tiger*: A Study in Systematic Marginality." Munich, GRIN Verlag, 2015. n. p. Accessed 15 May 2020. https://www.grin.com/document/293486

Mistry, R. *A Fine Balance*. Toronto: McClelland & Stewart, 2010.

Mukherjee, B. *Jasmine*. New York: Grove Press, 1999.

Murthy, U. R. Anantha. *Samskara*. Delhi: Oxford University Press, 1989.

Nambisan, K. *Mango-Coloured Fish*. Gurgaon: Penguin Books India, 1998.

Natarajan, S., et. al. *Bhimayana: Experiences of Untouchability*. New Delhi: Navayana, 2011.

Narula, S. "Equal by Law, Unequal by Caste: The 'Untouchable' Condition in Critical Race Perspective". *Wisconsin International Law Journal* 26, no. 2 (2008): 273.

Nayar, P. K. *Studying Literature: An Introduction to Fiction and Poem*. New Delhi: Orient Blackswan, 2013: n. p.

Olivelle, P. *Manu's Code of Law*. Oxford: Oxford University Press, 2005. 98, 111.

Pandita, S. "Caste Based Discrimination in India—Hidden Apartheid for Dalits." 1 January 2005. n. p. Accessed on 12 March 2017. https://amrc.org.hk/content/caste-based-discrimination-india-hidden-apartheid-dalits

Patel, T. *Single Woman*. New Delhi: Rupa & Company, 1991.

Patil, R. V. "A Feminist Approach to Manju Kapoor's "Difficult Daughters."" *Epitome Journals* 2, n. 8 (August 2016): 65-66.

Pawar, U. *The Weave of My Life: A Dalit Woman's Memoirs.* New York: Columbia University Press, 2009.

Rau, S. R. *Remember the House.* New York: Harper, 1956.

Rao, R. *Kanthapura* (1938). New Delhi: Penguin Books Limited, 2014.

———. "Javni". In *Twelve Modern Short Stories,* edited by Name Surname,166–185. Oxford: Oxford University Press, 2005.

Roy, A. "Caste and Class: An Interlinked View." *Economic and Political Weekly* 14, no. 7/8 (February 1979): 297.

Roy, A. *The God of Small Things.* New Delhi: Penguin Random House India Private Limited, 2017.

———. *The Ministry of Utmost Happiness.* Gurgaon: Penguin Random House India, 2017.

Marwah-Roy, A. *Idol Love.* New Delhi: Ravi Dayal Publisher, 1999.

Sarkar, S. *Gender Disparity in India: Unheard Whimpers.* Delhi: PHI Learning Private Limited, 2016. 320.

Sahgal, N. *Rich Like Us.* New Delhi: HarperCollins Publishers India, 2003.

Shankar, S. *Ghost in the Tamarind: A Novel.* Honolulu, Hawaii: University of Hawaii Press, 2017.

Shanmathi, R. and S. Shenbagavalli. "Gender Equality—Revisiting the Past and Identifying the Present Gender Biased Legal System in India." *International Journal of English Language, Literature and Translation Studies* 5, no. S1 (2018): 199.

Sharma, A. *Classical Hindu Thought: An Introduction.* New Delhi: Oxford University Press, 2000.

Sharma, D. I. C. S. *Mahabharata: Sanskrit Text and English Translation.* Edited by Om Nath Bimali. Delhi: Parimal Publications, 2004.

Smith, B. K. *Classifying the Universe: The Ancient Indian Varna System and the Origins of Caste.* New York: Oxford UP, 1994. 48.

Spivak, G. C. "Can the Subaltern Speak?" In *Colonial Discourse and Postcolonial Theory: A Reader,* edited by Patric Williams and Laura Chrisman, 66–111. New York: Colombia University Press, 1994.

"Status of Literacy." *Literacy Rate Census of India.* 2011. Accessed 20 April 2020. https://censusindia.gov.in/2011-prov-results/data_files/mp/07Literacy.pdf

Sudraka. *Mrichchhakatikam (The Little Clay Cart),* edited and translated by Arthur William Ryder. Harvard: Harvard University Press, 1905.

Taneja, P. "When I Hit You: Or, A Portrait of the Writer as a Young Wife by Meena Kandasamy—review." *The Guardian.* July 2017. n. p. Accessed 10 June 2020. https://www.theguardian.com/books/2017/jul/07/when-i-hit-you-meena-kandasamy-review

The Bengal Sati Regulation, 1829. Advocatetanmoy Law Library. Accessed 09 December 2021. https://advocatetanmoy.com/the-bengal-sati-regulation-1829/

The Commission of Sati (Prevention) Act, 1987, with *The Commission of Sati Prevention Rules, 1988.* New Delhi: Universal Law Publishiing, 2011.

The Constitution of India (As on 1st April, 2019). Government of India, Ministry of Law and Justice. Legislative Department, 2019. 04 & 25.

The Equal Remuneration Act, 1976. New Delhi: Universal Law Publishing, 2007.

The Dowry Prohibition Act, 1961: 28 of 1961. New Delhi: Universal Law Publishing, 1961.

Valmiki. *The Ramayana.* Translated by Ramesh Menon. New Delhi: HarperCollins Publishers India, 2010.

Williams, L. A. "Foodways and Subjectivity in Jhumpa Lahiri's *Interpreter of Maladies.*" *MELUS* 32, no. 4 (Winter 2007): 70.

PART I
Gender and Resistance

Chapter 1

Power Politics and Reclaiming Identity: A Study of the Transgender in Arundhati Roy's *The Ministry of Utmost Happiness*

Safiul Islam
Aliah University, West Bengal, India

Abstract

The hegemonic discourse of the establishment in religious structures and social, political, economic, and linguistic arenas has its roots in the old oppressive systems around the globe. Feminists made transgender people the victims of exclusionary politics during the 1980s and the 1990s by excluding them from the feminist movements. They have been deliberately marginalised and oppressed. Having been pushed to the fringe in every walk of life by the powerful class in society, transgender people have always fought back to get their rights. They strive in the quest for their essential selves or gender identities. This chapter will aim to delve into the lives of transgender people—their place in society, their untiring efforts to establish their identity, their insistence on voicing against humiliation and slurs, and their urge to live a life with human dignity like other normal human beings—through Arundhati Roy's second novel *The Ministry of Utmost Happiness* (2017). It also aims to deal with the sad plight, physical twinge, mental trauma, and the dreams, ambitions, and aspirations of the Indian transgender community.

Keywords: transgender, marginalisation, body, *hijra*, gender, trauma

* * *

The hegemonic discourse of establishing religious structures and social, political, economic, and linguistic arenas has roots in old oppressive systems worldwide. Transgender people have been deliberately marginalised and oppressed. Having been pushed to the fringe in every walk of life by the powerful class in society, transgender people have always fought back to get their rights. The present discussion endeavours to delve into the lives of transgender people—their place in society, their untiring efforts to establish their identity, their insistence on voicing against humiliation and slurs, and their urge to live a life with human dignity like other normal human beings. To achieve the target, this chapter will critique Arundhati Roy's second novel *The Ministry of Utmost Happiness* (2017), that is, perhaps, the only remarkable and pertinent Indian novel after Mahesh Dattani's play *Seven Steps Around the Fire* (2013), which deals with the sad quandary, physical twinge, mental trauma, and the dreams, ambitions, and aspirations of the Indian transgender community. The definition of 'transgender' changes through place and time. Susan Stryker in *Transgender History: The Roots of Today's Revolution* (2017) brings out the changing definitions of transgender:

> During the 1970s and 1980s, it usually meant a person who wanted not merely to temporarily change their clothing (like a transvestite) or to permanently change their genitals (like a transsexual) but rather to change their social gender in an ongoing way through a change of habitus and gender expression, which perhaps included the use of hormones, but usually not surgery. When the word broke out into wider use in the early 1990s, however, it was used to encompass any and all kinds of variation from gender norms and expectations, similar to what genderqueer, gender-nonconforming, and nonbinary mean now. In recent years, some people have begun to use the term transgender to refer only to those who identify with a binary gender other than the one they were assigned at birth—which is what transsexual used to mean—and to use other words for people who seek to resist their birth-assigned gender without necessarily identifying with another gender or who seek to create some kind of new gender practice. (Stryker 2017: 28–29)

According to "The Transgender Persons (Protection of Rights) Act, 2019" of India, a transgender person is one

> whose gender does not match with the gender assigned to that person at birth and includes trans-man or trans-woman (whether or not such person had undergone Sex Reassignment Surgery or hormone therapy or laser therapy or such other therapy), person with intersex variations, genderqueer and person having such socio-cultural identities as *kinner, hijra, aravani* and *jogta*. ("The Transgender Persons (Protection of Rights) Act 2019": 2)

The space for transgender people is socially, culturally, and politically determined. How could one wipe out one's memories related to gender? How far do laws and Acts show their power to change a child's psyche who, from the moment of his/her birth, is controlled by the psychic residue already existent in the collective unconscious? A majority of people rebuff giving transgender people human dignity. Not only adults and older people, but even children learn to take them otherwise. The mental condition of children regarding transgender people results in the 'Othering' of the 'third sex', and this has blatant social approval. From the moment transgender people are born, they grow up knowing that man and woman constitute the human species, and transgender people are like aliens who are thought to be just "clown[s] without a circus, queen[s] without a palace" (Roy 2017: 3). Anjum is one of the principal characters who, like other transgender people, "endured months of casual cruelty like a tree would—without flinching" (Roy 2017: 3). Anjum has been oriented with the sufferings of disgrace, humiliation, slurs, embarrassment, and physical anguish. Even a small boy throws stone at her that is very heart-rending and a blot on society, and she "didn't crane her neck to read the insults scratched into her bark" (Roy 2017: 3). People in the *Duniya* (world) push the lives of hijras (eunuchs) into risk and peril by spreading the iniquitous rumour that hijras are the kidnappers and castrators of little boys. But the hijras in Khwabgah emphatically proclaim that nothing happens there without *manjoori* (approval). Duniya unquestionably represents the society of ordinary human beings where hijras are invisible. Their existence in Duniya is illusory, and they are discernible only in *khwab* (dream).

Transgender people are the victims of power politics. Anjum thinks that she is neither merely a man nor simply a woman, but she is the combination of both. She boasts of both the qualities and values of both and believes that she is superior to any individual man and woman. "I'm Romi and Juli, I'm Laila and Majnu. And Mujna, why not? Who says my name is Anjum? I'm not Anjum, I'm Anjuman. I'm a *mehfil*, I'm gathering. Of everybody and nobody, of everything and nothing" (Roy 2017: 4). Society, however, relegates her to be 'nobody' and 'nothing.' She has no existence in the mainstream patriarchal society.

Transgender people—deliberately emasculated by the male members in society who are supposed to be strong—are purposely attributed as 'female' because they have, for ages, been considered weak, submissive, and powerless. They are also called by female names such as Bulbul, Heera, Baby, Nimmo, Mary, and Gudiya, and they call their dwelling house the *Khwabgah* (the House of Dreams), but feminists have made them the victims of exclusionary politics during the 1980s and 1990s. The American lesbian radical feminist Janice Raymond thinks that trans practices are inherently un-feminist. In her book *The Transsexual Empire* (1980), Raymond declares that trans women are servile constructions of a patriarchal medical system. This critique of trans women set off a politics of antagonism towards trans people. Jack Halberstam, the gender and queer theorist, and Surya Monro and Sally Hines, the researchers in gender, sexuality, and transgender studies, show how transgender people have been made to be the inhabitants of nowhere. They think that feminists consigned trans women as 'others', for they were not 'born women'. On the other hand, trans men were often observed as feminist conspirators because they transitioned from females to males for male privileges.

Power politics shows its varied colours in diverse situations. In one aspect, ordinary people, irrespective of religion, caste, creed, race, or economic status, belong to the side of the powerful, and hijras are on the powerless plane. Even poor people consider hijras as not worthy enough to help them. They have been by design marginalised and left out from lesbian/gay histories. The gender activists, R. A. Wilchins, in her book *Queer Theory, Gender Theory: An Instant Primer* (2004), and Sally Hines in her article "A Pathway to Diversity? Human Rights, Citizenship and Politics of Transgender" (2009) argue that although transgender people's role in the gay liberation uprising of the Stonewall riots (1969) and the formation of organisations such as the Gay Activists Alliance and the Gay Liberation Front is very significant and noteworthy, their contribution to lesbian and gay culture has not been fully conceded: "People who are today known as transgendered and transsexual have always been present in homosexual rights movements. Their presence and contributions, however, have not always been fully acknowledged or appreciated" (Devor and Matte 2006: 387). Hijras get a new kind of identity from rioters during the 2002 Gujrat pogrom. To the rioters, Anjum is '*Saali Randi Hijra*' (sister-fucking whore). The rioters do not kill Anjum because they believe that if they kill hijras that may bring them bad luck. Traveling by expensive cars such as Mercedes-Benz by the hijras also appears to be incongruous to the onlookers. It even creates anger in the bystanders.

Is it possible for a mother to be terrified of her baby, even when the baby is neither 'he' nor 'she'? The answer is not simple. Sometimes, motherly concern makes a mother apprehensive about her baby. Anjum's real name is Aftab. Aftab is a hijra or *kinnar*. Anjum's mother, Jahanara Begum, fears that her son may be isolated by other ordinary children and society's elders. She is fretful that her son's normal growth may be impeded. She is worried that her son would not get social recognition. She apprehends that her son may be deprived of society's basic privileges. She feels terrified because she thinks that her son would be an object of mockery and humiliation in the society. All these presumptions coerce her into reacting unconstructively. When Jahanara Begum discovers "nestling underneath his boy-parts, a small, unformed, but undoubtedly girl-part" (Roy 2017: 7), her reactions are noteworthy. She feels "her heart constricts and her bones turn to ash" (Roy 2017: 8). She even mulls over killing herself and her child. Finally, she decides not to tell anybody, not even her husband, anything about the gendered identity of the child for the moment. In the shrine of Hazrat Sarmad Shaheed, Aftab's mother's prayer "to teach me how to love him" (Roy 2017: 11) demonstrates the desperate attempt of her tormented self to keep aside the orthodox belief that a hijra can never be a human being to be loved like others. S. Hines and T. Sanger, in the introduction to *Transgender Identities: Towards a Social Analysis of Gender Diversity*, state:

> Locked into the notion of "gender dysphoria" is the idea of the "wrong body", which suggests a state of discord between "sex" (the body) and gender identity (the mind). In matching the gendered body and the gendered mind, surgery was (and still is) positioned as a route to gendered harmony. (Hines and Sanger 2010: 2)

The self-proclaimed 'sexologist' Dr Ghulam Nabi identifies Aftab as 'Hermaphrodite', who is not in a medical sense a hijra but a male body where a female has been trapped.

Jahanara Begum's apprehension regarding Aftab's future becomes valid. Her hopes for Aftab are smashed to smithereens when she observes that Aftab stops going to school for no apparent reason. He has a unique talent for music. Although in the beginning, he is appreciated and encouraged by the people for his extraordinary skill in Raag Yaman, Durga, Bhairav, Chaiti, and Thumri, later his life becomes hellish when other children begin to snicker and tease: "*He's a She. He's not a He or a She. He's a He and a She. She-He, He-She Hee! Hee!*" (Roy 2017: 12). They tease him even after Aftab stops going to music classes for this reason.

Hijras go through overt and covert humiliation and pestering. People's psyche towards hijras as the 'Other' covertly humiliates them. Within these adverse and humiliating circumstances, a sense of nostalgia regales Ustad Kulsoom Bi. Hijras were entrusted with the responsibility of security and administrative tasks in the Mughal harems. They were appointed as political advisers and generals. They were also competent figures in collecting taxes. Ustad Kulsoom Bi narrates the history of when the glory and dignity of hijras were at their acme. She feels proud of being hijra: "We are the *Hijras* of Shahjahanabad." (Roy 2017: 49)

In Hinduism, transgender people were acknowledged, accepted, and given a decent place in society. They were ensured human dignity and respect. They were allowed to enjoy fundamental rights and privileges. The ancient Indian Sanskrit text on sexuality and eroticism in the Kamasutra is regarded as the 'Tritiya Prakriti' (third sex). In the two great Indian epics, the *Ramayana* and the *Mahabharata*, a dignified presence of transgender people were documented. In the *Ramayana*, transgender persons were provided with a great place and honour in society by Lord Shri Rama of Ayodhya, the hero in the epic, for their loyalty and devotion to him. Lord Rama left Ayodhya for the Dandaka forest to spend a life of banishment for 14 years. While setting out for his journey to the forest, he saw at the gates of Ayodhya that his subjects were following him; he stopped and told the 'men' and 'women' to return to their places. After 14 years of exilic life, when Shri Rama returned to Ayodhya, he found that the hijras, being neither men nor women, had stayed there for 14 years. Shri Rama, being impressed by their devotion and loyalty to him, rewarded them a boon that they could convene benedictions on people on different propitious circumstances and rituals such as childbirth, weddings, and so on. From ancient times, hijras have been an essential part of Indian culture.

In the *Mahabharata*, some prominent characters played the roles of transgender people to attain some purposes. Arjuna, the great warrior, took the guise of a transgender person named Brihannala in his last year of exile. Mohini, an enchantress who snatched the pot of nectar from the demons and gave it to the gods, was the only female version of the Hindu god Vishnu. Shikandi, the great warrior in the *Mahabharata*, was a transgender person who killed Bhisma, one of the most powerful warriors and a statesman of the Kuru Kingdom. Gudiya, a hijra belonging to the Hindu religion and a resident of Khwabgah, reflects on how hijras were given both love and respect in Hindu Mythology. In this context, it could be said that transgender people in India are an affair from times immemorial. We can trace back their existence to the 13th and 14th centuries of Indian history when they were revered and believed to bring luck and provide extraordinary fertility power.

At the advent of British colonialism in India, *hijras* used to enjoy providing food and land, and later they were deprived of those benefits. In 1861, the British colonial administration implemented Section 377 of the Indian Penal Code (IPC), modeled on the Buggery Act of 1533, which criminalised non-procreative sexualities. Hijras, among others (gays and lesbians), were targeted. Such a 'legal panopticon' marginalised and stigmatised the Indian hijras, and even now, they are carrying the burden of that legacy. In 1994, the constitutionality of Section 377 of the IPC was challenged, but the challenge was dismissed on moral and ethical grounds. The Supreme Court of India upended Section 377 of the IPC in 2018 on the logic that it trashed the citizens' fundamental rights. During the colonial period, it was also believed that hijras were involved in castrating and kidnapping children.

The ordinary people from the Duniya have very little awareness about the struggles and sacrifices in building the Khwabgah. Khwabgah is their utopia, a house of dreams, where the guru, Ustad Kulsoom Bi, believes that "special people, *blessed* people, came with their dreams that could not be realized in the Duniya. In the Khwabgah, Holy Souls trapped in the wrong bodies were liberated" (Roy 2017: 53). To her, hijras are chosen people, beloved of God. The questions are: How satisfied are they with their life of isolation from society? Are they really happy in their Khwabgah or just pretending to be satisfied in the Duniya? To Nimmo Gorakhpuri, another resident of Khwabgah, Khwabgah is not a utopia but a dystopia where everybody lives a life of ceaseless torment. "Who's happy here? It's all sham and fakery, Nimmo said laconically, not bothering to look up from the magazine.... The riot is *inside* us. The war is *inside* us. Indo-Pak is *inside* us. It will never settle down. It can't" (Roy 2017: 23).

Nimmo even thinks that God created hijras as an experiment as He had a plan to "… create something, a living creature that is incapable of happiness. So he made us" (Roy 2017: 23). Roy gives a picture of one unexplored side of their life. No one feels the pain and agony, desire and ambition of hijras, some of whom, especially Anjum, want to be mothers, but destiny deprives them of this. Her heart and mind believe that she is born to be a mother, and she, one day, will be blessed with her own child by "Allah Mian" (Roy 2017: 83). Roy shows that in no way are hijras less humanitarian and less secular. A hand of trust and humanity is extended to the addicts and the homeless people living at the periphery of the graveyard who are invited to the feast and merriment organised to welcome Miss Jebeen the Second to Jannat Guest House, the new abode of Anjum and the other hijras. Anjum's adoption of the abandoned baby at Jantar Mantar during the 'Second Freedom Struggle' is not received warmly by the people who raise questions: "What will you do with her? You can't turn her into one of you, can you?" (Roy 2017: 119). They even accuse Anjum of kidnapping and then castrating male babies. Some people, such as the protester Mr. Aggarwal, consider that hijras cannot be a part of serious politics.

We cannot deny a fact relating to the professional activities of hijras: In this regard, they sometimes cross the limit of decency and civil manners. Moreover, sometimes these reach the level of mental and physical torture and humiliation. Their activities "ruin the occasion with curses and a display of unthinkable obscenity unless they [are] paid a fee" (Roy 2017: 24) which can no way be attuned with social acceptability. Razia, another resident of the Khwabgah who is not a hijra, calls these activities *badtameezi* (impoliteness). Nimmo Gorakhpuri, while referring to the *badtameezi*, says, "We're jackals who feed off other people's happiness, we're Happiness Hunters" (Roy 2017: 24). Being upset with a life of frustration, anxiety, and public mortification, they regard themselves as falling people who are neither real nor really exist. To Anjum, hijras are like aliens from the other world.

Throughout the 1990s, various activist and cultural groups and organisations, such as 'Transgender Nation' and 'FTM International' in the USA, and 'Press for Change' in the UK, have been formed to protect the rights and dignity of the transgender community. In the present day, different laws have been amended, and constitutional Acts have been made in different countries to give human dignity, human rights, ranks, and status to the lesbian, gay, bisexual, and transgender communities. "In the US, debate over the inclusion of gender identity in the 'Employment Non-Discrimination Act' (ENDA) continues, while in the UK, the 'Gender Recognition Act' (2004), enables transgender people to change their birth certificates and to marry in their gender of choice" (Hines and Sanger 2010: 10). 'Transgender Studies' as a distinct field of scholarship emerged in the late 1990s. The "social, cultural and legislative developments reflect how transgender is acquiring increasing visibility in contemporary society, and mark transgender as an important and timely area of social and cultural inquiry." (Hines and Sanger 2010: 11)

The Supreme Court of India on 15 April 2014 pronounced transgender people to be the 'third gender' who could enjoy the privilege of fundamental rights under the Constitution of India. They were also given the right to self-identification of their gender (as male, female, or third gender). Besides, they are given reservations in the admissions to educational institutions and jobs. In the census of 2011, for the first time in Indian census history, transgender people were counted in the 'Others' category under the 'Gender' option. Recently, many governments, semi-government, and private sectors have created a new option, 'transgender', along with male and female under the 'Gender' category in various application forms.

"The Transgender Persons (Protection of Rights) Act, 2019", commenced from 10 January 2020 in India "to provide for the protection of rights of transgender persons and their welfare and for matters connected therewith and incidental thereto" ("The Transgender Persons (Protection of Rights) Act, 2019": 1). The Act ensures the rights of transgender students who can learn together with other students without any fear, bigotry, disregard, intimidation, and so on. The Act also ensures the prohibition against discrimination in employment or occupation and healthcare services. As per the Act, they are given the rights of movement, rights to reside, rent, or otherwise occupy any property, rights to access service, facility, benefit, privilege, or opportunity dedicated to using the general public or customarily obtainable the public.

Arundhati Roy deliberately and intensely reflects on the accurate panoramic picture of the Indian transgender community relegated to the status of mere subalterns who are by design devoiced by the influential people of society. She pleads to the readers to be compassionate to *hijras*. Her message is that their mental and physical pain should be felt. *Hijras* wish that their unheard voice be heard. The government's sincere attempt to implement strictly and meticulously the law and policy made to protect the rights of *hijras* can undoubtedly bring some, if not in its entirety, positive results. Besides the government's initiatives, man's positive thinking and attitude can contribute towards the constructive blotch on the racial memories of the descendants, and soon, indeed, *hijras* would not be treated as the 'Other' anymore.

Bibliography

Dattani, M. "Seven Steps Around the Fire": *Collected Plays*. New Delhi: Penguin Books, 2000.

Devor, A. H., and N. Matte. "One Inc. and Reed Erickson: The Uneasy Collaboration of Gay and Trans Activism, 1964–2003." In *The Transgender Studies Reader*, edited by S. Stryker and S. Whittle, 387. New York and Abingdon: Routledge, 2006.

Hine, S. "A Pathway to Diversity? Human Rights, Citizenship and Politics of Transgender." *Contemporary Politics* 15, no. 1 (2009).

Hines, S. and T. Sanger, eds. *Transgender Identities: Towards a Social Analysis of Gender Diversity*. New York: Routledge, 2010.

Raymond, J. *The Transsexual Empire*. New York: Teachers College Press, 1994.

Roy, A. *The Ministry of Utmost Happiness*. Gurgaon: Penguin Random House India, 2017.

Sharma, Dr. I. C. S. *Mahabharata: Sanskrit Text and English Translation*, edited by Om Nath Bimali. Delhi: Parimal Publications, 2004.

Stryker, S. *Transgender History: The Roots of Today's Revolution*. New York: Seal Press, 2017.

The Constitution of India (As on 1st April, 2019). Government of India, Ministry of Law and Justice. Legislative Department, 2019. 04 & 25.

"The Transgender Persons (Protection of Rights) Act, 2019." *The Gazette of India*, No. 40 (December 2019): 1–2. Accessed 22 May 2020. http://socialjustice.nic.in/writereaddata/UploadFile/TG%20bill%20gazette.pdf

Thomas, M and I. Steger. "Section 377: The Former British Colonies with Laws against Gay People — Quartz India." 07 September 2018. Accessed 25 October 2021. https://qz.com/india/1380947/section-377-the-former-british-colonies-with-laws-against-gay-people/

Valmiki. *The Ramayana*, translated by Ramesh Menon. New Delhi: HarperCollins Publishers India, 2010.

Wilchins, R. A. *Queer Theory, Gender Theory: An Instant Primer*. Los Angels: Alyson Books, 2004.

Chapter 2

Redefining Women, Reconstructing Space in Attia Hosain's *Sunlight on a Broken Column*

Afsha Naaz
GGS Indraprastha University, Delhi, India

Abstract

In the present scenario of social consciousness, the intercultural and interfaith dialogue is increasing to understand the other by breaking the wall of stereotypes and decolonising the minds. There is a need to understand gender and its performance in the same way. Literature—being the tool of communication and space for the reflection of our lives—has played its part in creating a more profound understanding for people with different and diverse experiences. However, misrepresentation and misinterpretation have also caused a great deal of misunderstanding. There is a need to develop new ways of seeing and knowing others to defy these distorted interpretations. Therefore, this chapter, based on Attia Hosain's *Sunlight on a Broken Column* (1961), is one such attempt to investigate the lives of Muslim women represented by a Muslim writer. The chapter tries to deconstruct the diversity among Muslim women and their agency in the private and public space. A woman has to perform different roles, from being a mother to the house's matriarch. Simultaneously, we will also see how the domestic sphere or the *zenana* works as a space of resistance and power for women.

Keywords: domestic sphere, power for women, space, space of resistance, Muslim women

* * *

Introduction

> The domestic space as the space of the normalizing, pastoralizing, and individuating techniques of modern power and police: the personal-is-the-political; the world-in-the-home.
>
> —Bhabha 1994: 36

To define a woman is to fix her into a particular mold, giving her a specific shape, allowing her very little or no space for alterity. While there have been several such attempts in history, it has recently become a part of the discourse that gender is a social construct. The French feminist S. de Beauvoir, in her book *The Second Sex* (1949), says, "One is not born, but rather becomes, a woman …; it is civilization as a whole that produces this creature … which is described as feminine" (De Beauvoir 1949: 267). In her book *Gender and the Politics of History* (1988), J. W. Scott suggests gender as a fluid category with no fixed meaning: "'Man' and 'woman' are at once empty and overflowing categories. Empty because they have no ultimate, transcendental meaning. Overflowing because even when they appear to be fixed, they still contain within them an alternative, denied, or suppressed definitions" (Scott 1988: 49). Therefore, gender is not biological and physiological but rather a psychological and socially constructed phenomenon, which always remains in a state of constant flux or fluidity. As a part of their colonial agenda, the Western narrative has always shown persistence and rigidity in portraying the Orient's women. Such imagined narratives have misrepresented and misinterpreted the performance of gender in the public and private space, especially in the attempt to describe the minority community and its culture.

In his book *Orientalism: Western Conceptions of the Orient* (1978), E. Said exposed the perception of European writers towards the East. As a part of the post-colonial zeal, the natives who were still subjects of stereotypes started writing back in the coloniser's language. The emergence of the native's narrative gained momentum soon afterward, where the writers started defying the stock characters and stock situations through which they were portrayed in literature. Writers such as R. K. Narayan and U. R. Ananthamurthy initiated the insider's perspective of their lived experience in literature and showed things in a more flesh-and-blood way. One such stock character in a stock situation represents Muslim women with no agency, always staying behind the veil or in an oppressive private sphere. The Muslim women in the nineteenth-century have been depicted as victims in their private rooms (known as the harem/*zenana*).

In general, the stereotyping of Indian women in colonial writings, although with different narratives, leads to making them into a particular category, whether Hindu women or Muslim women. Each type represents traditionally oppressed women by men, in need of sympathetic outsiders to redeem them from their household. To counter these colonial narratives of 'female emancipation,' the new politics of nationalism arose. In *The Nation and Its Fragments* (1993), P. Chatterjee notes how nationalism allocated different social roles of gender into the *world* and the *home*. The *world* is where the earthly life is organised and is the domain of the male. The *home* is where spiritual identity is reared, and it is the female's responsibility to take care of this space. This space of the *ghar* (home) is the microcosm of the nation with its distinct Eastern culture and tradition. It was essential to learn their techniques and match their strength to overthrow the colonisers. There was a need for modernity in both spheres without altering the core of the national culture located in the home. The women's question once again arose here. A model of a 'modern' woman was created. However, Chatterjee defines this model of a middle-class 'new woman' as educated and cultural under a new kind of patriarchy. The first thing to note here is this model did not encompass non-elite women. Neither lower-class women nor Muslim women were included in this categorisation. Second, this was when women did not gain the consciousness to speak for themselves.

Therefore, this chapter explores the alternate narrative of a Muslim woman's experience while growing up during the nationalist struggle in India. Through her narrative voice, we will enter into the corners of her private sphere—the home/*ghar*—the home that encapsulates the heterogeneous characters of Muslim women with a unique identity of their own. It defies the norms of an oppressive private sphere by giving different house charges to other women. The home also becomes the space of negotiation between traditions and modernity, the microcosm of the nation. There will also be a rift within the gender and between the gender. Thus, the Muslim household stands in transience with the changing political and social times during the early twentieth century.

The post-colonial writer A. Hosain, through her novel *Sunlight on a Broken Column* (1961), takes us into the deep recesses of the lived experiences of Muslim women in the *zenana* and the public sphere. The performances of these women, which up till now were seen through a perforated sheet in bits and pieces, have come to light in a fully transparent and fluid manner. Here, the female characters are not like the shadowy figures of Salman Rushdie's *Midnight's Children* (1981), or Anita Desai's *In Custody* (1984), with no voice of their own; rather, the characters here speak, act, and negotiate amidst the different gender and cultural binaries existing in colonial India. If Rushdie says, "[T]here are as many versions of India as Indians" (Rushdie 1989: 323), Hosain has shown these many versions of women through the diversity in her female characters. Therefore, the narrative of *Sunlight on a Broken Column* speaks beyond the national and cultural boundaries, connecting different experiences at once, just like the metaphor of space working in the text. H. K. Bhabha has defined this spirit of speaking beyond in *The Location of Culture* (1994) as "the move from the specific to the general, from the material to the metaphoric, is not a smooth passage of transition and transcendence" (1994: 8). This chapter, thus, is an attempt to reinterpret these metaphors through the analysis of *Sunlight on a Broken Column*, consequently making new ways of seeing and knowing the women and the space they inhabit.

Women's Space in Home and the World

According to Bhabha, "The boundary becomes the place from which something begins its presencing" (Bhabha 1994: 7). If the boundary is not something where the presence ends, but instead from where the presence begins, we need to understand this fluidity of demarcation between the private and the public sphere; where do the home end and the world begin? Is home the new world? Are boundaries rigid? We need to understand these binaries by deconstructing women's agency in the text's private and public space. The personal and public can also be taken as analogous to the home and the world, the internal and external, and the feminine and masculine space. There is already a diversity in terms of female characterisation in the novel; we have different women with different agencies regarding domestic, social, cultural, and public roles that they have to perform at *Ashiyana* (home) world outside. *Ashiyana* is the imaginative feudal home of the protagonist in Lucknow, where the central narrative of the text has been located. The novel itself opens in the interiority of *Ashiyana*, with the mobility of women characters inhabiting the space. The space of *Ashiyana* is explored with the progress of the narrative is a hybrid space with multiple characters belonging to different classes, castes, genders, religions, and cultures. They range from the patriarchs Baba Jan, Uncle Hamid, and Uncle Mohsin to the matriarchs Aunt Abida, Aunt Majda, girls such as Laila and Zahra, maidservants Saliman and Ramzano, the washerman and his daughter Nandi, the courtesan Mushtari Bai, the aristocrat Thakur Balbir Singh, and the characters from the West such as Mr. Freemantle, Mrs. Martin among others. It is also a space where interfaith festivals are observed, such as Muharram, Eid, Shubrat, Holi, and Diwali. Thus, this diverse space of *Ashiyana* represents the nation in transition during pre-colonial times. The transformation happening in the nation is reflective of *Ashiyana*. This is the home where the world lies. The home is adopting new ways of thinking, thereby metamorphosing itself from the realm of tradition into modern. Here, in this transition, it is essential to deconstruct the multidimensionality of Muslim women's agency in the domestic space and the world outside to understand the personal and the political. There are three kinds of women in the novel, traditional, modern, and the ones in between, showing mobility in private and public spaces. The paper tries to focus on one from each.

The main character from the traditional women with the agency is Aunt Abida. She is crucial in the narrative because she looks after the protagonist Laila and teaches her their cultural and moral values. She is the one who holds the entire familial presence in *Ashiyana* in the absence of the authority of the male members such as Uncle Hamid. Though she believes in the ideological principles of religion and always practices her morals of *izzat* (honour or prestige) and *sharam* (shame), this never restricts her from fulfilling her social responsibilities. Even after practising *purdah* (a state of seclusion or secrecy), she looks after her father, Baba Jan's accounts, and deals with the men outside the *zenana*. For her, the mind comes first, then the heart, and that is how she makes decisions on business matters, which stands in complete contrast with the stereotypical portrayal of the women of the East, shown as irrational, sensual, and oppressed under patriarchy. *Purdah* for Abida is not a material veil to cover the woman from head to toe but a sense of security to which she returns. From the opening of the novel, we are introduced to the mobility of Abida, coming out of the *zenana* and moving towards *mardana* (manly). "The day my aunt Abida moved from the zenana into the guest-room off the corridor that led to the men's wing of the house, within call of her father's room, we knew Baba Jan had not much longer to live." (Hosain 1992: 14)

The *zenana* is the women's secluded place, like the room of one's own where one thinks, acts, and grows, just like the space for men is the *mardana*. The boundary of these gendered spaces is not associated with Muslim culture only; such descriptions can also be found in Rama Mehta's *Inside the Haveli* (1977) and Rabindranath Tagore's *The Home and the World* (1916). Hosain shows the fluidity between these spaces with the mobility of the characters. Reina Lewis in *Rethinking Orientalism* (2004) states that these gendered spaces "produce a series of spatial relations which map the bodies moving through and around them with force both socializing and symbolic" (Lewis 2004: 79). Just like the flexibility between the binaries of spaces, the characters' minds are flexible. Despite being a traditional Muslim woman, Abida stands as the matriarchal echo of Baba Jan and places her opinions in the marriage of Laila and Zahra when Uncle Mohsin tries to take over. "The walls of this house are high enough, but they do not enclose a cemetery" (Hosain 1992: 21). Abida herself is "a scholar of Persian poetry and Arabic theology" (Hosain 1992: 20), but she is equally dynamic in providing Laila with Western education. Abida has a stronghold on everything that is there in *Ashiyana*. The domestic space is the space of power and agency for Abida. She asserts her identity and proves to be a perfect social mother, a custodian of values, and an ideal public administrator.

The other traditional characters with agency are Hakiman Bua, who nurses Laila and Zahra; Ustan Ji, who teaches Urdu, Persian, and Arabic; and the courtesan Mushtari Bai, who is the custodian of culture and represents the decline of the Mughal civilization in Lucknow. She also has authority among her circle, which saves the life of Asad in the novel. In contrast to traditional Muslim women with agency in the domestic space, we have Aunt Saira representing modern Muslim women, a blend of Eastern and Western culture. Aunt Saira, Uncle Hamid's echo, stands shoulder to shoulder with her husband regarding social responsibilities. She is a part of a women's social club and has occasional hybrid meetings with other women. She has her liberal ways of education and understands changing marriage culture. Both Laila and Zahra are on the way to becoming modern women like Aunt Saira. They are in a state of transition where they negotiate between culture, religion, tradition, and their own identities at times. With the transition in the nation and the simultaneous change in *Ashiyana*, only the spaces are transformed; women's agency remains the same. The traditional and the aesthetic interiority of *Ashiyana* get replaced with the Western replica of the household, the cultural evening or *Sham-e-Awadh* of Lucknow has been replaced with Vice Regal's visit parties, and the space of socialisation gets shifted from the verandah to the women's club.

Sunlight on a Broken Column as a Female Bildungsroman

It is essential to see the narrative of *Sunlight on a Broken Column* in the light of a *female bildungsroman* to understand how emerging modernity affected the home. The new ways that took over the old in every aspect—West-influenced education, acts of resistance, mobility outside the house, fleeting traditions, love, and marriage. How much is the concept of a 'new woman' (discussed earlier) applicable here?

Bildungsroman, which was popularised by Wilhelm Dilthey, is a German term coined by the philologist Karl Morgenstern in 1819. As explained by Dilthey, *Bildungsroman* "examines a regular course of development in the life of the individual; each of its stages has its own value, and each is at the same time the basis of a higher stage. The dissonances and conflicts of life appear as the necessary transit points of the individual on his way to maturity and harmony" (qtd. in Trites 2014: 23). Here, the chapter formulates Dilthey's argument in conjunction with C. Lazzaro-Weis' model of the *female bildungsroman* for classifying Hosain's novel into this genre. Here, a few models of the *female bildungsroman* are taken and collocated with the narrative. As much as there is a need to unsee the stereotype of oppressed women characters in the text, there is a need to see the agency of these women in the different spheres, where the private or the domestic space works as the space of power and resistance. The figures portrayed earlier as rigid are now dynamic women characters raising their voices and adapting to the change. Here, we will see the character of Laila in the light of a female bildungsroman and also the phases of her becoming a strong woman: "I imagined myself a poetic rebel against false values" (Hosain 1992: 311). To consider this novel as a *female bildungsroman*, we need to see Laila's overall growth in the novel. We need to look at how this novel is an amalgamation of two sub-genres of *bildungsroman*: *Entwicklungsroman*, which is a development novel of the growth of a character from childhood to maturity, and *Erizehungsroman*, which focuses on the education of the character.

The narrative of *Sunlight on a Broken Column* is happening in between the life of a timid girl of 15 and her evolution towards a woman in her mid-thirties with a life of her own amidst the restricting aura of her family's tradition. It is divided into four parts with different phases of Laila's life. Part one (moving from childhood to adolescence) opens when Laila is 15 and an orphan living under the patriarchal fear of her grandfather Baba Jan, bedridden and about to die in *Ashiyana*. In the second part (adolescent years), Laila has moved with her uncle's family and begins her college education. The third part (adolescence to adulthood) deals with Laila's decision-making power when she begins her postgraduate studies and falls in love with a man belonging to another branch, for which she chooses to leave everything behind. In the last part (adulthood), she revisits Hasanpur in 1952 after Ameer's death and has already learnt to live independently.

The first aspect of *a female bildungsroman* is the assertion of a 'coherent feminine self' against a rigid patriarchal structure (Lazzaro-Weis 1990: 18); in the beginning, it is Baba Jan, the supreme patriarchal pillar of the family, then it is Uncle Mohsin, and finally Uncle Hamid. Laila feels oppressed from the very beginning. She describes "the sick air, seeping and spreading, through the straggling house, weighed each day more oppressively on those who lived in it" (Hosain 1992: 14). "Zahra and I felt our girlhood a heavy burden" (Hosain 1992: 14), from the fearful authority of Baba Jan. "The very silence of the room imposed immobility. So, too did, my fear" (Hosain 1992: 30). Then it is Uncle Mohsin making decisions for other people's lives, which makes Laila angry, but Aunt Abida calms her. Laila represses her anger at this initial phase of her life, which keeps on building for her later revolutionary self: "The cold stone inside me was now burning lead" (Hosain 1992: 23). When Laila gets a blow from Uncle Mohsin's stick while rescuing Nandi, she cries, "I hate you, I hate you" (Hosain 1992: 28), for which she is highly unapologetic. Later, she is labelled as a revolutionary for her behaviour.

After the death of the supreme patriarchal figure, Laila and her fears begin to liberate: "[F]or a moment the fear of Death left me" (Hosain 1992: 82), and she "felt a strange sense of release" (Hosain 1992: 85). This liberation is depicted with motion images of the cinema, shops, and the *bazaar* (market) when moving to Hasanpur from *Ashiyana*, where she is 'out of *zenana*.' The change begins to occur in her, and she feels more enlivened. Now, her fears are only 'acquiescent.' In the second part, she asserts her choices when she sits in a 'cotton sari' among her Aunt's assembly of ladies. She voices her opinions, which are not supposed to be uttered among those so-called modern and elite women. She expresses herself freely on 'love' which stirs everyone, and she is labelled as a 'socialist.' But Laila cares little about their opinions now: "[T]hey seemed like paper figure, as hollow as their words, blown up with air. There was nothing in them to frighten me." (Hosain 1992: 133)

In the family, where marriage is unquestionably the elders' decision, an individual's choices don't matter. Zainab wants to marry Asad, but Asad wants to marry Zahra. Still, he is economically unfortunate, while Laila chooses to marry the man of her choice despite his low economic and social status, against her family, community, and society. In asserting her potential in front of Uncle Hamid's decisions, defying Aunt Saira's traditional thinking of a suitable boy, and neglecting Aunt Abida's teachings of fulfilling her 'duty,' Laila marries Ameer and leaves everything behind. Her realisation and recognition of the outside world can be traced towards the end of the novel, where she attains a state of maturity: "I felt a kind of wonder, as if, layers of a mask were flaking off" (Hosain 1992: 192). She sees the humane side of her uncle, the fragile side of Sita, and different faces of politics from the one she uses to talk with Asad. Because Ameer advises her that the only duty is to herself, she gradually realises the change in herself. Laila's development in the novel from a fragile and feared girl to a revolutionary and rebellious woman, over 20 years with a shifting landscape, shows the transcendence that Hosain can portray. From Laila's childhood uncertainties and the growing differences with others to the assertion of her subjectivity and absolute alienation, she makes her identity. Laila's act of resistance against patriarchy and the larger society makes her an autonomous new woman who is educated, cultured, and knows when to speak.

Conclusion

By deconstructing Muslim women's diversity in the text, we need to understand how they are not a singular monolithic subject of an outsider's imagination. The women here are not subaltern; instead, they speak, act, and negotiate. There is no romanticisation involved in threading the narrative; this is the story of the everyday lives of these women, where flaws of culture are exposed in the same capacity as the way they give power in specific ways. Thus, there is a growing need to hear these voices and alternately see these spaces. Between stereotyping and glorifying, we need to start normalising the lives of Muslim women and their sovereignty in the private space.

Bibliography

Bhabha, H. K. *The Location of Culture*. London: Routledge, 1994.

Chatterjee, P. *The Nation and Its Fragments: Colonial and Postcolonial Histories*. Princeton, N. J.: Princeton University Press, 1993.

De Beauvoir, S. *The Second Sex*. Translated by H. M. Parshley. New York: Knopf, 1953.

Desai, A. *In Custody*. New Delhi: Random House, 1984.

Hosain, A. *Sunlight on a Broken Column*. New Delhi: Penguin Books India, 1992.

Lazzaro-Weis, C. "The Female 'Bildungsroman': Calling It into Question." *NWSA Journal* 2, no. 1 (1990): 18.

Lewis, R. *Rethinking Orientalism: Women, Travel and the Ottoman Harem*. New York: I.B. Tauris, 2004.

Mehta, R. *Inside the Haveli*. New Delhi: Penguin Publishers, 1977.

Rushdie, S. *Midnight's Children*. New York: Alfred A. Knopf, 1989.

Said, E. W. *Orientalism: Western Conceptions of the Orient*. New Delhi: Penguin Books Pvt. Ltd, 2001.

Scott, J. W. *Gender and the Politics of History*. New York: Columbia University Press, 1988.

Tagore, R. *The Home and the World*. London: Macmillan, 1916.

Trites, R. *Literary Conceptualizations of Growth: Metaphors and Cognition in Adolescent*. Philadelphia: John Benjamins Publishing Company, 2014.

Chapter 3

Women in Premchand's Stories Are Types, Not Individuals: A Contemporary Study of Select Short Stories of Munshi Premchand

Shreya Ghosh
Holy Cross College, Tripura, India

Abstract

Munshi Premchand is one the most celebrated and noted fiction writers in Hindi and Urdu, and he remains persistently popular to date. From curriculums to personal book lists, Premchand's novels and short stories in Hindi and translations continue to be widely read and relevant. His writings are notable for a powerful portrayal of the lives of the beleaguered and the marginalised sections of society. Premchand, writing in early twentieth-century India, was aware of the grim realities of life as faced by those who were conveniently trampled underfoot by the mighty on the grounds of caste and gender. Premchand's awareness of the plight of women is a widely known fact. Although his portrayal of women is grossly termed as conservative in most cases, in the long run, he has proven himself to be ahead of his time in being critically observant of the agonies faced by women in a patriarchal society. His brilliant portrayal of women in their various roles provides an opportunity to study those times and the society's ideology that shaped their characters. However, humanity has considerably evolved over the ages, the agony of the poor, the oppressed, and the weak. This chapter attempts to study the dusty or troubled reality of pre-independent India, emphasizing women as they were depicted in the select short stories of Munshi Premchand. It is interesting to see how the author created characters as types, not as individuals that remain etched in readers' minds.

Keywords: women, pre-independent India, patriarchal society, characters as types

***

The notion of gender difference is primarily propaganda produced, cultivated, and reaped by the patriarchal society. This difference is invariably interpreted as being rooted in the natural order of things and is widely circulated by the custodians of society to shape mass consciousness. The subordination of women and the notion of female inferiority give rise to a vast repertoire of images, ideas, or notions constructed to stereotype women. Women always struggle to fit into the definition of "normal" as society expects them to accept the norms designed to curb their will, emotions, and expressions. Munshi Premchand, one of India's most prolific writers, was socially aware and particularly sensitive towards the role and position of women in society. He was committed to speaking for those who were denied speech on the grounds of their caste and gender, and his vast repertoire of works reflects his social awareness. In his introduction to the book titled, *Premchand: Stories on Women*, the editor, M. Asaduddin, writes that unlike most of his contemporaries, Premchand continues to be relevant till date mainly "in the contexts of Woman Question (*Stree Vimarsh*), Dalit Discourse (Dalit *Vimarsh*), Gandhian Nationalism, Hindu–Muslim Relations and the current debates of the idea of an inclusive India" (Premchand 2018: vii).

The timeline in which Premchand composed the significant bulk of his work witnessed the call for modernist reform. This modernist wave also paved the way for the reformation of the position of women in India. Women in those times were primarily confined to the four walls of their domestic domain. But the new wave did open the doors of advancement in education and jobs for at least some sections of women in society. However, for Indian reformists, modernity did not mean compromising with the quintessential Indian sensibility. Indian thinkers and reformists wanted to project the new India as modern as well as essentially Indian. In this regard, the Indian woman and her domestic household were projected as the torchbearer of the nation's identity, tradition, and culture. Thus the notion of ideal Indian womanhood was intertwined with the more significant concept of the new age of India, which was ready to challenge its colonial rulers and chart its course as a newly independent nation. The urge to project this new nation required a certain degree of a reshuffle of gender roles. But within the domestic realm, Indian women and their households were still dominated by the traditional patriarchal system. The call for equality and emancipation of women did bring some visible changes. Still, it did not pave the way for any formidable changes as patriarchy hardly let loose its grip within the domestic sphere.

Literature was quick to respond to the call for women's reform, and Munshi Premchand emerged as a prolific figure in this field. In Premchand's works, women appear in all possible roles from different strata of the social circle. In most of his works, the writer advocated the ideals of progressive reform to emancipate women from various social evils of contemporary times. Being a realist, he depicted the prevalent problems faced by women and hinted at the way for desirable changes in the future. To understand Premchand's portrayal of women, a consistent focus on the position of women in Indian households of the times is imperative. Speaking about the feminine identity in India, Sudhir Kakar explains that the matrix of her life cycle shapes the identity of an Indian woman from childhood to adulthood. In his book *The Inner World: A Psychoanalytic Study of Hindu Childhood and Society*, Kakar notes that the identity of an Indian woman is "wholly defined by her relationship to others" (Kakar 1981: 56). He further divides an Indian woman's evolution into three stages: "First, she is a daughter to her parents. Second, she is a wife to her husband (and daughter-in-law to his parents). Third, she is a mother to her sons (and daughters)" (Kakar 1981: 57). The final stage is the most significant one since motherhood gave a certification to the identity of an Indian woman, especially if the child was a son. Within the domestic sphere, every Indian woman finds herself jumping from one role to the other under strict patriarchal surveillance.

Premchand explored all possible angles of a woman's life—familial relations, social conditions, marital household, economic empowerment, and so forth. For him, a woman in her multiple roles—as a selfless mother, loving wife, independent working woman, or helpless widow—embodies the primary emotions of human nature. He essentially portrays women as obedient, cooperating, and sacrificing, and their strength lies in love, compassion, and their sense of duty or service despite all the agony they face. However, he also emphasised self-respect, individuality, emotional and economic empowerment, and rational ability in women. In most of his stories, he celebrates the ideals of selfless love, patience, duty, purity, and so forth in a woman. Some stories depict the plight of a married woman, while some paint the struggles of widowhood. We find women who protest and those who suffer; some describe the poor mother while some present the modern working woman. While most of these women are oppressed and suffer because of their class and gender, some simply refuse to accept oppression and defy the authority of their oppressors. Their protest necessarily could not bring much change, but their triumph lies in their courage to voice a challenge against the superiority of the higher castes and patriarchal order. Such narratives furnish hope for possible changes in the future, and their beauty and scope lies in the fact that they are marked by the dynamic changes of the superior-inferior equation in society. Reading these stories today, a reader will find those times exceedingly oppressive and suffocating, especially for the marginalised sections of society. C. Gupta, in her article "Portrayal of Women in Premchand's Stories: A Critique", writes: "It is only in the understanding of the tensions and contradictions within both ideology and society during that time and their reflection on Premchand that one can make an attempt to try and understand his portrayal of women" (Gupta 1991: 89).

However, the significance of Premchand's portrayal of women is not just because of his reformist zeal or his sympathetic approach towards women of those times. His writings offer an alternative reading of history from a woman's perspective. A detailed study of his narratives will undoubtedly shift the focus to the position of Indian women within their domestic households. Women were disempowered and silenced but what needs to be understood is why and how were they silenced? Culturally and socially, the structure and functioning of an Indian household are administered by the patriarchal order. But the dynamics of the domestic sphere cannot be understood only in terms of the binary positions of patriarchal domination and feminine subordination. In his book, Kakar observes that the focus has always been on men, from myths to anthropological accounts. He points out that women, irrespective of their class and caste, always pray for their son, not their daughter. In her essay, "Can the Subaltern Speak?", G. C. Spivak argues that the male gets priority in subaltern studies while speaking of the subaltern. Spivak explained that because of the ideological constraint of gender, women are silenced. But the problem worsens when the subaltern woman faces double subjugation, first, on the grounds of her caste and then on account of her gender. Thus the whole narrative is not just about male dominance and female subjugation. A detailed study of Premchand's stories will expose the contradictions within the paradigm of patriarchal domination and feminine entrapment.

This chapter aims to understand Premchand's depiction of women to study the underlying complexities of female entrapment and silence. His stories are not mere tales of human agony as they provide scope to analyse contemporary times from a woman's perspective. This alternative take on history reveals the socio-cultural ideologies of those times and helps to understand the psycho-social matrix of female consciousness. Premchand's skilled depiction of life established candid pictures of almost all types of women who lived during the early twentieth century. From those who defied social taboos to those who were dominated as well as those who readily accepted social notions of womanly conduct and even oppressed other women, Premchand's canvas has it all. He has presented each woman with such precision that each character evolves as a type and not just an individual. Moreover, Premchand's female protagonists are such that they cannot be read in isolation and can only be understood in the light of contemporary times. In this regard, this chapter considers some short stories of Premchand in English translation that appear in different volumes published by Penguin and edited by M. Asaduddin. The chapter primarily deals with select stories: "Tulia", "The Goddess from Heaven", "The Widow with Sons", "Sati", and "The Condemned" included in *Premchand:*

Stories on Women, "Temple" from *Premchand: The Complete Short Stories: Vol. III*, and "Thakur's Well" from *Stories on Caste*.

At the beginning of the story "The Goddess from Heaven", Premchand writes: "At home, tolerance, forgiveness, and compassion were quoted as divine virtues…" (Premchand 2018a: 30). Home, household, and family—the terms may differ, but the essence or emotion associated with it is universal. For most women, home constitutes their entire world. For eons, women have dedicated themselves to the act of nurturing and sustaining their families. It is not surprising to see women in that role because they are biologically, culturally, and ideologically seen as the nurturing figure who builds and nurtures the family with selfless love, compassion, constant adjustments, and forgiveness. It is needless to say that women are assigned different roles in their lives, among which the role of a mother and a wife is of paramount significance in the domestic sphere. In fact, in Premchand's times, marriage and family were the primary concerns in most women's lives. In her essay, C. Gupta writes, "At this time the prime institution of a traditional female world was the household. This was the focal point of female reproduction, domestic labour and of kinship relations" (Gupta 1991: 91).

In the stories "Tulia" and "The Goddess from Heaven", we see the image of a submissive woman, the one who accepts her life in the name of fate and performs her duties towards the family that they are married into. "Tulia" is the story of a woman whose marriage was fixed at the age of five to a man who left home to earn a livelihood but never returned. She is a devoted wife who exhibits patience to wait for her husband in a marriage reduced to some mere letters received from a far land. She upholds her chastity and dignity by renouncing the temptations of other men who tried to win her. In "The Goddess from Heaven", marriage demanded all kinds of adjustments from Leela. First, she struggled to fit in as a dutiful daughter-in-law and later, after the tragic death of her children, she had to preserve and protect her marriage when her husband got lured by other women. At the end of the story, she emerged as a broadminded, understanding, and forgiving wife who wins her husband back.

In these stories, the image of an ideal wife and her unparalleled devotion to the institution of marriage is beautifully brought to life. Premchand also highlights the position of women in Indian households. In those times, the prevalent social order expected women to maintain the sanctity of marriage and the family's reputation. With a bit of scope of intellectual liberation and financial independence, women were expected to be patient and compromise to fit into the notion of an ideal wife. However, women somehow managed to survive through the trials of patriarchy. Tulia indeed draws our pity, but she also draws admiration for being kind and intelligent. She rejected Bansi Singh's advancements and helped his widow get her share of property from Bansi's younger brother by duping him with her charm. Tulia gives shelter to Bansi's widow, but the authoritative nature of the higher caste *thakurain* (land-lady) towards Tulia also hints at the prevalent casteism of the day.

In "Goddess from Heaven", Leela faces problems in the domestic setting of her marital home. Being submissive, she was an easy target for her mother-in-law. Even though she and her husband were aware of the harassment, they could not protest against the hierarchical family order. Later, when Leela's husband flouts his marital vows, he is forgiven by the understanding wife. In his case, society readily accepts the man despite his misconduct, but society would not have received any such delinquency from a woman. As a young lonely married woman, was Tulia in a position to accept Bansi Singh's proposal?

In most cases, women have to accept social norms with silence, or else society will close down its doors. For Tulia and Leela, silence worked in their favour, mainly because their social and economic sustenance depended on their marriage. Moreover, these women also exhibit a deep-seated sense of loyalty and duty towards their husbands. In the story "Sati", Mulia, the epitome of devotion and faithfulness, is a poor victim of her husband's insecurity and suspicion. All these women felt it to be their utmost responsibility to support their husbands no matter how they conduct themselves. Thus, Premchand's female protagonists are not just individuals; they are embodiments of love, patience, loyalty, and forgiveness when it comes to family and marriage.

In some stories, the reformist in Premchand presents the stark reality of oppression faced by women, particularly the widows. In "A Positive Change", Bhungi, a needy, lower-caste woman, exhibits extreme courage to fight the oppressive higher caste *zamindar* (landlord). Living in extreme poverty, she chose hard work over begging to make ends meet. The zamindar's incessant tortures made her life miserable, and one day, Bhungi threw herself into the fire to put an end to her tormented life. The story ends on a positive note with Bhungi being saved and taken care of by the *zamindar*, but what makes her character remarkable is her undaunted courage even in the face of extreme adversity. "The Widow with Sons" depicts the life of an old widow facing injustice at the hands of her children. In this story, Phulmati's role and position in the family suddenly revert from being the driving force of the household to being nobody. Apart from being disrespectful and negligent, she also found her sons cheating their sister on her rightful share of the jewellery. Phulmati accepted a life of disgrace as the laws did not guarantee her any survivor benefits. In the end, she gets respite by drowning herself in the Ganges. Although Phulmati draws our sympathy, she also draws respect for her sense of dignity. She did not appear weak and worked as a maid to feed herself in a house where she was reduced to a non-entity.

In this story, Premchand raised the cause of a widow's financial and social security after her husband's demise. The cause of widow remarriage was also highlighted in his writings. "The Condemned" narrates the sad story of a young widow, Maani. Being an orphaned widow, she lived with her cruel uncle and aunt and later got married to her cousin Gokul's friend, much to the displeasure of her uncle and aunt. But her remarriage led to a massive brawl between Gokul and his family, following which the former left the house. Maani could not endure the harsh accusations of her aunt and committed suicide. The letter recovered after her death points at how society stigmatised a young widow and her choice to remarry. Unlike the docile-forgiving woman, Premchand presents a woman of courage in these stories. He was an advocate of various reforms for widows. But society in those times was not progressive, and the ending of the story "The Condemned" shows the conservative stance associated with widow remarriage.

Moreover, in most cases, married women oppressed widows within the domestic household. Neither did Phulmati's daughters-in-law stand by her, nor did Maani's aunt encourage her remarriage. However, even in their suffering, these women exhibited courage. With no scope of self-liberation, they had to accept the hardship, but they did not surrender to their oppressors. Bhungi did not leave the village to escape the tortures of the zamindar, while Phulmati chose to do all the household work for the food and shelter she received from her sons.

While most of these women discussed so far were victims of the matrix of dominance- subservience, some women characters of Premchand also put up a strong resistance against patriarchy. When we talk of women in early twentieth-century India, any discourse about the paradigm of oppression and resistance will expose its complexities. Women, especially those who belonged to the lower castes of society, faced double subjugation on the grounds of their gender and class. In her essay "Can the Subaltern Speak?", G. C. Spivak points out that women were silenced because of the ideological constraint of gender. Speaking about the position of the subaltern concerning the historiography of Indian nationalism, Spivak criticised the attempts made by the subaltern studies group to speak for the subalterns. She argues that the claim of speaking for the subalterns, in reality, silences them. She explains that the issue of gender further accentuates these complications. Problematising the historian's place, Spivak argues that in subaltern studies, while speaking of the subaltern, it is the male who gets priority both as the object of colonial historiographies and as the subject of insurgencies. She emphasises that the subaltern woman is deeply in the shadows because she faces double subjugation, first on the grounds of her caste and then on account of her gender.

Moreover, the notion of the oppressed native women was necessary to justify the emergence of the progressive modern man. The native woman called out for liberation, but Spivak explained her true voice was ventriloquised as she was always spoken for. In fact, the nationalists resurrected the voice of the native woman for their ends. Thus, the voice of the native subaltern woman got effaced in the discourse of both nationalism and colonialism.

Premchand's story "Temple" and "Thakur's Well" offer exciting insights into this connection. "Temple" narrates the story of Sukhiya, a poor, broken, widowed mother with a sick son who decides to perform a puja at the local temple for the recovery of her son. However, the custodians of religion and society did not allow people from the lower castes to enter the temples. Being a tanner woman, she could not enter the temple nor offer puja since this would make the deity "impure." But determined to seek blessings, Sukhiya protested with raging questions: "Is he only their thakurji? Doesn't he have any relationship with the poor like us? Who are these people to stop me?" (Premchand 2018b: 3). The story ends with the tragic death of Sukhiya and her son after they were beaten mercilessly for trying to enter the temple secretly. In "Thakur's Well", Jokhu and his wife Gangi belonged to the lower castes of society and were restricted to draw water from the well of the higher caste Thakurs. Gangi knew that the bad water they had access to is hazardous for them, and so driven by her sense of duty towards her sick husband, she decided to take the rebellious step of drawing water from Thakur's well. However, she braved all odds to draw water but eventually failed to succeed. On her return home, she found her husband drinking the same foul water.

Both stories depict the stark reality of class prejudice. If Sukhiya and Gangi were born into the higher castes of society, they would not have had faced any restrictions with performing puja or collecting water. Their gender, too, makes them easy targets of patriarchal and social oppression. But Sukhiya and Gangi do not accept authoritarianism of the patriarchal order with silence. Although they are entrapped within the system that has been operational for ages, they vehemently denied it. Without fearing the consequences, Sukhiya dared to enter the temple while Gangi went to the Thakur's well. Although their defiance could not enforce any desirable change in their situation, their acts of courage empowered them as individuals and added dignity to their characters.

Moreover, their defiance might be understood within the matrix of their sense of duty. In their respective roles of a mother and a wife, they were driven by service sentiment towards their families. The stories also reflect upon the hidden complications of the patriarchal social order. Spivak has rightly explained how women from higher castes are subaltern on the grounds of their gender and not by class. While Gangi was waiting for the right time to fetch water, she overheard the conversation between two women who belonged to the Thakur class. Their conversation exposed the state of disparity within the domestic domain, where they were treated as slaves by their husbands. But owing to their higher rank, they did enjoy some advantages compared to the likes of Sukhiya or Gangi. These complexities of the socio-patriarchal order provide a vivid picture of contemporary times, particularly in the context of the emancipation of women. But the stories also focus on the extent of change that Premchand envisioned for women in India, especially for those at the periphery of society.

Besides the weak and passive woman, Premchand also portrayed the strong and assertive woman in some of his stories. "Miss Padma" is a story of a modern, independent working woman. The story is worth mentioning for the character of Miss Padma, who chose to live with the man she loved without marrying him. In a country like India, marriage is perceived as a holy union, while society despises and stigmatises the concept of live-in relationships. Premchand was ahead of his time to portray a woman in a live-in relationship. Although the relationship was not successful, the idea was path-breaking when seen from the perspective of those times. Another important story is "Anubhab", which focuses on Mrs. Gyanchand in the backdrop of the nationalist movement. She decided to give shelter to a nationalist's wife after being alone with no social and monetary help. The story highlights the significance of women supporting other women in distress.

Being true to his art, Premchand thus provides a realistic picture of the poor state of women in the early half of twentieth-century India. This chapter attempted to study and understand the position of women in Indian households of the time. Premchand's narratives, known for their sympathetic portrayal of women, offer an alternative understanding of those times from the woman's perspective. In India, the focus has always been on men, and nothing much has been documented on women. But his women-centric narratives break this norm to bring the Indian woman from the periphery to the center. His portrayals of a submissive wife, a helpless widow, or a selfless mother were true to life. These stock images of womanhood provide a comprehensive idea about ideal Indian womanhood as projected by the patriarchal social order. But the interesting aspect of his stories is that Premchand focuses on the deviations from the popular notion of womanhood to root for desirable changes in the future. Moreover, it is interesting to understand the complications and the contradictions involved within the space between patriarchal dominance and feminine entrapment.

Bibliography

Gupta, C. "Portrayal of Women in Premchand's Stories: A Critique". *Social Scientist* 19, no. 5/6 (1991): 89–91.

Kakar, S. *The Inner World: A Psychoanalytic Study of Childhood and Society in India*. New Delhi: Oxford University Press, 1981.

Premchand, M. *Premchand: Stories on Women*. Edited by M. Asaduddin. New Delhi: Penguin Random House, 2018a.

———. *Premchand: The Complete Short Stories, Vol. III*. Edited by M. Asaduddin. New Delhi: Penguin Random House, 2018b.

———. *Stories on Caste*. Edited by M. Asaduddin. New Delhi: Penguin Random House, 2018c.

Spivak, G. C. 'Can the Subaltern speak?' *Die Philosophin* 14, no. 27 (1988): 42–58.

Chapter 4

The God of Small Things: Revisiting the Bible of the Indian Feminist Movement

Mohosin Mandal
Aligarh Muslim University, Uttar Pradesh, India

Abstract

The God of Small Things, Arundhati Roy's debut novel, stirred the Indian academic discourse after being published in 1997. Roy, a very talented writer, did not leave any issue untouched that Indian women face in their lives, such as marriage, motherhood, divorce, female education, domestic violence, or discrimination inside the home. Roy's female characters challenge the old patriarchal systems and expose the unholy nexus among the institutions. She ventures to talk about inter-caste love and the sexuality of mothers. She chooses issues such as motherhood and makes the audacious attempt of raising the theme of the sexuality of a mother, which no Indian author had dealt with before. Roy, through her narrative, has proposed the way out of patriarchy.

Keywords: Marriage, motherhood, sexuality, patriarchy, resistance

* * *

Arundhati Roy's debut novel, *The God of Small Things*, a milestone in the history of the Indian feminist movement, stirred the Indian academic discourse after being published in 1997. Roy broke the taboos of inter-caste relationships, extramarital affairs, female sexuality, and divorce. Further, she exposed the hypocrisy of society so vividly that the conventional readers were not prepared to witness it. Roy shook the readers' conscience and did not leave any issue untouched that Indian women face, be it marriage, motherhood, divorce, female education, domestic violence, or discrimination inside the home. The male-dominated society monitors female sexuality to maintain the male monopoly, and myths, religious scriptures, laws of the society, and value systems function together to assert sexual dominion. "Sexual dominion obtains nevertheless perhaps the most pervasive ideology of our culture and provides its most fundamental concept of power" (Millett 1990: 25). "Multiple, local and unstable relations of power are seen as inherent in all human interactions, and as constituting the foundation for global states of domination such as Capitalism, patriarchy and racism" (Deacon 1998: 113). Roy's female characters challenge the old patriarchal system and expose the unholy nexus among the institutions.

Roy made the audacious attempt to raise the theme of the sexuality of a mother, which no Indian author had dealt with before. "The sacralised attitude towards mothers and the unwritten taboo on exploring sexuality have almost silenced Indo-English women's writing on sexuality and therefore on exploring motherhood" (Chanda 2002: 74). She chose motherhood to glorify and divulge how patriarchy operates at different levels and wrote about "women from three generations with a purpose to focus on three types of women characters — submissive, rebellious, and transgressive" (Islam 2012: 111) in *The God of Small Things*. They could not overturn the age-old traditions, but they (particularly the women of the second and third generations) convulsed the base of the patriarchal structure. Ammu, the tragic heroine, had a very traumatic childhood as domestic violence spoiled her childhood imagination. Her father abused her mother physically, which had a distressing effect on her psychology.

In India, there is a long social history of family's obstructing women's aspirations for knowledge. Roy raises the issue that a girl's education and aspirations to pursue an academic career have no significance for the chauvinistic male society. The larger institution of patriarchy also controls education. Like other institutions, it frames the psyche of women in favour of domination. Women are supposed to play the role of a mother, daughter-in-law, and wife. The institution deliberately keeps them illiterate and forces them to spend their entire lives in the service of the male members of the family. Ammu is the victim of gender discrimination in her own family, whose higher education is considered a waste of money by Pappachi (her father).

In contrast, Pappachi sends his son Chacko to Oxford for higher studies. The discrimination between Chacko and Ammu reminds us of Virginia Woolf's hypothetical comparison between Shakespeare and his imaginary sister in *A Room of One's Own*: "What would have happened had Shakespeare had a wonderfully gifted sister, called Judith" (Woolf 2000: 48). Thus Woolf starts and goes on imagining her possible fate:

> She was as adventurous, as imaginative, as agog to see the world as he was. But she was not sent to school. She had no chance of learning grammar and logic... Soon, however, before she was out of her teens, she was to be betrothed to the son of a neighbouring wool-stapler. She cried out that marriage was hateful to her, and for that, she was severely

beaten by her father. Then he ceased to scold her. He begged her instead not to hurt him, not to shame him in this matter of her marriage.... How could she disobey him? How could she break his heart? The force of her gift alone drove her to it. She made up a small parcel of her belongings ... took the road to London ... she had the quickest fancy, a gift like her brother's, for the tune of words. Like him, she had a taste for the theatre ... she wanted to act, she said. Men laughed in her face. The manager [said]... no woman ... could possibly be an actress. She could get no training ... who shall measure the heat and violence of the poet's heart when caught and tangled in a woman's body? —killed herself one winter's night and lies buried at some crossroads. (Wolf 2000: 48–49)

In a patriarchal society, marriage is an indispensable event in a girl's life. Preparing the psychology of girls in favour of marriage starts at the very earliest stage of their lives. All the social institutions, cultures, and traditions join hands in this process. Ammu, too, experiences the same fate. She has nothing to do at Ayemenem other than waiting for marriage proposals. In our social setup, as said by S. de Beauvoir in *The Second Sex*, "for girls marriage is the only means of integration in the community" (de Beauvoir 1953: 447). Still, no proposal comes her way because her father does not have enough money to raise a suitable dowry.

Long-suffering Ammu becomes frantic. All she wants is an escape from the stagnant life. One day she gets a chance to spend a summer with a distant aunt in Calcutta, where she meets a young man who proposes to her. Ammu accepts the proposal, although she knows him very little because she had no choice but to take a stranger as her husband. She thinks that it is better to marry him than to return to Ayemenem, but she realises very soon that she has made a wrong choice. Her husband loses his job is an alcoholic, drinking drives him into an alcoholic stupor. His boss Mr. Hollick, has an evil eye on his beautiful wife. He suggests that Ammu's husband go on leave and send Ammu to his bungalow. Her husband, who has no sense of self-dignity and self-respect, agrees to send his wife to the pervert boss to save his job. This inhuman decision by her husband traumatises her. Out of humiliation and anger, she is wholly numbed. Her husband grows uncomfortable and starts abusing her physically. However, Ammu is not one to receive a blow passively like her mother. She hits back and takes the heaviest book she can find on the bookshelf, and hits him back with it as hard as she can on his head, legs, back, and shoulders. He apologises for the violence when he regains consciousness but insisted on saving her transfer. She leaves him and returns to her parental home.

When a woman leaves for her in-laws, the doors of her parental home are closed for her permanently. After coming to her parents' house, Ammu realises that she is a woman of nowhere and has escaped individual torture to be subjected to collective rage. Baby Kochamma, Mammachi, Chacko, and Police Inspector Thomas Mathew all join hands to torture her physically and mentally. They constantly force her to accept her position in her parents' house as a divorced woman. As she married a person who was outside her caste and religion, her situation is worse. According to Baby Kochamma, a daughter, after marriage, has no place in her parents' home, and a divorced daughter who dared to make love marriage without the consent of family and that too with the man from another caste has no position at all.

Though Ammu undertakes as much responsibility in the factory as Chacko, he always refers to it as his factory, pineapples, and pickles whenever he is dealing with food inspectors or sanitary engineers. Legally, this is the case because Ammu, as a daughter, has no claim on the property. Chacko declares that Ammu has no claim over the properties, "what's yours is mine and what's mine is also mine" (Roy 2002: 57). The rebellious spirit in Ammu does not allow her to accept the limits of her divorcee status. She breaks the age-old love laws, shows the courage to reclaim her body, and dares to enter into an illicit sexual relationship with an untouchable Paravan, who is socially, culturally, and economically inferior to her. The subaltern male and the subordinated female in *The God of Small Things* become comrades-in-arms in a losing battle against the forces of oppression. In this context, Nivedita Menon, an Indian feminist scholar, writes about accepted sexual behaviour in society and remarks that compulsory heterosexual marriage is the only mode of union for couples. Any deviation is considered a threat to the established order. The hierarchy is well-maintained inside the family: "a Man, his wife, his children" (Menon 2012: 5).

When the relationship is revealed, Ammu has to go through extreme physical and mental torture at the hands of Mammachi and Baby Kochamma, who lock her up. Inspector Mathew's harassment of Ammu shows how patriarchy works at the administrative level. He humiliates Ammu and hurls insults at her. He says police administration serves only to protect the dignity of modest women, not the women of ill reputation. On the contrary, he thinks that society has given him the right to abuse Ammu sexually. The police inspector instead of assisting her, touched her improperly as if men with higher authority have the licence to exploit women physically. M. Foucault observed that there is no such thing as power, but power exists through relationships. In *Discipline and Punish: The Birth of the Prison,* he aptly remarks: "[I]s it surprising that prisons resemble factories, schools, barracks, hospitals which all resemble prison?" (Foucault 1995: 228).

Manusmriti, the Laws of Manu, which has a tremendous effect on Indian society even now, instructs women to be chaste even after the death of their husbands. It says, "A virtuous wife who after the death of her husband constantly remains chaste, reaches heaven…" (Manu 1886: 160). Otherwise, suffering and punishment wait for a widow if she is found guilty of following her carnal desires after the demise of her husband. Patriarchal institutions exercise violence to establish and maintain hegemony. Michel Foucault in *The History of Sexuality* comments that "[m]odern society has attempted to reduce sexuality to the couple—the heterosexual couple and in-so-far as possible, legitimate couple" (Foucault 1998: 45). A patriarchal society is the state's concern too, which imposes a cycle of prohibitions and even uses violence as a tool to control sexuality. All the patriarchal institutions (state, educational institutions, religious institutions, and medical sectors) are entrusted with monitoring sexuality. Chako asks Ammu to get away from the house; otherwise, he would assault her bitterly. Helpless, Ammu had no other option but to leave Chacko's house and dies at the age of 31 in a grimy hotel room. Even death does not end her humiliation as a church repeatedly denies to bury her. Nobody from her family except Rahel and Chacko is present at the funeral. Finally, she becomes a number, Receipt No. Q 498673.

Although her lone battle against patriarchal norms failed, she deserves to be acclaimed. She confronted the androcentric notions of society by refusing a surname for Estha and Rahel because she thought that choosing between her husband's and father's name did not give a woman the right to choose her own identity. She also rejected the patriarchal notion that a single mother could not raise her children properly and that a child must need a father. She tries her best to teach her children good manners to avoid the lack in their upbringing. She gives them the love and care of a father and a mother, defying the societal notion that a woman cannot rear up a woman singlehandedly, for right upbringing, one needs a father.

Ammu's daughter, Rahel, the third-generation woman in the novel, is far different in temperament and attitude from Ammu and Mammachi. She defies the authority of the father, husband, and brother. She is the symbol of an emancipated woman, fond of living her own way and confronting all the traditions, customs, and laws designed to suppress women. When she meets Larry McCaslin, a research scholar of Architecture from Boston, she does not think twice about marrying him. However, Rahel's married life does not run smoothly. Larry fails to understand his wife; whose eyes offend him.

Finally, Rahel divorces Larry when she understands the futility of their relationship. Divorce is not a scandalous affair for her. She casually informs K.N.M. Pillai about her divorce: "[W]e're divorced." (Roy 2002: 130), and she pronounces the word divorce, a thing society considers such a scandalous thing in such a light manner as if it has no considerable bearing on her life. She is an optimist and not in despair. What Larry sees in her eyes is a kind of obligatory optimism. The optimism in Rahel makes her confident enough to choose her career independently and the separation from Larry never leaves her depressed. Ammu has to pay with her life for defying the laws of love imposed on her by patriarchal society. Rahel knows very well about the destructive consequences of doing anything that the orthodox community does not approve of. Despite this, she is considered more dangerous by society's moral radar than her mother. She forms an incestuous relationship with her brother at the age of 30, which society cannot bear at any cost. J. Butler in *Gender Trouble* analyses that "the taboo against incest and implicitly against homosexuality is a repressive injunction which presumes and original desire localized in the notion of 'dispositions' which suffers a repression..." (2015: 89). Rahel does not care a fig, and here lies the victory for women, which Rahel wins.

Besides presenting these two rebellious women, Roy offers some token women characters in the form of Mammachi and Baby Kochamma. Mammachi, a woman of the first generation in the novel, is a role model for the traditional Indian woman. She is submissive, gentle, tame, and meek. Women such as Mammachi are not uncommon in Indian society. They are subject to constant ill-treatment and torment by their husbands, who think of their wives as their legal, economic, and sexual property. She is treated as an object and not a human being who might have emotions and feelings and wishes to live in her own way. Pappachi, a sadist, beats Mammachi regularly every night with a brass flower vase. Mammachi suffers this disgrace and dishonour regularly till one day Chacko stops her by twisting her vase-hand around her back and warns to never happen it again. It is a great irony that Mammachi escapes from the cruel clutches of her savage husband only to enter into the new trap of her son, another agent of the patriarchy. He dispossesses her from her pickle factory.

Mammachi's suffering at the hands of her sadist husband stimulates the readers' sympathy, but her change of mentality and negative attitude towards her daughter also shocks the readers. In collaboration with her son, she and Chacko do to Ammu what her husband did to her. She starts acting as an agent of this male-dominated society. She perpetually makes Ammu realising that she, being a divorcee, has no right in the Ayemenem House. Although both Ammu and Chacko are divorcees, Mammachi treats them differently. Her attitude towards Chacko is submissive and obedient, but towards Ammu, she is dictatorial. Mammachi approves of Chacko's illicit sexual relationship with pretty women working in the factory as it is well accepted in the society. However, her attitude towards Ammu in a similar situation is just the opposite. She brutally punishes Ammu when the latter satisfies her women's needs. Mammachi's attitude towards Margaret Kochamma (daughter-in law) also shows the patriarchal bent of her mind. She sees Margaret not just as a woman coming to meet her ex-husband for a purpose other than sex, but labels her a whore. Actually, in patriarchy, women who themselves are victims of the structure unknowingly became carriers of the system. Foucault describes the concept of 'Panopticism' in *Discipline and Punish: The Birth of the Prison*. He says that sometimes the victims are "caught up in a power situation [in the power structure] of which they are themselves the bearers" (Foucault 1995: 201).

Baby Kochamma, another woman, acts as a vile agent of the male chauvinistic society. She is the culprit who ruins the lives of Ammu, Estha, Rahel, and Velutha. She is the victim of patriarchy. In her youth, she had fallen in love with father Mulligan, a handsome Irish monk. To be with him, she converts to the Roman Catholic belief against her father's will so that she can be near to Father Mulligan. When she realises the futility of her efforts to get to her loved one, frustrated Baby Kochamma comes back home to her father. It is interesting to note that Baby Kochamma's father could not understand his young daughter's motive for converting to the Roman Catholic faith. Baby Kochamma's father realises that his daughter has developed a 'reputation' and is better to let her pursue education, as there is no possibility of getting her married. Thus, he makes arrangements for her education at the University of Rochester in America. This passage voices patriarchal prejudice, which considers the daughter's education a poor substitute for marriage, not as something desirable and valuable for its own sake.

Roy suggests that tyrannising women was so common that it was uniformly seen among the rich and the poor. We get the reference of the Kathakali men who beat their wives. We also get the reference of the Naxalites who raped the tribal women. Arundhati Roy shocks and delights her audience by rejecting traditional expectations, especially those related to the myths of patriarchy. The masculine complacency is shattered in the novel when marriage becomes deromanticised. Ammu's wedding with a person, after a period of courtship that lasts for five days, best exemplifies this. Roy achieves the same effect again while describing Rahel's marriage: "Rahel drifted into marriage like a passenger drifts towards an unoccupied chair in an airport lounge with a sitting down sense." (Roy 2002: 18). While the first instance reflects the hollowness of the marriage system, the second one shows its triviality. R. E. Karen, in "Feminism and Fairy Tales", reflects that "culture's very survival depends upon a woman's acceptance of roles" (Karen 1986: 210). Both Ammu and Rahel refuse to accept the prescribed behaviour and venture to talk about inter-caste love (especially when the woman is from a higher caste as the core of Brahminical patriarchy is dependent on control over women's sexuality).

Bibliography

De Beauvoir, S. *The Second Sex*. Translated by H. M. Parshley. New York: Knopf, 1953.

Butler, J. *Gender Trouble*. New York: Routledge, 2015.

Chanda, S. G. "Mapping Motherhood; The Fiction of Anita Desai." *Journal of the Association for Research on Mothering* 4, no. 2 (2002): 74.

Deacon, R. "Strategies of Governance: Michel Foucault on Power." *Theoria: A Journal of Social and Political Theory*, no. 2 (December 1998): 113–148.

Foucault, M. *The History of Sexuality*. London: Penguin Books, 1998.

———. *Discipline and Punish*: The Birth of the Prison. New York: Vintage Books 1995.

Islam, S. "What's Your is Mine and What's Mine is also Mine." *International Journal of English and Literature* 2, no. 3 (Sep. 2012): 111.

Manu. *Manusmriti*. Translated by George Buhler. Oxford: Clarendon Press, 1886.

Menon, N. *Seeing Like a Feminist*. Gurgaon: Penguin Random House India, 2012.

Millett, K. *Sexual Politics*. New York: University of Illinois Press, 1990.

Rowe, K. E. "Feminism and Fairy Tales." In *Don't Bet on the Prince; Contemporary Feminist Fairy Tales in North America and England*. Edited by Jack Zipes, 210. Aldershot: Gower, 1986.

Roy, A. *The God of Small Things*. New Delhi: Penguin Books India, 2002.

Woolf, V. *A Room of One's Own*. London: Modern Classics, 2000.

Chapter 5

Bodies that Matter: Interrogating the Discourses around the 'Body' in Samina Ali's *Madras on Rainy Days*

Hasina Wahida
Aliah University, West Bengal, india

Abstract

The 'body' has long been a discourse site in our understanding of social and cultural theory since the emergence of feminist studies or feminist reflections in the western world. The centrality of the 'body' as the locus of relationships in the heteronormative social structure has baffled readers and critics alike. Many writers have tried to scrutinise the cultural implications surrounding the 'body' and have endeavoured to reflect upon the possibilities beyond the socially registered heteronormative framework. This chapter aims to look into the myriad possibilities and presences surrounding the 'body' and project the problematics regarding the various concerns of the body's identity through Samina Ali's novel *Madras on Rainy Days*.

Keywords: 'body', feminist studies, heteronormative social structure, the identity

* * *

In her novel *Madras on Rainy Days*, Samina Ali offers a multidimensional view of the concept of the 'body' as recognised and understood in human society. It is challenging to pin down the discussion on the novel to a single standpoint, as the idea of the 'body' traverses beyond the conventional understanding of the female body. In the story, the very notion of the 'female body' is asserted because here 'body' iterates the picture of a naked 'female body' with breast and vagina, which are the signifiers of the class feminine. Critic such as S. Ortner and J. Butler have interrogated the relationship of the sexes with the idea of nature and culture. While Butler is of the notion, unlike Simone de Beauvoir, that both sex and gender are culturally constructed, Ortner in the article, titled "Is Female to Male as Nature is to Culture?" talks about female appropriation and inclusivity in social roles to minimise and obliterate women's objectification. Samina Ali's novel *Madras on Rainy Days* penetrates the 'body', both male and female, and interrogates the nature and the identity of the subject.

The narration circles around four individuals, two of the female sex and two of the male sex, and probes their true *identity* beyond that designated by society. The emphasis is on identity because the characters are in a quest to recognise their own selves. While the female self of Layla tries to negotiate with the religious, social, and cultural identities ascribed to her, Sameer and Naveed try to resolve the crisis of their sexual identity. Layla's relationship with her cousin Henna, founded on a bond of sisterhood, has in it subtler implications that give them shelter and repose, which is eventually lost through the rape and murder of the pregnant Henna. The rape of the 'female body' could be another dimension towards the identification of feminist discourse.

The trope of 'place' becomes a signifier as Layla sees America as a life of luxury and unboundedness (though her own premarital and mother's life had not been enjoyable, even in America). Sameer sees it as untied, boundless, and free (free from social shackles and the enforced stigma). The characters revolve around the innumerable binaries between the cultures in India and America on the outside and between their sexual identities on the inside. This chapter shall endeavour to look into the various concerns of the identity of the body or, to borrow from Butler's book *Bodies that Matter*, the idea of bodies that matter and try to situate Samina Ali into the new tradition of feminism. Butler writes in her "Preface" to *Bodies that Matter*:

> I began writing this book by trying to consider the materiality of the body only to find that the thought of materiality invariably moved me into other domains.... Not only did bodies tend to indicate a world beyond themselves, but this movement beyond their own boundaries, a movement of boundary itself, appeared to be quite central to what bodies 'are.' (Butler 2011: viii)

The centrality of the 'body' as an agency operates throughout the novel: first, in the form of male domination and assertion over the female body; second, through the religious dimension as the female becomes the subject and tool of sacred concoction or interpretation; third, through the cultural dimension where the narrative traverses between life in India and America; and finally, through the twist with the male too becoming a victim of patriarchy. Therefore, the narrative navigates through cultural, religious, and natural domains of sexual identity, offering a multifaceted understanding of femininity in the novel.

Butler uses the term 'policing gender' that is sometimes used as a way of "securing heterosexuality" (Butler 2010: xii) in her 1999 "Preface" to the book *Gender Trouble: Feminism and the Subversion of Identity*. Butler points out that the enforcement of sexuality is a social and cultural practice by heteronormative society or the society that accepts normative heterosexuality as the only standard. Sameer's gay identity needs to be shielded or masked, and to do that; society keeps up its vigil. Despite knowing that Sameer is homosexual, his parents marry him off to Layla. The world is shown the bloodstained handkerchief on the day after the *nikaah* (marriage) as a sign of victory for Sameer having had sex or intercourse with a virgin wife. However, the truth is that it was needed to ensure that he has succeeded in having physical consummation with someone of the opposite sex, which is considered to be normal in a heteronormative power structure. Like the Ixion's wheel, Layla, Sameer, and Naveed bound together are destined to spin for eternity on the wheel of patriarchy. The discussion may be carried further by dividing the chapter into religious, cultural, and sexual aspects to examine the underpinnings in the writing of Samina Ali. The novel *Madras on Rainy Days* is set in a Muslim household in Hyderabad with Layla growing up in between America and India, born to a doctor father who has divorced her mother and has taken a second wife. The novel centers on the marriage of Layla. The chapters are named "*Mungni*" (Engagement), "*Shaitan*" (The Devil), "*Mehndi*" (The bride's hand-dyeing ceremony), "*Sus'ral*" (In-Laws Place), "*Aysh*" (Enjoyment), "*Myka*" (Mother's place), and "*Ghum*" (Disappearance).

The novel begins with Layla objecting to the marriage. She is an American girl perplexed by the contrast between the liberty given to the American people and her Indian Muslim identity that requires adherence to some moral codes of conduct and ethical practices. There is a strange amalgamation of religion and culture to limit the boundaries of a woman. Being a Muslim girl of a conservative family, it is imperative to consent to the marriage fixed by her parents and relatives. The exciting part is that Islam guarantees the right of choice, and in Islamic practice, a woman's prior consent is mandatory before the marriage is solemnised. However, society and culture have their interpretations. While Islamic jurisprudence is followed, invisible surveillance hardly allows women to deny a marriage proposal. There is a close relationship between religion and understanding of gender, but the homogenisation of experiences based on some universalistic constructions tends to endanger the subject position of the person under question. In the book *Troubling Muslim Youth Identities: Nation, Religion, Gender*, B. Crossouard et al. have pointed out how building up an identity is based on many localised factors. The discourses and particular histories of a place play a crucial role in the identity claims of belonging and distinction.

As far as Layla is concerned, she was lying on her aunt's marriage bed. Marriage is associated with the body—the consummation leading to the ultimate surrender of the woman, which implicitly announces the victory of patriarchy. Interestingly, the girl is burdened with social stigma even before marriage. The question of choice is severely mocked when the girl denying the marriage is labelled a whore or a prostitute by her mother. Sex is the central point of control of patriarchy. While sex before or without marriage is considered taboo, marrying an unknown person and surrendering the body to him is deemed 'marital sanctity' and a white flag of the woman's surrender and man's victory. Lying on her aunt's bed, Layla picturises her aunt's surrender to her husband and his family:

> … She saw my uncle's face for the first time that evening when he made love to her—not on the soft red velvet that covered the mattress for this celebration, but carefully positioned on top of the two-by-two-foot white sheet that would give more validity to this union than her wedding necklace or their vows. The next morning, he hung the red spotted cloth on the clothesline and it fluttered in the wind for all to see, a white flag of her surrender and his victory. Then she, having proven herself worthy of him, began the long process of forgetting her own family to become integrated with my own. (Ali 2004: 8)

The centrality of a woman's existence is her body. Thinkers such as S. de Beauvoir, K. Millett, or G. Greer, and even Shulamith Firestone have developed their understanding of the female body by infusing in it the social and political context. While de Beauvoir considers sex as biological and gender created by patriarchy to discriminate, women must be aware of the difference meted out to them. On the other hand, Millett examines the writings of male writers such as Henry Miller, Norman Mailer, and J. Genet and formulates a sexual overview of patriarchy as a political institution. Germaine Greer in her book *The Female Eunuch* observes that "a systematic deconstruction of ideas of womanhood and femininity. She argues that women are forced to assume submissive roles in society to fulfill male fantasies of what being a woman entails" (qtd. in Booner 2019: 151). Layla wants to make a difference by having sex with a white boy in America, but it results in her getting pregnant and her subsequent abortion. These are considered unethical according to the dictates of Islamic law and are also not recognised in the Indian tradition. However, though Layla defies such conventional and religious ethics, she agrees to the marriage decided by her family.

Moreover, she must also visit an *alim* instead of a regular doctor. Interestingly, the word *alim* (all-knowing) is one of the names of God in Islam. Layla visits along with her mother and Abu uncle cannot provide medical relief to her abdominal pain and continuing periods but seems to know what she has been through. Ali here makes a strange case for religious faith and truth where the blind *alim* is presented as a visionary. Ironically, the *alim* becomes true to his name (the all-knowing) as he unknowingly says that the American way of life is strange and not according to the dictates of Islam and that the girl needs medical attention and not any spiritual tonic. He also makes an uncomfortable disclosure when he remembers that Sameer is a boy with a limp on his feet who had an accident in his teens. His mother has brought him to the *alim* for a cure instead of visiting a regular doctor. Layla's mother is in disbelief, and she denies that her daughter will marry the slightly physically challenged boy.

Economic dependence is one of the prime reasons women cannot fight the injustices that are meted out. Many feminists of the first wave and the second wave have talked about the need to bring women out of the male economic power apparatus. As believed by many, women should come out from the confined role of the housewife and join the workforce outside, but others are skeptical about the feasibility of this approach. Socialist feminists, for instance, believe that patriarchy and capitalism are combined into one system. They assert the need for change in public attitude so that women can be integrated into all levels of society. It is already stated that Layla's father has divorced her mother and has taken a second wife, but they are economically dependent on him for their sustenance. Even the family and relatives in India are unaware of this divorce. It is not that the disclosure would bring any discredit to the father whose second wife and children are readily and unquestioningly accepted in the household because Islam, after all, consents to four marriages. But that the first wife is separated from her husband and lives with her daughter alone in America would raise questions. Layla's mother alone has to bear the brunt of all the caustic comments and be socially ostracised. The father, therefore, comes to attend his daughter's wedding arranged by the mother.

Interestingly, though legally they are divorced, the man still holds his authority over the physical 'body' of the mother and the daughter. When Layla, on the day of her marriage, insists that her mother does away with her father, the man overhears and comes to assault Layla physically: "...his light eyes dark with anger. The demon in him coming out" (Ali 2004: 86). The cruelty and power of patriarchy silence the woman and make her invisible. A father is even calling his daughter a *randi* (whore), and that too on her wedding day. The plight of a woman is transferred from the domination of one to the other. The essence of feminism is choice, the right to choose one's way of life not dictated by any laws.

Interestingly, as Ali points out in several of her lectures, Islam does give reverence to women. Still, it is through the deliberate misrepresentation and misinterpretation of its dictates that patriarchy is exhibited. Women should know less of their rights so that they could be kept under control. It is her silence, her crippled existence, which leads to her invisibility. Sameer is crippled physically, while Layla and her mother are crippled psychologically.

P. Myrne, in her chapter "Women and Sexual Rights" in *Female Sexuality in the Early Medieval Islamic World*, brings in the observation of Ali Ibn Nasr, who ideates a logical clarification for sexual discrimination in the matter of intercourse between man and woman. While it is allowed for a man to have intercourse with four wives, why is the same forbidden in the case of women, although it is believed that "women have nine shares of sexual appetite whereas men only have one share?" (Myrne 2020: 67). Ali Ibn Nasr explains that this is because "it would not be possible to know the father of the child, and thus lineage becomes corrupt as well as the heritage" (Myrne 2020: 67). Even the Arabic word *nikaah* for marriage in the Quran signifies sexual intercourse and, thus, the focal point of the relation being the 'body' or the 'flesh' is undeniable.

Layla sleeps with Nate before marriage because she wants to be the owner of her sexuality before submitting it to her husband. There is no condition attached to the encounter, and she wants to defy the custom silently through this premarital realisation of her sexual appetites. Islam considers it sinful: "A sexual relation before marriage was seen as a sexual violation, regardless of if she went into it willingly. The crime was a crime against the 'owner' of her sexuality, her father or close male relative" (Myrne 2020: 70). The word 'owner' itself bears the concept of the objectification of woman as a property to be possessed— "my heart was unusually calm, as it had been the night I had let Nate into my room, my body tamed by its habitual surrenders" (Ali 2004: 94). The same commodification is evident when Sameer sends erotic letters to Layla before their marriage. That he imagines Layla as a 'body' is evident when she finds inside Sameer's trunk many erotic magazines with nudes and lurid pictures of women. The pornographic representation of the woman that the man is going to marry. However, it is later revealed that being gay, Sameer cannot imagine the female body, so he needs the erotic pictures to inject in himself the heterosexual drive.

Ali's novel offers several twisted relationships through various understandings of the 'body' has been used in different contexts, especially in post-1960s feminist discourse. "[I]t is perceived as an inert, receptive surface; the layered site of all sorts of social, cultural, discursive markings that produce a useful, disciplined, normalized subject" (Margaroni 2019: 84). Let us first examine the essence of womanhood through the relationship between Layla and her cousin Henna. In a society where a woman's identity is politically influenced and charged, the essential womanliness remains invisible. Many radical, cultural, and even post-structural feminists have tried to celebrate the female consciousness through mothering, childbearing, child-rearing, or through a shared bond of companionship among women. In her "Compulsory Heterosexuality and Lesbian Existence", Adrienne Rich talks of the means towards achieving a lesbian orientation. She calls the 'lesbian continuum' to deconstruct the clinical definition of lesbianism. She also talks of a female friendship, or what she calls a 'female erotic.' Thus, though Nafiza is uncomfortable seeing the physical proximity of Henna and Layla in adolescence, their togetherness gives them a mental calmness that cannot be defined in societal terms. That is why Henna, who is in a long-distance relationship with her husband, wants to "know what he felt when he touched [her]" (Ali 2004: 70). As both the women talk about individual sufferings and longings a few lines later, Layla expresses how she had longed to be one with Henna, even "secretly claiming it (Henna's child) as my own" (Ali 2004: 72).

Here we see a different understanding of the body beyond the stereotyped and prevalent biological assumptions. The notion of the desire in erotica gets deconstructed as the erotic description now becomes an essence towards expressing belonging, a shared identity, and a shared identification. This is not lesbianism, but a connection, a oneness, a new understanding of the self. Both Henna and Layla are victims of a dictating and traditional autocratic society or power structure that seeks to presume the feminine identity in the genitalia and the gratification of sexual desire. Layla and Henna find in themselves the precious bond of understanding and connection that dismisses the epistemology of the knowledge of sexuality. When Henna is raped and killed by some unknown men in front of her husband, Sameer watches dumbfounded from a distance, helpless and unable to help. Eventually, Sameer's witnessing of the deed is revealed before Layla. The loss is irreparable; it is the loss of a connection and a bonding as if stripping Layla of her own body. Through the relationship between Layla and Henna, Ali seals a beautiful bond of friendship and understanding above the level of materiality and sexuality.

In the final section, the relationship between Sameer and Naveed should be analysed as it opens up another discourse on the 'body.' Even though we tend to focus on normative heterosexuality in our understandings of the bodily discourses or the relation between two female bodies, the relationship between two male bodies cannot be completely ruled out. While the Henna–Layla relation goes beyond the bodily dimension in representing the relation between Sameer and Naveed, Ali expresses the fluidity and flexibility of bodily discourses. This queerness shall be approached from a religious dimension and the socio-cultural one in this chapter.

The marriage between Layla and Sameer and the homosexual relationship between Sameer and Naveed are entrapped in a circuit of social recognition and non-recognition. Any relationship desires social and religious sanction, and the society and culture of a particular place bring in the ethical and religious question to perpetuate or inhibit relationships. Religion is used as a tool by society to resist several acts, homosexuality being one of them. The question of concern here is not so much about whether homosexuality is prohibited in Islam or not, but more about the desire for universal recognition. Butler points out in *Undoing Gender*:

> The desire for universal recognition is a desire to become universal, to become interchangeable in one's universality, to vacate the lonely particularity of the nonratified relation, and, perhaps above all, to gain both place and sanctification in that imagined relation to the state. Place and sanctification: they are surely powerful fantasies, and they take on particular phantasmatic form when we consider the bid for gay marriage. The state can become the site for the recirculation of religious desires, for redemption, for belonging, for eternity. (Butler 2004: 111)

This explains Sameer's desire to go to America. It would give state sanction to his homosexual desires, which cannot be realised in the conservative framework of Muslim culture in Hyderabad or, say, in India.

Since an effort is made to particularise the Sameer–Naveed relationship, it is pretty clear that there is something beyond the normative dimension. Sameer and Naveed are childhood friends, and it is on their wedding day, Layla first sees Naveed dancing erratically before their flower-decked car from her mother's place to her in-laws' home. She sees her mother-in-law, Zeba's face somewhat clouded and offended by Naveed. Next, Naveed meets them at home one day after Sameer and Layla return from an outing. Nafiza, the servant, understands that the relationship between Sameer and Layla has not still attained communion. She knows the truth about Sameer's whereabouts and the truth of the tale of his giving tuitions. The ugly side of the relationship between Sameer and Naveed is exposed when Sameer and Layla go to Madras for their honeymoon and get a visa for their final departure to America. In a nasty encounter, the truth of the relationship between Sameer and Naveed is revealed, and Layla returns alone. After that, she takes the final decision and leaves Sameer to become free and independent of all the clutches of society.

Ali puts in some powerful lines which shall be quoted to reflect upon the volley of questions that come forward. After Layla returns, she confides in Roshan, Nafiza's daughter, the truth of her husband. The interaction between the two women brings puts forth some crucial observations. Firstly, Layla should leave her husband because Islam prohibits homosexuality; secondly, Layla, no doubt, loves Sameer because he is her husband (as if it is imperative on a woman to love her husband compulsorily); thirdly, Layla should be compassionate and understanding because society would question her commitments and loyalty, not her husband's homosexuality. Society would say Layla's failure as a wife leads her husband to choose the sinful (according to Islam) path; and lastly, Sameer tries his best to accept a heterosexual partner but cannot. Now, the first three observations show Layla, the woman, to be in a more flawed disposition according to the dictates of society. Though religion has given her freedom to leave, the laws of society always come with a clause. How this condition and decision affect a woman is no doubt an often-debated issue of discussion, but what strikes her the most is the last line where Roshan says, "He must have believed he would be able to touch you ... until he found he couldn't" (Ali 2004: 237). This last line comes with the twist which posits man too as the victim of patriarchy. Sameer wants to go to America because it sanctions same-sex marriages or relationships. There is a peculiar tug of war between religion and society; culture in the West and religion; culture in the East.

Kecia Ali, in the chapter "Don't Ask Tell: Same Sex Intimacy in Muslim Thought" from *Sexual Ethics and Islam*, begins with an excerpt from Ibn Hajar Haytami's list of *enormities*, which has some of the sexual sins according to Islam, which includes "...anal intercourse between men (*liwat*) and tribadism (musahaaqat al-nisa), which is a woman doing with a woman something resembling what a man would do with her" (Ali 2006: 75) among others. However, the second sin mentioned above has been dealt with differently from Henna and Layla from a feminist perspective. According to Islam, emotional proximity through the body is considered sinful. Islamic jurisprudence terms illicit relationships as sinful, and in tribadism, the sin consists in its lack of a lawful tie between the concerned parties. Islamic scholars like Ibn Hajar and others consider same-sex relationships to be an impossibility, unlawful, illicit, and sinful. However, as Kecia Ali points out, some self-identified queer Muslims challenge this concept and aver that sexual orientation is divinely granted. Therefore, there must be provisions in Islam towards recognizing same-sex relationships.

However, there happens to be no such evidence in Islamic discourse as Kecia Ali points out, though there are instances of same-sex intimacies in Muslim majority societies in the medieval era. In various interpretations of the Quran, while some interpreters believe that it completely shuns homosexuality, others believe that the sacred text is not explicit in its statements on desires or identities. From an Islamic perspective, the homosexual relationship between Sameer and Naveed is sinful and, therefore, unacceptable. The novel shows

Sameer's struggle to accept the female partner, but his libidinal drive makes him choose otherwise. The 'body', therefore, becomes the centre of discourse. In the chapter, we observe various cultural, social, and religious discourses surrounding the very pivot of the 'body.' For this purpose, the chapter constantly shifts between different feminist premises from Butler's 'gender performativity' to Rich's 'lesbian continuum', social sanction, and finally to Islamic jurisprudence. Moreover, to channelise the discussion to the relationship between Islam and gender only would be to overshadow the role of the state and the culture of a particular society, which too partakes in gender identity formations.

Bibliography

Ali, K. "Don't Ask Tell: Same Sex Intimacy in Muslim Thought." In *Sexual Ethics and Islam: Feminist Reflections on Qur'an, Hadith and Jurisprudence*, 75. Oxford: Oneworld Publications, 2006.

Ali, S. *Madras on Rainy Days*. New York: Picador, 2004.

Booner, M. *Media and Gender Equality*. Essex, UK: ED-Tech Press, 2019.

Butler, J. *Bodies that Matter: On the Discursive Limits of "Sex."* Routledge: Taylor and Francis e-Library, 2011.

———. *Gender Trouble: Feminism and the Subversion of Identity*. London: Routledge, 2010.

———. *Undoing Gender*. Abington: Routledge, 2004.

Crossouard, B. et al. *Troubling Muslim Youth Identities: Nation, Religion, Gender*. London: Palgrave Macmillan, 2017.

Greer, G. *The Female Eunuch*. London: Fourth Estate, 2020.

Margaroni, Maria. "Body." *The Bloomsbury Handbook of 21st Century Feminist Theory*, 82. (ed.). Robin Truth Goodman London: Bloomsbury, 2019.

Myrne, P. *Female Sexuality in the Early Medieval Islamic World: Gender and Sex in Arabic Literature*. London: I.B. Tauris, 2020.

Ortner, S. B. "Is Female to Male as Nature is to Culture?" In *Woman, Culture and Society*, edited by M. Z. Rozaldo and L. Lamphere, 68–87. Stanford: Stanford UP, 1974.

Rich, A. "Compulsory Heterosexuality and Lesbian Existence." *Signs: Journal of Women in Culture and Society* 5, no. 4 (Summer 1980).

Chapter 6

Body on the Market: A Marxist–Feminist Study of the Novel *Masooma* by Ismat Chughtai

Md Mizanur Rahaman
Samuktala Sidhu Kanhu College, West Bengal, India

Abstract

This chapter examines the mechanism of the commodification of the female body and its various ramifications concerning the novel *Masooma* by Ismat Chughtai. It also considers the corrosive consequence of this capitalist 'reification' in the forms of the identity crisis and the inhuman corporeal experiences of the protagonist. A renowned feminist writer of modern Urdu literature and a prominent figure of the Progressive Writers' Movement, Ismat Chughtai was always vociferous about the causes of female emancipation. A lifetime iconoclast, Ismat Chughtai often spoke against the dominant ideology of patriarchy and its complex power relation in which males occupy the center and thus women permanently inhabit the periphery. In the matrix of patriarchy's 'endogamous ties', a colonial discourse is established that endows males (sometimes females too) privilege and power to exploit, subjugate, and commodify female bodies. *Masooma*, a scathing critique of society and its people, is a story that unravels the corruption and hypocrisy of middle-class gentility. It depicts the predicament of its protagonist, Masooma, and her family, her transformation from the shy, pretty Muslim girl Masooma to Nilofar, often treated as an exchangeable commodity. Her existence in the unsavoury world of Bombay talkies is equated with her body, a commodified body that becomes property of various people.

Keywords: commodification, endogamous ties, identity crisis

* * *

> We live in a predatory capitalist society in which everything is for sale. Everybody is for sale, so there is ubiquitous commodification—be it of music, food, people, or parking meters.
>
> —West 2014: 56

Let us begin with particular examples from the contemporary world of consumption; a commercial advertisement presents a succulent female body on the big television screen to attract the audience's attention. At the same time, the spectacle of the famous Bollywood item-song *shila ki jawani* (Shila's youthful body) lasciviously flaunts a much-coveted beautified body. There is also the bleak and tragic picture of a girl abducted and trafficked into the narrow slum of shame. So what is the invisible thread that presents a commonality between all these incidents? The simple but not simplistic answer is the reduction of female bodies into a commodity and the inhuman negligence of the capitalist society that, by denying the dignity of human relationships and values, measures everything in terms of economic gain and exchange value. Capitalism survives by its unstoppable and predatory logic of evaluating everything in monetary value, be it personal relationships, rituals, or human bodies. Ismat Chughtai's *Masooma* is such a novel that depicts the predicaments of its titular character, Masooma, who is a victim of such an exploitative society.

I. Chughtai was a prominent writer of modern Urdu literature, whose bold and innovative prose style has placed her along with eminent writers such as Sadat Hasan Manto, Krishan Chander, and Faiz Ahmed Faiz. A prominent figure in the Progressive Writers' Movement, Chughtai was born in 1911 into a middle-class liberal Muslim family and had an upbringing in an atmosphere in which she savoured the liberal taste of European literature. She started to write in a profoundly patriarchal era, where the women were hemmed up within the four walls of the *zenana* (part of a house for the seclusion of women) and often ostracised from the socio-political discourse of the time. Her unorthodox, bold, rebellious texts created tremors among the orthodoxy. Her fictional world concerned the psychological experiences and the socio-cultural and sexual realities of the subaltern in society, challenging the stereotypes and clichéd feminine roles imposed by the patriarchal structures that claim women should be passive, docile, modest, and obedient. She also exposed the corruption, hypocrisy, and double standards of morality of the upper-middle class *sharif* (exalted) society where the women are neglected, their voices muzzled. Their sexuality is also silenced or often treated as a commodity. Her association with the Progressive Writers' Movement (est. 1936), which was committed to communist and socialist causes, acquainted her more clearly with the miseries experienced by the marginalised and the prevailing exploitation and inequality in society. In an interview, Chughtai speaks about the intellectual background which influenced these writers:

> The Progressives were very concerned with inequality. It was the inequality among men that they wished to put an end to ... the Communist domination of the movement came to be strongest after the British left, after we got freedom. (Chughtai 1871: 177)

However, before examining the novel Masooma as an epitomic text that critiques the capitalist tendency to transform its protagonist into a commodity, it is legitimate and relevant to ask what a commodity means. What are the attributes which qualify a thing as a commodity? Moreover, what are the physical and psychological effects that result because of commodification? K. Marx, in his *Das Capital* (Vol. 1), has well postulated the definition and attributes of a commodity:

> A commodity is, in the first place, an object outside us, a thing that by its properties satisfies human wants of some sort or another. The nature of such wants, whether, for instance, they spring from the stomach or from fancy, makes no difference. (Marx 1887: 26)

A commodity plays the dual role of 'use-value' and 'exchange value', and consumption is at the core of this capitalist mode of production. Within the capitalist mode of production, commodification refers to the transformation of nature, goods, ideas, people, relations, and trade and economic exchange. While defining a commodity, A. Appadurai asserts that it is "anything intended for exchange" (Appadurai 2005: 25). This obscene aspect of capitalism has been analysed and criticised by many thinkers and philosophers. I. Kant has carefully observed that a nasty part of capitalism is its relentless drive to reify everything and warns us by saying, "act in such a way that you treat humanity, whether in your own person or the person of another, always at the same time as an end and never simply as a means" (Kant 1997: 38). This view of Kant, which upholds humanity as an end, differentiates human beings from other objects and never to be reified to fulfill someone else's selfish desires. However, capitalism survives only through its indefatigable spirit to transform everything into a commodity, including human beings and human relationships.

M. Nussbaum, drawing her ideas from the dignity of human beings as an end in itself, has presented a penetrating analysis of seven different methods involved in transforming not an object into an object:

- Instrumentality. The objectifier treats the object as a tool of his or her purpose

- Denial of autonomy. The objectifier treats the object as lacking in autonomy and self-determination
- Inertness. The objectifier treats the object as lacking in agency, and perhaps also in activity
- Fungibility. The objectifier treats the object as interchangeable (a) with other objects of the same type and/or (b) with objects of other types
- Violability. The objectifier treats the object as lacking in boundary integrity, as something that it is permissible to break up, smash, break into
- Ownership. The objectifier treats the object as something that is owned by another, can be bought or sold, etc.
- Denial of subjectivity. The objectifier treats the object as something whose experience and feelings (if any) need not be taken into account.

Nussbaum 1999: 213–214

Ismat Chughtai's *Masooma* is looked at from the perspective hitherto elaborated. Luce Irigaray's seminal text *This Sex Which Is Not One* is very instrumental in understanding the nefarious mechanism of commoditisation of female bodies in the fictional world of *Masooma*. Contemporary literature abounds and explores such damaging aspects of modern capitalist society from Margaret Atwood's *The Handmaid's Tale* (1985), or *The Edible Woman* (1969) to Mahasweta Devi's short story collection *Breast Stories*. They all picturise a world of female bodies that are somehow colonised and commodified. Female characters' bodies are discursively manipulated, made docile, and tortured to conform to the dominant structures of power. In *The Handmaid's Tale*, Offred, a handmaid in the Republic of Gilead, is forcefully abducted, and the theocratic state uses her body to populate/bless the system. Jashoda from *Breast Giver* becomes a milk mother to suckle the children of other families but ultimately dies of disrespect and oblivion when her body is no longer helpful.

In *Masooma*, we find the process of thingification, or capitalist reification of the protagonist, Masooma. It is the darkest of all of Chughtai's writings. The writer has related her direct experience of the dark, gloomy, and corrupted world of the film industry of metropolitan Bombay through the parable of Masooma, a neighbour of the narrator of the story. "[The] book was not written for the faint-hearted … A gritty anger and a biting realism combine with a keen eye for detail, not merely to depict the dark underbelly of Bombay [cinema] but also to scratch the mask of sharif culture" (Jalil 2012: Para. 1). Masooma is born into an aristocratic family. Her birth is celebrated with much furore because she was the only daughter to her parents after two sons. The soothsayers prophesied that she would bring prosperity to her family. Her mother dreamt of arranging an extravagant marriage ceremony with all the traditions of the time. However, all hell broke loose when Majid, her father, was compelled to migrate to Pakistan with his two sons. He promised to come back to take them but never returned. At first, Masooma's mother tried to survive by selling whatever little wealth and jewellery were left. Still, when everything was finished, she decided to migrate to Bombay. She was told that Bombay gives reasonable prices for a good thing, a foretelling of the future awaiting Masooma. In Bombay, she and her family attracted the pimp Ehsaan Sahib and the Seth Ahmad Bhai, who wanted to consume the delicate and fragile body of Masooma. Ehsaan Sahib helped the family only to gain a profit in the future. Masooma's mother tried her best to feed and protect the family amidst all these miseries, but when she learnt that her husband had married a new girl of 18 and was sending the divorce papers, she cried the whole night and understood utter futility of marriage. Here the writer has criticised the institution of marriage, which though sanctified with all the religious ceremonies of eternal bonding, brings, in many cases, miseries and misfortunes to the women:

> To hell with the nikah! What's in nikah? Her own nikah had been conducted by the Bade Qazi sahib, the one who had conducted innumerable nikahs for a rich old man. Today that nikah had become even more insignificant than these grains of sand. (Chughtai 2018: 42)

This catastrophe made Masooma's mother adamant to "trade" Masooma to Ahmed Bhai. She had been given 5,000 in advance, a flat in Dadri, and 1,000 per month. The repercussions of abominable economic transaction metamorphose Masooma into Nilofar, a denigrated prostitute, who satisfies the perverted desires of the eminent respectful people of the gentle (*sharif*) society. A harlot, who provides her mother and her family all the sustenance and luxury, roams in the narrow subterranean world of darkness and rummages to find some peace in her life. This incident of financial exchange between Masooma's mother and Ahmed Bhai, of which Masooma is kept in ignorance, corresponds with Martha Nussbaum's elaboration on capitalist reification and its ramifications. It renders Masooma bereft of any individual determination or agency and autonomy. She becomes just an instrument or a means to an end in the hands of various people. In such a capitalist society, where Ehsaan Sahib and Ahmed Bhai are its dwellers, everything is regarded as an object to be consumed. Ehsaan Sahib convinces Ahmad Bhai that Masooma is a high-bred fruit that cannot be easily plucked. He says, "[H]ow long can ripe fruit stay on the branch? Trust me. You won't find high-quality goods lying on the footpath. Be patient and wait a few more days" (Chughtai 2018: 8).

Even Masooma's mother, who always speaks to protect the honour and guard her virginity, does not mind selling her daughter to Seth. She feels quite satisfied with Masooma's condition. She has grown fat and embellished herself with costly jewellery. Once she had implored Ahmad Bhai for Masooma's marriage, but now she denies such proposals by Ahmad Bhai because if Masooma gets married, she will be deprived of the extravagant life she leads. She does not think twice before buying Benarasi saris and gold jewellery as birthday gifts for just about anyone anymore. However, all this comes with the great price of the loss of identity for Masooma. Her complicit role in degrading and exploiting her daughter and mother resembles a "patriarchal motherhood" (O'Reilly 2008: 20), who, instead of fighting patriarchal subjugation, actively participates in reinstating and strengthening the hegemonic institution. The very concept of the inner world and the outer world, private life, and public life cease to exist for her since she becomes a means for economic profit for various people. Transforming her into a profitable commodity violates her very integrity.

Masooma's travails take a new turn with the appearance of Surajmal Kanodia, a ruthless movie producer and promoter. In the circumscribed life with Ahmed Bhai, she becomes coarse and peevish because of living with him for a long time, but Surajmal is gentle and modest enough; he does not mistreat her. So gradually, Masooma also learns this manner of behaving gently and speaking softly. However, this is all just the outward appearance of Surajmal; under this veneer of gentility and modesty, he is the most crooked Machiavellian and very vile. To change the monotony of his married life, he kept three or four mistresses with him. He also did business in their names, took contracts, and opened factories, and so on. However, the girls were not intelligent enough to understand this crooked policy of his. Of all the characters in this novel, he is the cruelest who only cares for his money and business. One day, we know that Masooma is legally married to Ehsaan Sahib, not to Surajmal. The daughter she has with Surajmal legally belongs to Ehsaan, which means her mother's lover is her husband—what a travesty of fate. Despite all this, she fell in love with Surajmal and wanted to be with him. One night she and Surajmal are compromised, and they travel, but when she opens her eyes, she finds that she is no longer in Bombay but in Poona, sold to or handed over to Raja Sahib. She understands what has happened to her and why Surajmal was so good to her that night. This incident explicitly supports the argument proposed above that Masooma is a commodity with an exchange value and fungibility, and she can be easily exchanged for monetary gains. Surajmal sustained her and fed her when he thought she is crucial but sold her when she became rebellious.

Raja Sahib, another important character in this novel, has lost his state and harems but still managed to survive in the modern-day world of capitalism by hoarding fortunes in Bombay and other big cities. Though his harem was banned, he did not lose his interest in women. His growing interest in film actresses and girls from good-but-ruined families is evident in his persistent entreaty to Surajmal to hand over Masooma to him. When Surajmal fed up with her, he made an economic deal with Raja Sahib that he had to buy the production of Surajmal's upcoming film along with Masooma. She became a mistress to Raja Sahib and accompanied him to the eminent *sharif admi* (honest man). She again is transformed from Nilofar to Masooma Jung by Raja Sahib. However, whatever she does, she cannot find peace and solace of mind. She starts drinking while living with Ahmed Bhai and is addicted to marijuana and drug injections at the Poona hotel. She supports her family, provides the dowry for her sister's marriage, but she is empty and dreams of death and snakes that chase her everywhere. The jewels that adorn her and the garments she wears laugh at her:

> As always she woke screaming. In the semidarkness of the room, she saw Raja sahib's moon-shaped necklace shimmering on her bosom. She lowered her head and the moon-shaped necklace laughed. The pearls smiled one by one. The heads of the labourers and the skulls of little children laughed loudly on her naked chest. (Chughtai 2018: 139)

Necklace and pearls, which appear as emblematised feminine beauty to her, had lost their glimmer and became instruments of suffering. These instruments also insinuate Raja Sahib's atrocious business enterprises thrive upon exploiting working-class people as reflected in the symbol of the skulls of little children. Her screaming at night reflects upon her physical and psychological alienation. Also, the author hinges upon class exploitation through the character of Raja Sahib. Masooma's fateful journey from Ahmed Bhai via Surajmal to Raja Sahib denigrates and dehumanizes her. They regard her as a mere doll to be used, from an economic paradigm that Luce Irigaray has defined as the endogamous ties in her *Commodities among Themselves*. According to her, this same paradigm is equally applicable in all patriarchal capitalist societies:

> The exchanges upon which patriarchal Societies are based take place exclusively among men. Women, signs, commodities, and currency always pass from one man to another; if it were otherwise, we are told, and the social order would fall back upon incestuous and exclusively endogamous ties that would paralyze all commerce. Thus the labour force and its products, including those of mother earth, are the object of transactions among men and men alone. (Irigaray 1985: 192)

Here, 'endogamous ties' refers to the process of the economic transactions of women as goods (as in the title) who are to be circulated in a chain of monetary transactions. In this process, the women lose their individuality and are reduced to a mere commodity. The titular Masooma is haply reduced to signs, goods, currency in a patriarchal capitalist society.

The novel ends on a very tragic note; there is no beacon of hope and light. Everyone thrives in this morally corrupt world except Masooma, who is the sole subject of infamy. Society does not raise a finger at those people who compelled Masooma to perish in this dark galley of prostitution which turned Masooma to Nilofar and then to Masooma Jung. To this *sharif* (irony intended) society, this world is not corrupt, but it is Masooma who is morally corrupt:

> who, as if crushed between the two stones of grinding mill, is not a human being but an insignificant grain of wheat which endured Ahmad Bhai, suffered Raja sahib and Surajmal who made a compromise with living death, with arsenic and dhatoora, who mixed together all the poison produced by the lives of her family and gulped it down. (Chughtai 2018: 142)

I. Chughtai has posed many questions regarding the status of women, the institution of marriage, which, nonetheless, are still relevant in contemporary society. Masooma remains a subaltern in a patriarchal world that is dominated by the capitalists, such as rajas (kings) and pimps. She has been deprived of agency of her 'self' and her body and the right to truth and life. Her miserable condition and dislocation reflect the hypocrisy of the accepted norms. In most of Chughtai's short stories, the victims are from the lower classes and are servants and maids in the households of upper-class families. However, Masooma is from a respectable family who is not given leeway to live her own life. She is never allowed to be an individual with a body and a soul in such a society. She is just an entertainer, a commodity to satisfy the lust of various people, a body in the market. The fictional world of Masooma is an allegory of modern capitalist society, a warning to the dangers of life in a capitalist society, and a critique of the dehumanising effect of patriarchy. Masooma can be anyone and everyone, and her predicament is a warning to posterity.

Bibliography

Appadurai, A. "Definitions: Commodity and Commodification". In *Rethinking Commodification: Cases and Readings in Law and Culture*, edited by Martha Ertman and Joan C. Williams, 25. New York: New York University Press, 2005.

Atwood, M. *The Handmaid's Tale*. New York: Penguin Random House, 1998.

———. *The Edible Woman*. Toronto: McClelland and Stewart, 1969.

Chughtai, I. *Masooma*, translated by Tahira Naqvi. Delhi: Speaking Tiger, 2018.

Devi, M. *Breast Stories*. Translated by Gayatri Chakravorty Spivak. New York: Seagull Books, 2018.

Irigaray, L. *This Sex Which is Not One*. Translated by Catherine Porter. New York: Cornell University Press, 1985.

"ISMAT CHUGHTAI: A Talk with One of Urdu's Most Outspoken Woman Writers." *Mahfil* 8.2-3 (Summer-Fall 1972): 177.

Jalil, R. "Masooma by Ismat Chughtai—a Review." *Hindustani Awaz: Literature, Culture and Society* 10 July 2012. Accessed 23 September 2017. http://hindustaniawaaz-rakhshanda.blogspot.com/2012/07/masooma-by-ismat-chughtai-review.html

Kant, I. *Groundwork of the Metaphysics of Morals*. Translated by Mary Gregor. Cambridge: Cambridge University Press, 1997.

Marx, K. *Capital: A Critique of Political Economy*. Translated by Samuel Moore and Edward Aveling. Vol. I. IV vols. Moscow: Progress Publisher, 1887.

Nussbaum, M. C. *Sex And Social Justice*. Oxford and New York: Oxford University Press, 1999.

O'Reilly, A. *Feminist Mothering*. Albany: State University of New York Press, 2008.

West, C. "Interview Magazine." 2 Novermber 2014. Accessed on 13 December 2018. 56. https://www.interviewmagazine.com/culture/cornel-west

Chapter 7

Searching for Self and Autonomy, Breaking Claustrophobic Domesticity: A Critical Analysis of Kavery Nambisan's *Mango-Coloured Fish*

Tanbir Shahnawaz
Rishi Bankim Chandra College, West Bengal, India

Abstract

Individual freedom is not a decorative piece or a reward that can be showcased in a dining room. On the contrary, it is a hard-earned thing and requires the commitment and energy of a long-distance run. It is something to be achieved with much toil. Everyone wants freedom of speech, thinking, and participation in this world, including choosing whatever one likes. From time immemorial, these two groups have been coexisting. If anyone in these groups is harmed or mistreated, humankind is harmed overall. It is a common practice that women have been usually subjugated and dominated throughout the history of all ages and all countries. However, as time progressed, women have also vented their expressions, ideas, and dreams and participated in various protests, movements, and written literature. Such a story is our concern in this chapter. *Mango-Coloured Fish*, a powerful novel written by an emerging woman novelist, Kavery Nambisan, a surgeon who practices specifically in the rural areas of India, worked on a principally feminine premise in the novel. The novel's protagonist is Shari, who goes or instead flees to her brother's house just two weeks before her marriage ceremony to a person she does not like. She is in a moral dilemma about her choices as she loves another man. So she does not want to sacrifice herself for her parent's will and, thus, suffer all her life. She wants to break away from the claustrophobic domesticity and violence, which awaits her and wants to live her life according to her will. The journey is a symbolic journey into the nooks and crannies of herself. It is a novel about exquisite self-discovery and about focusing on insight into others and oneself.

Keywords: feminism, patriarchy, coexistence, claustrophobic, domesticity.

* * *

Introduction

The progress of any civilization and society depends upon man and woman, the two primary groups of humankind, coexisting from time immemorial. From the beginning of the world, the man-woman relationship and their conjugation are considered to be essential. Without their conjugation, not only humankind but also the other creatures would not have multiplied in the world. Our contemporary literary writers are conscious about the matter and stress the need for the coexistence of men and women in their literature. It is common and familiar that patriarchy as a social system has been tormenting and exploiting women. The movement of feminism stems from such deprivation, humiliation, and an ardent desire for liberation. K. Nambisan, a practising surgeon-cum-writer from Palangala in Kodagu (Karnataka State), stresses the philosophy of man-woman coexistence in her novel *Mango-Coloured Fish* (1998). It is the story of a single girl Shari or Sharada, 22-years-old, the narrator, and the novel's protagonist. She is the exceptional daughter of her family at the crossroads of life. She rebels against the statutory hypocritical rules and regulations of family and society to carve out a path of her own. As has already been stated, achieving freedom is not easy; the way is replete with difficulties and humiliations. The novel has two prologues that enlighten us about the themes: a quest for happiness and satisfaction in this imperfect world, where nothing is perfect or ideal, especially marriage relationships. The first prologue is from H. G. Wells' comic novel *The History of Mr. Polly* (1910), which unambiguously says, "a living does not matter unless there were things to live for..." (Wells 2005: 142). The second prologue is taken from the Bible, which clearly states, "Better is a dinner of herbs where love is, than stalled ox and hatred therewith" (Stuart 1852: 284). So, it is clear that the search is for love, a genuine kind of love, an ideal though imperfect quest; this quest for love and freedom guides the 22-year-old heroine Shari through the narrative.

Shari is the third and youngest daughter of her "close-knit family" (Nambisan 1998: 9). K. Nambisan has applied the stream of consciousness technique in the narrator-cum-protagonist Shari's quest for self-entity, happiness, and identity. The narrative moves backward and forwards frequently to provide us an insight into the working of Shari's inner psyche. The novelist has aptly used the stream of consciousness technique here in the way each thought flows and melts into another. The protagonist's thoughts flow into something that reminds young Shari of her ex-lover. Throughout the story, she grapples with her memories. It is about Shari and her journey to discover herself through thorough introspection and contemplation just weeks before her planned wedding with Gautam.

The novelist Nambisan has depicted the multitudinous thoughts and feelings which pass through the mind of the narrator-protagonist. By bringing her heroines into self-inspection and self-reflection processes, Nambisan transforms them into more liberated and empowered individuals than what their biological existence or society has endorsed. Nambisan explores the field of women's emotions closely. Shari describes her family in the following lines: "That is, Mother, Father, and Chitra are close. Krishna and I hover at the periphery of things. We are the stitches that slipped out of a cosy pattern" (Nambisan 1998: 10). She is attached emotionally to her elder brother Krishna more than anyone else. She is not very attractive, but she has a mind of her own. She is tired of the domesticity of her family life and cannot bear the dominating attitudes of her family members. She wants to come out of the established family and societal norms to attain her individuality and satisfaction. She dislikes her parent's marriage, where her father has yielded his individuality to his wife shamefully and has become a sort of henpecked husband. He has compromised with her choices from the beginning of their marriage just to stabilise their marital relationship. Shari is disgusted with such an artificial union. Her mother is a Tamilian but hates everything about Tamils and prefers Delhi as the center of culture and sophistication. Shari thinks it to be shocking as they are Chettiars from Madras. Her family settled in Delhi when her grandfather established Madras Stores at Khan Market, and ever since, they have underestimated everything south of Nagpur. This is ironic because they owe all they have to South Indian spices.

On the contrary, Shari considers Paru Uncle and Paru Aunty as her surrogate parents, for they have been closer to Shari than her parents. Shari has considered for years that she has "two sets of parents" (Nambisan 1998: 13). Paru Uncle calls her "Puttu Mari" (Nambisan 1998: 13) in Kannada, which means little darling, a particular word for endearment he has for Shari. Her elder sister, Chitra's marriage, is similar to her parents' marriage; she is a shadow and a perfect replica of her mother, who has cultivated all social graces, is a well-maintained coquette a socialite. Shari knows quite well that Chitra's "dead-end marriage [is] a cul-de-sac in which they have folded themselves until they stick together" (Nambisan 1998: 72). Shari dislikes Chitra and her mother for intervening in her life and planning it to have a good marriage. However, Shari is quite confident about the marriage between Krishna and his wife Tejaswini or Teji as both are doctors, and "Teji and Krishna's is special. Deep down, their marriage is sound..." (Nambisan 1998: 231). Shari feels solace only in Krishna, who is also her mentor. She is convinced that although Krishna and Teji married against the will of their parents, they still have a better understanding. Their marriage is a true union between two minds like Paru Uncle and Paru Aunty, and their relationship will survive to the end despite all its ups and downs. About Teji, Shari feels: "She speaks honestly, without smugness. It hasn't been easy for her, accepting Krishna's strange combination of talent and lack of ambition" (Nambisan 1998: 25). A few weeks before her marriage to Gautam, she flees to Krishna's house at Vrindaban to sort herself out. Krishna and his wife Teji advise Shari "not to do anything for the wrong reasons" (Nambisan 1998: 66). When she goes to marry Gautam, Krishna feels dissatisfied and irritably advises her: "[Y]ou are not a fool, but you are foolish" (Nambisan 1998: 66). Krishna has always been an inspiration and philosopher for Shari, and urges her to reconsider her relationship with Gautam, "[H]e glitters like the ring on your finger. He is the type of guy who thinks the world needs him" (Nambisan 1998: 66). She considers this remark of Krishna as male jealousy or ego and takes the side of her fiancé. She asserts that Gautam possesses a so-called impressive presence; Krishna agrees with her views but adds that he is anxious she would be sick and tired with the kind of person Gautam was. To be fatigued in marriage is the worst part. Nothing can protect a man who is deep down fed up. He is frightened Shari will be washed and pressed and moulded into something Gautam's looking for to consummate his cherished image. Thereafter she will be like the stereotyped Sher Singhs and Chitras.

In the novel, we find Gautam vain, egotistical, and materialistic. He wants to get ahead in life, and dreams of a successful career and desires wealth. He is confident of "moulding" Shari to his own way of thinking. To him, without wealth, success is ineffectual. His father was successful, but he felt no resentment for a man who, although a university professor, could just afford a two-wheeler, and lived in a rented house. Success yoked with wealth provides dignity and which is peerless. He wanted, Shari, to be the most coveted person in the world. He wants to manufacture or mould Shari in his way, but Shari thinks: "Moulded. How? Pulled, pushed, elongated, flattened, hammered, punched and gouged out until I was the right specimen, the perfect wife?" (Nambisan 1998: 76). She cannot "change physically into the most pleasing woman" (Nambisan 1998: 10) to be tender and desirable like her mother. She also resists Gautam's attempt to have premarital sex, and Shari's resistance shocks him, but she looks forward to life with him after they are married properly. Her mother is certain that Gautam will bring happiness, security, and order to Shari's life. She believes Shari should have a purpose in life, which she lacks, but Shari is not confident enough whether she loves Gautam or just an infatuation after meeting him. She, after all, does not want to please him and live her life to other's expectations. Shari does not want to sacrifice her life to a false sense of responsibility.

However, Shari feels shocked when she observes the apparent happy life of her school friend Yashoda or Yash, who is married to a microbiologist, and realises that this marriage is a compromise between them like the one between Shari's father and mother. Yash often cheats on her husband, Satyamurthy (statue of truth), whose lovemaking she considers mechanical and formal, without any pleasure or sincerity. She is fond of late-night parties and amusements but leads a dead-end marriage. Shari counsels her that she is a failure because she does not even try to make a success of their marital life, to which Yash says that Satyu (her husband) although having every potential, is dim. She not only cheats him, she receives letters from multiple lovers scattered around the house, and he never suspects. Just because Yash smiles and waits for him and cooks his favourite dishes. He believes his wife buys all the perfumes to excite him. It's pathetic. She thinks that his love is also shallow and superficial. He doesn't know about her mind or body. It was three weeks after marriage that they ultimately consummated infidelity. He hadn't, in fact, looked at her, didn't know that her left breast was a little bigger than the right one. He chews her like a hungry calf, crashes in and crashes out which is unbelievable.

Yash believes adultery to be "vile, it's a daily humiliation" (Nambisan 1998: 123) and feels like a Pomeranian who is kept as a pet. Shari is disgusted by such a hollow relationship and takes lessons from this type of artificial union. Shari shudders to think of marriage where there is no understanding between the husband and the wife. Shari comes across such a kind of dysfunctional marriage between Naren's Hindu father and a Christian mother. He is Shari's unrequited love; he is aware of Shari's love for him but fears any intimacy with her. His mother is a religious fanatic and compels her husband to live according to her will till he dies of a bursting stress ulcer in his stomach. In her journey for her existence, apart from the marriage of Paru Uncle and Aunty, the union that touches Shari is between George and his dead wife Portia. The specialty about this relationship is that George comes to Delhi every year to celebrate and commemorate his love for his dead wife, who died here seven years ago on their thirtieth wedding anniversary. Needle to say, Shari is overwhelmed. This is, at least, one marriage that has worked—even beyond death. George speaks blithely about Portia without a touch of emotion in his voice: "My children think I come here to grieve. I come to celebrate. I sing her name, touch her with my mind. Everything was good, only death was ill-mannered as not to give so much as a warning" (Nambisan 1998: 164).

George inspires Shari to begin her life anew and encourages her to set out on her quest for happiness again. She boldly decides to put off her forthcoming marriage with Gautam against her family's will, as she thinks that he chooses to marry her as long ago, years before they met, he had determined, in that sure certain way of his, on the kind of woman who would be his obedient wife. He had his future presented in front of him like a panorama. She is uncertain whether things will be normal with Naren, but she decides to set her concerns and anxieties aside. She misses Naren desperately and cherishes spending all her life with the blind school teacher Naren; she decides to give herself more time and space to sort out herself. In the meantime, she decides to restart her job as a KG teacher and waits for what lies ahead.

This is probably what gives Shari satisfaction and happiness, and purpose for her own future without carrying any past burdens. Yash lauds her decision positively. She comes across a glass bowl with fishes "darting about in the glass bowl like shafts of gold" (Nambisan 1998: 237) in the bedroom of Yash. But all this, as the title of the novel indicates, is a subject of perspective, from which point one view marriage and at what time or stage in one's life. Yash calls the fish her "best friends" (Nambisan 1998: 93). The reason behind it is that "they don't try to understand me. I look into their fish eyes and feel comforted. They are so perfectly formed they don't seem alive. And every time I look at them they are a different colour" (Nambisan 1998: 93). Shari is surprised in finding the fish changing their colour every time she looks from different directions: "I thought they were red and gold. Look, they are green now, with a tint of violet" (Nambisan 1998: 92), but it is the sunlight that reflects off the glass and water that makes it so. Myna, the four-year-old girl child of Yash, childishly replies that these are "mango-coloured" (Nambisan 1998: 93). This strikes the mind of Shari about the many perspectives on marriage, which, therefore, remain as a kind of mirage for her; she views it as the mango-coloured fish of Yash's bowl, the beautiful little fishes who keep changing their colours and patterns.

More than marriage, she values friendship, and she feels the blind Naren tops the list more than anyone else. Her determination to live and choose as per her own will draws a likeness with the memorable heroine Anna in Leo Tolstoy's eponymous novel *Anna Karenina* (1875). The story begins with the sentence, "happy families are all alike; every unhappy family is unhappy in its own way" (Tolstoy 2008: 3), which bears the key to Anna's sheer frustration that comes out of an unhappy marital relationship. It is not easy to judge the authenticity of the explicit statement that all happy families are the same, as we do not come across any delighted families in *Mango-Coloured Fish*. Almost all the families—Shari's parents, Krishna and Teji, Paru Uncle and Paru Aunty, George and Portia, and Naren's family—are torn apart by various problems, such as domination, or mutual misunderstanding between members of a family, lack of communication or expression, mechanical love, jealousy, and frequent quarrels, or evil. Our encounter with all the families and characters generates mixed reactions in us; we all want to be happy at any cost, but we do not want to be like everyone else in the same manner. The only way to nurture our distinctiveness in our own way is by accepting unhappiness.

This difficult circumstance is the similar dilemma that the would-be bride of Gautam, Shari, feels when she struggles between domestic peace, on the one hand, and the intense desire for freedom and individuality, on the other. Both Shari and Anna Karenina are rich in complexity: Shari, like Karenina, is guilty of defiling her marriage and her home. She shudders to think of playing the role of a sophisticated and obedient wife with great composure and refinement. Shari, a passionate spirit, determines to live life on her own terms. Although both are humiliated, they dare to face society and decline their moral outlook because of which they have been doomed, joining their friends and trustworthy relatives when they know very well that they will meet with nothing but contempt and disdain. Shari is worried that Gautam does not desire her sincerely but wants to remain with her out of a sense of duty to excel in his career. Her rejection of the claustrophobic domestic responsibilities and societal norms throughout the novel is a symbolic denial of all the societal conventions imposed by patriarchal society.

Moreover, Shari, a woman searching for autonomy and passion in a male-dominated society, contrasts with the epitome of living only for his family and husband's will, which other women in Indian society generally embrace. At the end of the novel, Anna succumbed to her fate and committed suicide, whereas Shari decides to control her life herself and that committing suicide is not a solution. Shari, in the end, comes out of her existential crisis and starts leading her life anew. We are always our own worst enemies when we cannot escape our situation, as in Anna's case, but Shari here proclaims the central place of the self in existence. The difference is that Shari finds herself not to be a punisher or oppressor, as Anna does, but a nurturer that pours value into life. Unlike Anna, Shari puts seeds into the ground of her life to make it fertile or meaningful. Anna's self is an annihilator, while Shari's is a creator. Shari's self is of the highest importance in defining the reality of her existence. This focus on the self as the centre of existence links Nambisan with other literary modernists and helps explain her enormous influence on twentieth-century literature and thought. Such kinds of women struggling against their social situations and forceful obligations can be found in Nambisan's other novels too, such as *On Wings of Butterflies* (2002).

In this novel, Nambisan has dreamed of a world where women are allowed to do what they please, and men are set apart like others. Some determined women set out to build the most incredible community of oppressed women, and they trigger vibrations in the hearts of thousands of such women throughout the country. They associate peevish career women, self-satisfied homemakers, mentally plagued teenagers, and oppressed women. A group of passionate, bold, and strong-willed women leads the battle from the front against men and society. Some prominent heroines are the brave, man-hating Lividia, politically shrewd Kripa, the verbose police officer Tara, the torrid Rani of Kantipur, and their energetic mentor Evita. Evita is mentally tormented by the sexual harassment of her mother in her childhood and is resolute in her commitment to vengeance. In the novel, all of these determined women join together from various parts of the country and baffle the rest of the world that watches them in intoxicated reticence. They are resolute in winning their war for justice, and in their course of action, they never allow fate or men to intervene again.

In another novel, *The Hills of Angheri* (2005), Nambisan presents a Shari-like character in Nalli. The hills of her village that have frequently appeared alive in the stories of her grandfather appeal to her to do something that she likes and what she wishes. She is a 12-year-old girl who is restless in pursuing her dreams, which is impossible for her to execute at the same time in a traditional family and restrictive society to which she belonged. Her friend Jai is pursuing an MBBS degree, and she wants to be a doctor like him to fulfill her dreams of a career apart from the employment of household chores of post-marriage life. She also has a vision of founding a hospital of her own in her village. She adamantly resists all her family restrictions and travels to Madras. Later, she also gets an opportunity to pursue her higher degrees in London, a dream she never thought of achieving. She gets acclimatised with her medical profession, and gradually with the help of her friends, she learns to live by her own skills as a surgeon. But all these successes and adventures do not make her complacent. The sight of the hills of Angheri still haunts her—god of Ajja, advice of Appa, her dream of founding a hospital of her own money in her village, which she desperately cherishes to be realised. But the episode of her return to her family is replete with sorrow and disdain; after being humiliated, she sets off again.

This time she travels to Keshabganj, searching for serenity and the realisation of her heart's desire. This engaging, elegant, touchy, and feminist novel tells the story of a young lady surgeon who desperately tries to deal with the hazards and impediments of her life and career. But just like the *Mango-Coloured Fish*, Nambisan uniquely binds the individual self with the universe from which they belong to. It will be an injustice if we do not mention her debut novel *The Truth (Almost)About Bharat* (1991), a bizarre story of youth and adventure. The story is set in contemporary India. Bharat, also known as Viswanath, a medical student, is heartbroken due to his unrequited love and falls into depression. Out of frustration, he leaves his everyday life and undertakes different adventures, and experiences quirky incidents at other places with different people and women. This is the tale of rebellious youth and a brilliant MBBS student who sets out on a countrywide road trip on his motorbike. The time of the novel spans three months in the life of Bharat, and it has been presented from a male point of view. In 2019, a movie was released titled *Kabir Singh* with Shahid Kapoor as the protagonist with traits of toxic masculinity, resembling Nambisan's novel.

Nambisan's novel has been written from a feminist point of view, as has already been mentioned. Nambisan aims to make her readers understand the covert mechanism of gender disparity and deftly emphasises sexuality. She has provided a critique of these social relationships throughout the narrative. She attempts the advancement of women's rights and interests through the mouthpiece of her protagonist Shari. In an attempt to recommend a formal estimate of feminism, Susan James, a British professor of philosophy, describes feminism's in the following words:

> Feminism is grounded on the belief that women are oppressed or disadvantaged by comparison with men, and that their oppression is in some way illegitimate or unjustified. Under the umbrella of this general characterization there are, however, many interpretations of women and their oppression, so that it is a mistake to think of feminism as a single philosophical doctrine, or as implying an agreed political program. (James 1998: 576)

Kavery Nambisan uses the ideas of intimidation as a proxy for more emphatic accounts of prejudice over which feminists disagree. However, Nambisan suggests that women's position is subordinate to that of men in the novel. Patriarchal society and ideology continue because both men and women want to perpetuate patriarchy. Men want to dominate women, and women placidly admit to being subjugated by men. However, in the case of the *Mango-Coloured Fish*, Shari, the protagonist, explores alone the world of realities and is in search of something or someone. Shari knows that after the discovery of her choice and self, no one would welcome her, no one would miss her at home. Her nonperformance in all domains has transformed her into the least important in her family. When she returns home; father, mother and Chitra get by very well without her. She can perceive them acutely. The members of family evoke no affection or fury. Just an ambiguous concern. Like her mother and sister, she represents the traditional model of living being dutiful toward husband and children. Chitra, Shari's sister, gets married to Anand, not by choice, but by her parents' wish. Chitra is unable to resist the conventional mode of life and marriage, whereas Shari can do so.

Thus, by appealing to the exploration of the past and the present and the oppression of the disadvantaged and the marginalised, Nambisan consistently points to the fact that any act of reading of her works has significant social and political implications. The novel primarily focuses on the second-and the third-wave feminism movement's issues to encourage women's self-identity. The trauma of subjugation drives Shari to quest for her identity. The haunting of her memories, which the novelist has poignantly delineated through the stream of consciousness method, makes her a self-dependent woman. "The journey of Shari ends with her transformation from an absent-minded, quirky woman to an independent woman" (Padmavathy 2017: 17). In *Mango-Coloured Fish*, it is not only Shari who is the victim of the so-called well-wisher for women, society, and patriarchy and norms, even her mother, her sister Chitra, her sister-in-law Teji, and her school friend Yash have also more or less been subjugated.

Nambisan's writings effectively address the problems of other thematic representations by constructing a new language to provide artistic expression and view modern culture as a reality. Kavery Nambisan's writing is still relevant for her depiction of the difficulties of the youths. She swims in the inner psyche of women and projects their thoughts wonderfully. For her, literature is not a way to escape life but an investigation and a survey. She likes to delve deep into the private sphere and escape the traditional grounds of external fact and the physical world. In particular, her genuine interest is to explore the human psyche, the internal environment, and she reveals the mystery of her characters' inner existence. She usually writes for the urban middle class; the social stratum she is acquainted with. Tradition and societal dominance confine her characters entirely to the cruelty of their men who, in exchange, do not allow them to look for their individuality and identity. They face adversities, and they are obliged to renovate themselves to a greater degree of consciousness. The dilemma of identification is a common issue in these novels. The incapacity to adapt in the correct position to the scheme of things, often situational and sometimes inflicted; the individual and culture, the person in society, shape the persistent interests of the novels. Kavery Nambisan's stories deal with the politics of the female predicament and women's pursuit of ever-elusive bliss and enthusiasm of life. In all her works, we find a clear sense of optimism through transformation. The novel carefully identified several vital stages of change from being bonded to being born in another world. All women are happy in their own domestic lives and compromised themselves to the cages of society, families, and husbands because they have no other options. Only Shari comes out victorious and paves the way for women's emancipation from the bondage of society, family, and patriarchal rules and regulations. Hence, the *Mango-Coloured Fish* is not only an adventure story of a liberal-minded, courageous woman's life but also about the social and political implications of the dominated, discriminated sections of society. As a consequence of that, their freedom, decisions, and choices make it a pathbreaking novel that will inspire other women.

Bibliography

James, S. "Feminism." In *Routledge Encyclopedia of Philosophy*, Vol. 10, edited by Edward Craig, 576. London: Routledge, 1998.

Kabir Singh, (Film). Directed by Sndeep Reddy Vanga, T-Series, 2019.

Nambisan, K. *Mango-Coloured Fish*. Gurgaon: Penguin Books India, 1998.

———. *On Wings of Butterflies*. New Delhi: Penguin Books, 2002.

———. *The Truth (Almost)About Bharat*. New York: Penguin Books, 1991.

———. *The Hills of Angheri*. Delhi: Penguin, 2005.

Padmavathy, G. "Feministic Views – Seeking Self-identity of the Protagonist with Reference to Kavery Nambisan's Mango-Coloured Fish." Special Issue Published in International Journal of Trend in Research and Developement (IJTRD), ISSN: 2394-9333, Special Issue ICART-17 (August 2017): 17. URL: http://www.ijtrd.com/papers/IJTRD10884.pdf

Stuart, M. *A Commentary on the Book of Proverbs*. New York: M. W. Dodd, Brick Church Chapel, 1852.

Tolstoy, L. *Anna Karenina*. Translated by Kyril Zinovieff and Jenny Hughes. London: Oneworld Classics LTD., 2008.

Wells, H. G. *The History of Mr. Polly*. New Delhi: Penguin Books Private India Lmt., 2005.

Chapter 8

Technocracy versus Theocracy: A Critical Study of *Sultana's Dream*

Abdul Mabood
Chandigarh University, Panjab, India

Abstract

Asian people, especially among Bengalis in Bangladesh and India. She was a litterateur, educationist, social reformer and has been revered as a pioneering Bengali Muslim feminist. At the time when Muslim women were suffering at the dirty hands of patriarchy, the *ulema*, and colonialism in the subcontinent, she started writing. She used various forms of literature to express her thoughts against them. She wrote short stories, poems, essays, novels, and satirical pieces. The present chapter intends to deal with Hossain's imaginative and ambitious *Sultana's Dream*, a short work of science fiction and a feminist utopia. In this novella, she emphasises running the world peacefully; we do not need masculine power but the human brain. She strongly advocates the use of harmless science and technology in everyday life. Originally written in English, this piece is known as the best one among her literary works.

Keywords: education, religion, women, patriarchy, science, technology

* * *

R. S. Hossain (1880–1931) was born in a small village called Rangpur in the British colonial province of Bengal Presidency, which is now situated in the northern part of Bangladesh. She was born in a highly educated *zamindar* (landlord) family, and of course, the educated members in it were only the men. In those days, the existing culture did not allow women to receive education, especially in Muslim families. Still, if one wished, and the respective family was kind enough, a woman could learn Arabic and Urdu to read the Quran and some religious texts. Learning English was not allowed. He was highly ambitious regarding his children's education, but only of the sons and daughters. As a result, her daughters were denied modern education, including English.

Unexpectedly, Hossain proved herself to be a different woman of that age. She was an iconoclast and broke all notions of claustrophobic domesticity and conservative ideas. Out of her own will, she learnt English secretly and started writing in English against the tyranny in operation. She refuted the idea of keeping women confined and attacked the patriarchal mindset with her writing. She openly condemned the practice of keeping women away from the modern educational system. Women could never enjoy the advancement of science and technology, so she slammed the society she lived in to teach them only religious topics. Putting aside all the stereotypical attitudes, she raised a strong voice in support of female education. Also, unexpectedly, keeping in view the contemporary conservative mindset, she got her brothers different from others. They were inspired by Western culture, which helped them overthrow the staunch patriarchal mentality. They decided to help her in learning English clandestinely. Moreover, apart from her brothers, her husband, Khan Bahadur Syed Sakhawat Hossain, was also very open-minded, and he wholeheartedly supported her in her modern education and writing.

Hossain did not stop with writing only; she even established a school for Muslim girls who were banned from getting an education. She termed her newly founded school after her husband's name, whom she lost within a short span of time. She initiated her great endeavour with five students only in Bhagalpur, a Muslim majority area. Later, it was shifted to Calcutta. She was very devoted and adamant about bringing Muslim girls to school. It was challenging to cross the social norm to break the age-old taboo. She went from door to door to collect students, gave lectures, and tried to make people understand the importance of female education. She was not against religion; she instead advocated the concept that *purdah* or the veil and education can go together:

> Despite her outspokenness on issues such as purdah, her actions as a reformer were invariably tactful and strategic. All her life, she herself used the burqa (the full covering of the body) when she appeared in public. In her school and among friends and relatives, she covered her head with the end of her sari. She pointed out that some form of veiling or protecting oneself from public exposure was common to all civilised societies of her time. (Sabir 2014: n. p.)

Her hard toil proved to be fruitful. Persuaded by her, many Muslim families agreed to send their girl children to her school and educate them in modern society.

Along with teaching Muslim girls by herself, she also kept nurturing her writing talent, and she did wonders in this field. She started her literary career by publishing a Bengali story named "Pipasa" ("thirst") in 1902. Just after few years, she published another notable work *Sultana's Dream* (1908). Her other works that moved the readers are "Padmarag" ("Essence of the Lotus") (1924), "Nari Sristi" ("Creation of Women") (1918) and "God Gives, Man Robs" (1927), "Abarodhbasini" ("The Zenana Women") (1931), and so forth. Her other writings which are required to be mentioned are "Stri-jatir Abanati" ("Woman's Downfall"), "Ardhangini" ("The Female Half"), "Home" ("Griha"), and "Borka" ("The Cloak"), etc. published in 1903-1904. Hossain used her pen essentially to criticise social prejudices. Her writing reflected her anguish against the contemptuous social practices like the *Purdah* system, child marriage, polygamy, prohibition of women from education, suppression of women, etc. She brought the best out of herself through her literary piece *Sultana's Dream* (1905), in which she criticized patriarchal discourse existing in society. In the book, she dreams of a reversed society altering the role of men and women and a sensible merger of technology and religion. She tried to convert the history of conflict between science and religion into a coexistence. They might not mix; they might not become homogeneous, but they might give human beings two windows to look at the same creation. She understood that there was a need to develop a consensus between these two entities constantly at war. Through the story, she tried to establish a narrative that one needs not be anti-science while believing in religion. In her story, no one is executed for harbouring scientific views, and also, no one is frowned upon for being religious.

In *Sultana's Dream*, Hossain imagines a land where people would live with science and technology but not at the cost of religious faith. She also emphasises the power of intellect and reduces the brute male power, conferring females with more authoritative sovereignty. The story begins with the narrator Sultana who seems to have fallen asleep while taking a rest in her "easy chair." In her semi-sleep state, while contemplating the condition of women in India, she feels like visualising someone who resembles her friend, Sister Sara. In her dream, she starts walking with Sister Sara and sets foot in a world that turns out to be a never-seen-before place. Describing the strange site, Sister Sara tells Sultana that they have entered a country called "Ladyland", a utopia run by women. She adds that this manless world is a place of love and laughter without any conflict and violence. The Queen of this place has set up separate universities specifically for women, who have developed devices to regulate the weather. In contrast, men's universities are dedicated to focusing on the development of weaponry.

According to Sister Sara, the land was attacked by a neighbouring country, and a war ensued. The army, which consisted of men soldiers, was defeated humiliatingly. Hence, the responsibility was shifted to the women of the land.

The women came forward and took up the job to save their country. In doing so, the God-obeying pious women asked men in the land to confine themselves into the zenana - a part of a house where women are secluded - to protect their modesty. The women in charge, using their brains, did a new thing the men could never think of. With the help of a giant reflecting glass, they directed the concentrated beams of solar light and heat towards the enemy. "The heat and light were too much for them to bear. They all ran away panic-stricken, not knowing in their bewilderment how to counteract that scorching heat" (Hossain 2005: 10). The post-war scenario was changed in the land. Seeing the success of the women in the battle, the men of the land decided to stay in the *zenana* only like women used to do till then, and the name of the *zenana* was changed into *mardana* (coming from the word "mard" means man). Women started ruling the country, which ultimately became Ladyland. Since then, its men lived inside and now were used to it. They lived there cosily and had ceased to complain. The rest of the day was used to develop more valuable stuff, such as art, science, etc. The whole country was a giant, beautiful garden where women have created scientifically advanced machines. There were no asphalt or concrete roads. People travelled by aircraft only.

In Hossain's time, the Muslim community as a whole was lagging many years behind, and the status of the Muslim women was appalling. They were kept within the boundaries of the home to do household chores only. Except for a few scattered examples, most Muslims were unaware of the advancement of science in those days. Moreover, it was taboo in the community to consider anything that came from the West. During that time, all scientific experiments and developments had been taking place mainly in the West. The patriarchal society forced the women of those days to receive religious learning only, strictly prohibiting them from acquiring any form of modern-day knowledge. Hossain understood that society's development is impossible without girls' education and that their education must include science knowledge. When we read and analyse Hossain today, what gives her more credibility is her thinking about pollution-less technology. Today, the world is dangerously polluted, and Hossain many years ago had warned her readers that human beings have no option but to embrace pollution-less technology to survive. She advocated the use of modern apparatus that would not harm the ecological balance of the earth. Today, we have come so far using and taking the help of science, but simultaneously we cannot ignore the damage caused by it. She speaks of utilising science but not of the present day, polluting the environment and posing a threat to the planet. She talks of air cooling systems but not today's air conditioning machine, emitting poisonous gases. Moreover, she indicates using an architectural air cooling system with a "corrugated iron roof" (Hossain 2005: 6).

Hossain envisages a disease-free country, and in her utopia, nobody dies of any illness except a natural death caused due to aging. People of that country are free from pests and insects. Hossain's thought would intrigue us to look for a panacea that would cure all diseases and prolong a healthy life. As a far-sighted woman, Hossain understood that in the future, the use of renewable energy would provide substantial benefits for our climate, health, and economy. This reliable and resilient energy system will be affordable, less risky, and will rarely fail. People in Sister Sara's world do not pollute the air and water by using fossils and coals while cooking but rather replace those fuels with solar energy and keep the environment clean, reducing premature mortality.

Hossain also refers to cloud seeding, a very advance scientific process of weather modification, through which rainfall can be controlled or regulated over a particular place. Being ahead of her time, Rokeya had tried her best to bring the unbelievable technology in front of common people. The writer describes what she saw in Ladyland: "[T]he captive balloon which they managed to keep afloat above the cloudland, they could draw as much water from the atmosphere as they pleased. As the water was incessantly being drawn by the university people, no cloud gathered and the ingenious Lady Principal stopped rain and storms thereby" (Hossain 2005: 8). They do not suffer from drought as they have developed the "balloon" that can collect effluent water from the clouds themselves. Indeed, it is an extraordinary visionary device that can push the human race much forward if used at the mass level. Then, there is the beautiful description of an air-car that flies but does not pollute the air like today's jets do. It works with the help of "hydrogen balls" (Hossain 2005: 13) and "wing-like blades" (Hossain 2005: 13). With a square wooden plank with seats to carry passengers, the balls are fastened to help them overcome gravity and float in the air. Today, a similar type of mechanism is used mainly in flying parachutes. The use of solar energy is a reason for keeping the place of Sister Sara cool. Human activity and present-day science overload our atmosphere with emissions that cause global warming by trapping heat and making the environment increasingly hotter. However, in Ladyland, no use of dangerous machinery would emit greenhouse gases. In the story, the solar beam used to fight back the enemy of another country may seem hilarious, but it fosters significant ideas.

Though the plot and technique may evoke laughter, concentrated solar power is essential science equipment in real life. This system generates solar power by using giant mirrors or lenses to concentrate a large area of sunlight onto a small space. By this process, a huge amount of electricity is produced. Hossain emphasises the use of the brain rather than the brawn. In the inverted world of *Sultana's Dream*, men who use the muscle rather than the brain are confined to the *mardana* performing their daily boring activities, while the women, headed by their Queen, run the country wisely and well. Hossain condemned male militarism as her thought is visible in Sister Sara's words: "We have no hand or voice in the management of our social affairs. In India man is lord and master, he has taken to himself all powers and privileges and shut up the women in the zenana" (Hossain 2005: 5). Sister Sara further says that "[A] lion is stronger than a man, but it does not enable him to dominate the human race. You have neglected the duty you owe to yourselves, and you have lost your natural rights by shutting your eyes to your own interests" (Hossain 2005: 5). The visitor to Ladyland is shocked at how could it be possible to be confined in the *mardana* from men's viewpoint whose brains are "bigger and heavier than women's" (Hossain 2005: 9). Again, Sister Sara replies with a very logically convincing answer: "Yes, but what of that? An elephant also has got a bigger and heavier brain than a man has. Yet man can enchain elephants and employ them, according to their own wishes" (Hossain 2005: 9). She here rejects the traditional notion of men having superior brains. While denying brute male power, she does not discard the ethics of her religion. Though she is in Ladyland in her dream, still she feels uneasy about roaming around unveiled on the way lest she should encounter any male, which, in her religion, is considered to be an unbecoming phenomenon. Perhaps, Sister Sara also adheres to these religious beliefs as, for example, "men had been asked to clear off" (Hossain 2005: 7) when she took the writer to the kitchen in the dream. As assumed from the text, it can be said that the people of Ladyland do abide by a religion that is, though not named, but common to all religions in real life, as Sister Sara, in reply to one of Sultana's queries, says, "[O]ur religion is based on love and truth. It is our religious duty to love one another and to be absolutely truthful" (Hossain 2005: 11–12). Even when men are not around, their reserved behavior may prove them to be verecund, but Hossain advocates that it is not the men but God that the women feel accountable towards.

Hossain wanted to give education to Muslim women and to be vested with more power. She wanted to create a scientific temperament among Muslim women through modern education. It was a tough job to go against one's own community, but she did. It was challenging to raise her voice against male power, but she realised that it was the need of the hour. In her work, she is "playing with conventional religious and cultural justifications for the seclusion of women.... She's also alluding to a conundrum that all feminist utopias that have any men in the picture at all have to address: the 'brute strength' problem" (Singh 2006: n. p.). She learnt English, acquired knowledge, and tried to spread it as wide as possible. She understood the importance of the language of the native people. She emphasised that Bengali language — not Urdu which was then choosen and spoken by the aristocratic Muslims — should be the medium of expression because the majority Muslims used it for speaking. She had mastery over Bengali and strappingly promoted its use at the Bangiya Nari Shikkha Sammelan (Convention on Women Literacy in Bengal) in 1927. She demanded the progress of the country and community only with the intellectual development of the people through modern education. She showed her concern about how Muslim women could adapt to the modern intelligentsia and reconcile their tradition with Western education throughout her life. Hossain had a brave heart that openly challenged the morality of colonisation. Though Hossain had adapted the modern attitude of the people from the West, she was not a blind follower or supporter of them. She did not spare the opportunity to criticise them when needed. Hossain was furious against the use of colonial power, which subjugated and suppressed the people. At the time of writing, she was very aware of British power. Yet, she was not afraid of standing against it. She directly scoffs at the British Raj when, through the Queen of Ladyland, she tells the narrator:

> We do not covet other people's land, we do not fight for a piece of diamond though it may be a thousand-fold brighter than the Koh-i-Noor, nor do we grudge a ruler his Peacock Throne. We dive deep into the ocean of knowledge and try to find out the precious gems, which nature has kept in store for us. We enjoy nature's gifts as much as we can. (Hossain 2005: 14)

Though the story is staunchly women-centric, there is a message for all human beings that women should be empowered to uplift society. Women have been in confinement, and they have got accustomed to it. They are there for so long that the majority of them have almost forgotten about their right. Consciously or unconsciously, they have accepted it as their reality:

> The messages in Sultana's Dream are not meant for men alone. The men of Ladyland, used to their seclusion and sidelining, have become used to their own subjugation, uninterested in rebellion, obsessed with the cleanliness of their kitchens and the petty details of their invisible lives. In the condescension she heaps on them in Sultana's Dream, Rokeya Sakhawat Hossain is careful to underscore how the toleration of suffering enables its persistence. The women who bear it in silence allow the perpetuation of oppression and are complicit in its persistence. (Zakaria 2013: n. p.)

Along with significant and crucial scientific inventions like cloud seeding and weaponry, Hossain also emphasised the scientific evolution of things used in domestic life, mainly by women. Being religious herself, she fills her story with a scientific temper: "Science plays a central role in this utopia; it allows the women to come to power in the first place, to eradicate disease, and to cultivate plenty of food despite the elimination of half the workforce" (Subramanian 2013: n. p.). She attacks patriarchy and decries colonialism. She keeps religion where it should be kept and embraces science. In *Sultana's Dream*, Hossain has shown a picture of possibility. It is a picture of a land where women can become leaders, religion and science can forget their antagonism, and people can live in absolute peace.

Bibliography

Hossain, R. S. *Sultana's Dream* and "Padmarag". New Delhi: Penguin Books, 2005.

———. "Abarodhbasini" ("The Zenana Women"). *The Essential Rokeya: Selected Works of Rokeya Sakhawat Hossain (1880-1932)*, edited, translated, and with an introduction by M. A. Quayum. Netherlands: Brill, 2013.

———. "Ardhangini" ("The Female Half"). *The Essential Rokeya: Selected Works of Rokeya Sakhawat Hossain (1880-1932)*, edited, translated, and with an introduction by M. A. Quayum. Netherlands: Brill, 2013.

———. "Borka" ("The Cloak"). *Begum Rokeya Rachanabali* (*Complete Works of Begum Rokeya*). Edited by Mostofa Mir. Dhaka: Bornayan, 2010.

———. "God Gives, Man Robs." *The Essential Rokeya: Selected Works of Rokeya Sakhawat Hossain (1880-1932)*, edited, translated, and with an introduction by M. A. Quayum. Netherlands: Brill, 2013.

———. "Home" ("Griha"). *The Essential Rokeya: Selected Works of Rokeya Sakhawat Hossain (1880-1932)*, edited, translated, and with an introduction by M. A. Quayum. Netherlands: Brill, 2013.

———. "Istri-jatir Abanati" ("Woman's Downfall"). *The Essential Rokeya: Selected Works of Rokeya Sakhawat Hossain (1880-1932)*, edited, translated, and with an introduction by M. A. Quayum. Netherlands: Brill, 2013.

———. "Nari Sristi" ("Creation of Women"). *The Essential Rokeya: Selected Works of Rokeya Sakhawat Hossain (1880-1932)*, edited, translated, and with an introduction by M. A. Quayum. Netherlands: Brill, 2013.

Sabir, A. "The Champion of Women-education-Rokeya". 30 November 2014. Accessed 11 June 2020. https://www.linkedin.com/pulse/20141130233822-243100982-the-champion-of-women-education-co-founder-rokeya-sav-international

Singh, A. "Where Women Rule and Mirrors Are Weapons". 14 May 2006. Accessed 22 July 2019. http://www.lehigh.edu/~amsp/2006/05/where-women-rule-and-mirrors-are.html

Subramanian, A. "Sultana's *Dream* by Rokeya Sakhawat Hossain". 30 September 2013. Review of *Sultana's Dream. Strange Horizons*. Accessed 10 May 2019. http://www.strangehorizons.com/reviews/2013/09/sultanas_dream_.shtml

Zakaria, R. "The Manless World of Rokeya Sakhawat Hossain". 13 December 2013. Accessed 23 June 2019. https://www.dawn.com/news/1072250/the-manless-world-of-rokeya-sakhawat-hossain

PART II
Caste-Gender Intersectionality and Resistance

PART II

Chapter 9

Individual and Agency in Derozio's "The Fakeer of Jungheera"

Siddhartha Chakraborti
Aligarh Muslim University, Uttar Pradesh, India

Abstract

Henry Derozio's long narrative poem "The Fakeer of Jungheera" has often been read as an indictment of the practice of sati and as an example of Derozio's own modest attempt in raising public opinion against the horrific practice. Alternatively, it is an early imitative Romance, or even an Orientalising work, exoticising sati for the West. However, the poem is not as straightforward as it may first appear. This chapter proposes to read the poem to interrogate how the poem foregrounds the question of individual agency in the assertion of self, life, and love in the face of bigotry, patriarchy, and religious oppositions. In what may very well be the first recorded instance of inter-religious love to be recorded in Indian English. This chapter, through close reading, hopes to find and uncover the timeless tropes which continue to inform narratives of purity, community, and honour that colour the imaginations of *"ghar wapsi"* (homecoming) and "love jihad" today. The chapter questions existing scholarship by attempting to historicise the poem in order to argue that it is a sustained work aimed at inspiring individual assertion in the times of the poet.

Keywords: Derozio, inter-religious love, individual agency, sati, patriarchy

* * *

The debate on sati has primarily been dominated by the binary of the legal and sacred, as famously argued by G. C. Spivak in the essay "Can the Subaltern Speak?" Interestingly, the death/suicide of the nationalist revolutionary Bhaduri is counterpoised to remind us of the many possibilities of the death/suicide beyond the banal and the quotidian, the obvious, and in the articulation of the exception, which demands a relook at the question of choosing death over life. The question of choice in itself reflects an agency, no matter how illusory, at least when the option is one of death over life and not merely a selection of commodities. The chapter will proceed to focus on this agency (or the denial of it) in a sustained rereading of Derozio's "The Fakeer of Jungheera" (1828), the only long narrative poem of Henry Louis Vivian Derozio, the young, firebrand teacher of the erstwhile Hindu College of Kolkata.

Also, a rereading it must be, for this chapter is nothing but a complete negation of existing popular and scholarly articles that have propped up the text either as an early imitative verse curiosity—a product of the existing debates on sati from the time that initially banned the practice through Western colonial diktats—as a romantic reworking or a collection of smaller works, and so on. Even more so, this chapter proposes to un-read the detailed sordid personal narrative of Derozio, the subverser of young Hindu boys, or hunt around in his already (over) written about short life for any authorial intention. Instead of such broad concerns, the chapter proposes to close read the text from an admittedly restricted vantage of choice, of possibility, of agency, for it is not the most exciting word of Spivak's title, "Can", also the most overlooked?

The real question that engulfs us from the beginning of the poem's narrative is the question of agency. Can Nuleni escape the flames? Can the Fakeer rescue her? Can they live happily ever after? Can the Fakeer defend them from the wrathful state instigated into action by a father seeking honor restoration? Can the doomed love of the unfortunate pair transcend into another age? To miss the question of the individual's agency will be to misread the poem—either as a romantic imitation, a sort of Orientalist mimicry by a half breed keen to further his position or a query of a pre-nationalistic eastern cosmopolitanism. If not for the question of agency, Derozio can be safely locked away as an individual moment of history rather than be recognised for inspiring the history of momentous individuals. Indeed, the key to the Derozian spirit that informs the Young Bengal Movement is this possibility of assertion against the norms—the assertion of the individual will rather than the subsumption of the individual identity into an organised group. While the underlying focus was the assertion against blind faith and societal restrictions, the vessel of that assertion was the individual rather than any collective. Because of this expectation, readers usually approach the text through their preconceived notion of Derozio as an anti-sati colonial-era reformer. Derozio is usually pre-read and through these expectations fueled further by the popularity of his proto-nationalist sonnets like "To India - My Native Land" and "Harp of India", both widely taught in Indian schools and colleges. However, the text of "The Fakeer of Jungheera" does not allow such a simplistic reading. The ambivalence that Derozio brings into his description of sati is also enforced by his short notes accompanying the text. In his note on Hindu Widows, he comments in the beginning:

that the Hindu Widow's burning herself with the corpse of her husband, is an act of unparalleled magnanimity and devotion. To break those illusions which are pleasing to the mind, seems to be a task which no one is thanked for performing, nevertheless, he who does so, serves the cause of Truth. (Derozio 2001: 162)

But the same note goes on to say:

The philanthropic views of some individuals are directed to the abolition of widow-burning, but they should first ensure the comfort of these unhappy women in their widowhood—otherwise, instead of conferring a boon upon them, existence will be to many a drudge, and a load....We are not the advocates of Concremation, or any of the doctrines of the superstitious Hindoos; but as we are perfectly convinced of their right to the peaceable enjoyment of this their particular, though inhuman ceremony, we have ventured to submit our sentiments with candour and boldness. It is however our firm, and sincere wish that the day may soon come when the rays of intellectual greatness will awaken the benighted natives of India from their long trance of bigotry and error. (Derozio 2001: 162–163)

Therefore, while it is clear that Derozio does not support sati as a practice, he is also not of the opinion that it can be merely banned forcefully. He is convinced of the right of the people to their rituals. Instead of direct colonial proscription, he is hoping for a change of attitudes through education and enlightenment. Sati in "The Fakeer of Jungheera" is not to be read from the binary of sacred or legal, but from the vantage of enlightened individual will. It is only through this understanding that we can relate Derozio's later paean to W. Bentinck, who abolished the practice in 1829, titled "On the Abolition of Sattee." While the poem is seen as a confirmation of Derozio's support for the governmental decree, we can nonetheless note that the poem is more concerned with the glorification of the individual Bentinck. The poem itself speaks of the yet-to-come day when women will be freed from injustice—implying that the mere decree will only do so much. Indeed, this is prophetic, since even after independence, the Indian government still had to pass The Commission of Sati Prevention Act, almost 142 years after Regulation XVII or the Bengal Sati Regulation of Bentinck stray cases of sati have continued to be reported into the twenty-first century.

This exaltation of the individual who will be battling despite all odds is not Romantic—and by this, we must understand that it is not merely a product of an esemplastic imagination. The poem in the collection is prefaced by an indicative sonnet, "To India - My Native Land", which clearly outlines what the poet is attempting in his collection. The poem's sestet states:

> Well—let me dive into the depths of time
> And bring from out the ages, that have rolled
> A few small fragments of these wrecks sublime
> Which human eye may never more behold. (Derozio 2001: 99)

While the sonnet has been panned by critics in its placement as an introduction to "The Fakeer of Jungheera" since prima facie, neither the collection of poems in general nor "The Fakeer of Jungheera" in particular qualifies as a small fragment of these wrecks sublime in the expected sense of past glory. Paranjape notes that the only allusion to some sublime impact lies in the allusion to *Vetal Pachhisi*. The section "The Legend of the Shushan" can be traced back to the *Kathasaritsagara* of Somdeva. The expectation is that the 'wrecks sublime' refers to some 'golden era' incidents such as King Vikramaditya from Hindu Indian mythology. Instead, we are presented with some failed love adventure from the period of Shah Shuja. The poetic imagination is to be historicised to understand the poem's mythopoeia—not that the poem is resurrecting a particular myth that historicises the country's present nationalist imagination. The poem must be read not only through an understanding of the times of the poet (as those times probably serve as the reception culture of the poem, not our times), but rather through an understanding of medieval Bengal under Shah Shuja.

In his second volume of *The History of Bengal*, it is, therefore, a little ironic that R. C. Majumdar refers to Bengal during the period of Shah Shuja's administration as a 'country without a history', quoting Gibbons to mean that this was a period of great peace and prosperity. He notes how the prince's position immediately below the Emperor awed intending rebels into submission and envious rivals at court into silence. There was no foreign incursion worth noticing in the province during his viceroyalty. Interestingly, the period immediately before Shah Shuja's rule had seen the culmination of multiple power struggle from within and outside Bengal, with the subjugation of Pathans landlords and Hindu kinglets united in a confederacy known as the Baro Bhuiyans by Raja Man Singh, the checking of Arakan pirates and Portuguese influence, including the capture and destruction of the fort of Hooghly by Qasim Khan, besides the conquest and addition of Assam to the Mughal sphere completed under Alayar Beg. The period also saw the gradual increase of influence of other European powers. Besides the Portuguese, Spanish, English, Dutch, French, Swedes, and even Austrians attempted to get into the rich trade opportunities that Bengal provided. Bengal was the wealthiest province in Mughal India and possibly one of the most affluent regions in the world. That Shah Shuja chose to flee and seek shelter with the Burmese Buddhist king on his defeat during the succession struggle shows a healthy exchange even with Buddhist Burma. The atmosphere of Bengal was, therefore, already multicultural, multiethnic, and cosmopolitan. There was a healthy mix of various religious, racial, cultural, and language groups in its major cities and ports, including Dhaka, Hooghly, and Rajmahal. It is into this medieval melting pot that we must situate the action "The Fakeer of Jungheera."

The action of "The Fakeer of Jungheera" itself can easily be criticised for being unrealistic, especially if they are read from our times. In a world where inter-religious love between Hindu women and Muslim men is decried as 'Love Jihad', it is difficult to believe that in medieval Bengal (and indeed most of India), it would have been common for rich and powerful landlords to marry and seek women from other religious communities as well. Not only could such courtship be acceptable, but it would also indeed be a matter of creating political alliances. Can we forget that even the great Mughals had Hindu wives? On the other hand, we also have examples of Hindu kings, Rajputs, and Marathas who married Muslim women. While not a norm as such, inter-religious marriages for political considerations was not uncommon. Indeed, Shah Shuja himself had married the Hindu daughter of Raja Tamsen of Kishtwar. The father of Nuleni, himself a Hindu Brahmin, approaches the Muslim noble for help and arms against a Muslim Fakeer at the Muslim capital of Rajmahal. This, too, would seem odd if read from our times when the flouting of social morality is invariably met with a communal response. Considering the history of the Baro Bhuiyans and resistance to Mughal rule, where Bengali Hindus and Muslims would have acted in accordance, this no longer seems improbable. Indeed, the unity of the state and the patriarchal authority in demanding retribution for lost honour is probably the only artifact that easily transcends the space-time of medieval Bengal to this age. The Fakeer meanwhile declares in the arms of Nuleni:

> No more to Mecca's hallowed shrine
> Shall wafted be a prayer of mine;
> No more shall dusky twilight's ear
> From me a cry complaining hear;
> Henceforth I turn my willing knee
> From Alla, Prophet, heaven, to thee. (Derozio 2001: XXVII)

By turning away from the Muslim creed of God and his prophet Muhammad, the Fakeer is doing a sort of idol worship, where Nuleni becomes a replacement of the almighty. Almost like a sort of a 'ghar wapsi, the Muslim Fakeer becomes a Hindu. If this rescue of the widow from sati is a holy war, the end of this love jihad is not through the victory of jihad but love. The saintly Fakeer from the beginning of the poem, who is described as 'holy' and 'hallowed' after the assertion of his 'self' through love, becomes the Robber-chief of the Robber band after giving up his communal religious identity. This contrasts with how Shuja's halls harbour profane and worldly nautch girls from Kashmir, besides minstrels singing of tantric sanyasis, through their aid of the father searching for vengeance, become "the stars of the Moslem Chivalry" (Derozio 2001: IX). They carry out "god's decree" (Derozio 2001: IX). The assertion of the Fakeer is against not only the norms of society in interrupting the ritual of sati, but goes on in the assertion of a forbidden love and finally climaxes in the assertion against religion and God. This transgression must be punished swiftly and leaves both the Fakeer and Nuleni dead in each other's arms. We must piece for ourselves the rest of the tale. How did Nuleni know the Fakeer from before her marriage? Did the Fakeer become a Fakeer because of the impossibility of his love being fulfilled? Is the Fakeer also of the same military aristocratic background, so far as he is not only well trained in fighting and horsemanship but also commands a sizeable, well-trained cavalry? Derozio links up the fragments from the wrecks in Canto 2 VII:

> I've gazed on many a ruined wall
> And shattered tower at Rajmahal;
> I've looked on many a battlement,
> By time destroyed or tempest rent;
> And as their fragments round me lay,
> Those mighty wrecks did I survey. (Derozio 2001: VII)

Here we realise that the fragments from the 'wrecks sublime' in the introductory sonnet are linked inextricably with Rajmahal, the capital of medieval Bengal, the wealthiest province of Mughal India, over 12 percent of the world's total GDP. In other words, Derozio, the 'East Indian', is probably not even thinking of some Indian glorious past but rather is thinking of medieval Bengal. As such, to bring in expectations of a modern national imagination into our reading of the poem will be ill-placed.

The poem, therefore, is less about sati or inter-religious love than it is an assertion of individual agency. It can be argued that Nuleni merely delays her death by escaping from the funeral pyre or that the choices of the Fakeer come to nothing since, in the end, they all die. However, that is the point of the poem—to bring to light fragments of sublime wrecks. It asserts how once in Bengal, it was possible to dare to go against the strictures of society, that too in the face of death—because the independence of thought and individual agency were alive. Derozio was undoubtedly hoping that by igniting that passion for freedom, he would inspire others to carve out their unique voices in their times as well.

Bibliography

Derozio, H. L. V. "The Fakeer of Jungheera". *Songs of the Stormy Petrel: Complete Works of Henry Louis Vivian Derozio*, edited by Dr Abirlal Mukhopadhyay et al. Calcutta: Progressive Publishers, 2001.

———. "The Harp of India". *Songs of the Stormy Petrel: Complete Works of Henry Louis Vivian Derozio*, edited by Dr Abirlal Mukhopadhyay et al. Calcutta: Progressive Publishers, 2001.

———. "On the Abolition of Sattee." *Songs of the Stormy Petrel: Complete Works of Henry Louis Vivian Derozio*, edited by Dr Abirlal Mukhopadhyay et al. Calcutta: Progressive Publishers, 2001.

———. "To India - My Native Land". 12 August 2021 (last modified). Accessed 07 December 2021. https://www.literaturewise.in/mdl/mod/page/view.php?id=321

Majumdar, R. C. *The History of Bengal*. Vol. II. Dacca: University of Dacca. 1948.

Paranjape, R. M. "East Indian Cosmopolitanism: The Fakeer of Jungheera and the Birth of Indian Modernity." *Interventions* 13, no. 4 (2011): 550–569.

Spivak, G. C. *Can the Subaltern Speak? Reflections on the History of an Idea*. New York: Columbia University Press, 2010. 94-104.

Chapter 10

Understanding Dalit Feminist Perspective through Bama's *Karukku*

Fouzia Usmani
Aligarh Muslim University, Uttar Pradesh, India

Abstract

Bama Faustina Soosairaj is a Dalit woman writer whose autobiographical work *Karukku* (1992) is not only a significant contribution to Dalit literature but has also been received well globally for the considerable energy and universality at its core. Having a subaltern identity herself as a Tamil Dalit Christian, Bama's works raise their voice against all forms of oppressing forces worldwide. The socio-political conditions of Dalit Christians, who embraced Christianity just to come out of their subaltern position within the Hindu religion, form the backdrop of Bama's literary ventures. After their conversion, Dalit Christians lost the privileges that they were entitled to as Hindu Dalits. Their status as low caste people remained unchanged even within Christianity. Bama has also emerged as a Tamil Dalit feminist for voicing against the traumatic life of Dalit Christian women in particular. In her works, Bama unfolds how caste, class, and gender intersect to exercise power and control at all levels. Dalit feminists address three different modes in which Dalit women are oppressed: first, as a Dalit by the upper caste community; second, as low-paid workers exploited by the upper caste landowners; and third, as women subjugated by the male members of their own community. The matrix of power exercised in all spheres of life is well articulated in her autobiography, *Karukku*. It is through her own lived experiences that Bama presents: first, what it is to live at the most outside layer of the hierarchical organisation of the Indian society; and second, it offers a fresh Dalit feminist perspective that refuses to identify with mainstream life, on the one hand, and asserts the identity of a Dalit woman empowered by education and awakened self-respect, on the other.

Keywords: caste, class, gender, Dalit Christian woman, Dalit feminism

***

> My final words of advice to you are Educate, Agitate and Organize; have faith in yourself. With justice on our side I do not see how we can lose our battle. The battle to me is a matter of joy. The battle is in the fullest sense spiritual. There is nothing material or social in it. For ours is a battle not for wealth or for power. It is a battle for freedom. It is a battle for the reclamation of the human personality
>
> Qtd. in Keer 2005: 351

Many female writers appeared in the 1970s, whose contribution to the women's movement in India is undoubtedly significant. Neera Desai, Maitreyi Krishnaraj, Jasodhara Bagchi, Iravati Karve, Vena Mujumdar, Susie Tharu, Vandana Shiva, and others were associated with the woman question in India. However, they followed the Western feminist perspective largely informed by Simon de Beauvoir's book *The Second Sex*. They did not pay much attention to the fact that the problems faced by Indian women are more complex and intrinsic, which cannot be understood through the lens of Western feminism solely. The issues need to be looked at within the context of the highly layered and hierarchical structure of Indian society. Sharmila Rege, a known woman scholar and associated with the second generation of feminists, came forward to address the problem across cultures, religions, classes, and communities. She knew that the Western perspective was not sufficient to address the concerns of Indian women as it failed to see it within the matrix of gender, caste, and religion. In her well-received work *Writing Caste/Writing Gender: Reading Dalit Women's Testimonies*, Rege opened a window to understanding the gender–caste interface. This book contributes to "the creation of caste-specific feminist organization and movements" (Ambewadikar 2016: 3). Dalit feminism is one such movement that takes to dealing with Dalit women's problems. Rege's work also plays a significant role in addressing the issues of Dalit women as it "explains the Dalit feminist standpoint using the life-narrative, or testimonies, of eight Dalit women from the 1920s until today" (Ambewadikar 2016: 2). Life narratives and testimonies of the Dalit women give an insight into the most authentic and barefaced reality of Dalit life. This point of view gives a boost to the autobiographical works of many Dalit women writers.

Bama Faustina Soosairaj, well known as Bama, is a Dalit woman writer whose autobiographical work *Karukku* (2000) awarded the Crossword Award for translation in 2001 contributes to Dalit literature and is received globally for marked energy and universality at its core. With casteism at its centre, the book has its relevance primarily within India, but its insistence "on humanism which crosses all boundaries" (Shameemunsia 2014: 101) makes it work worth reading around the world. Though this work is the life narrative of a Dalit Christian, it represents all those who have been oppressed culturally, economically, and politically. Thus, all the marginalised people are Dalits by implication, as affirmed by Gail Omvedt. According to M. S. Wankhede, "Dalit Literature is an umbrella term, which may be substituted by subaltern studies." (Wankhede 2017: 141–142)

Having a subaltern identity herself as a Tamil Dalit Christian, Bama's works articulate all forms of oppressing forces surrounding the marginalised community of Dalit Christians. The socio-political conditions of Dalit Christian, who embraced Christianity to get rid of their subaltern position within the Hindu religion, form the backdrop of Bama's literary ventures on the whole. After their conversion, Dalit Christian lost the privileges they were entitled to as Hindu Dalits. Their status as low caste people remained unchanged even within Christianity. Besides dealing with the ordeals of being Dalit Christian in general, Bama has also emerged as a Tamil Dalit feminist for voicing the traumatic life of Dalit Christian women:

> A recent wave of Dalit literature emerged as Dalit Feminism. Bama is a representative novelist of Dalit Feminism. Caste and Gender are the two important identity-building mechanisms that create a Dalit feminist perspective. Dalit feminism redefines women from the socio-political perspective of a Dalit, taking into account the caste and gender oppression (Kumar and Sabeetha 2017: 92).

Bama's works reveal the complex hierarchical structure of Indian society. People of Tamil Nadu are commonly considered inferior on a regional basis. A Dalit Tamil is a low caste among Tamils. Within the Dalit community, Paraya is the lowest in the order based on caste. The Paraya males further marginalise Paraya women. Herein, gender also has a role to play. In this labyrinthian structure of Indian society, Bama unfolds how caste, class, and gender intersect to exercise power and control at all levels. Dalit feminists address the three different modes in which Dalit women are oppressed: first, as a Dalit by the upper caste communities; second, as low-paid workers exploited by the upper caste landowners; and third, as women subjugated by the male counterparts of their own community. The matrix of power exercised in all spheres of life is well articulated in Bama's autobiography, *Karukku*, told through her own lived experiences as a Dalit woman.

Bama begins her autobiography with a detailed account of her village and its beautiful surroundings. The natural resources were also in full sway in her village. People earned their livelihood from the land as well as the woods. Before moving to the grim realities of caste and communities, she talks about the mesmerising beauty of nature, on the one hand, and the arrangement of lives around lands and woods, on the other in such a way that it engendered a class culture in the village. Dalits were not living a marginalised life on the grounds of their caste only, but they were also economically deprived. Bama highlights how the utilisation of natural resources was trapped in the hierarchical organisation of society. The upper caste was the privileged one and benefitted from most of the natural resources. The upper community occupied most of the lands, and the lower caste people were forced to work in their fields at very cheap labour rates. Parayas worked day and night to produce grains for the upper caste people, but they never had enough food to survive. Bama is also perplexed to see that men and women were paid differently. This is a sad state of affairs that a Dalit woman is paid less despite her equal contribution in production and fieldwork. What adds to her miserable condition is that she has to run the family alone with that meager amount that she earns. In her community, it is not the man who is the sole breadwinner in the family, but a woman too works to carry the financial burden. Moreover, they do it without any contribution from the male counterparts to the domestic expenditure. A Dalit woman, thus, faces marginalisation on the pretext of caste, gender, and class.

Bama resolved to write *Karukku* when she had forsaken "the life of renunciation and came out into the world" (Bama 2012: ix). She, thus, refused to live on the margin. She decided to become a nun to elevate her status and that of others but renounced this life after witnessing a similar pattern of power relations prevalent in the church. She became a nun to work for the poor but soon realised that the nuns, who had pledged to live a life renunciation, lived with all sorts of comforts and operated solely for the wealthy and the upper-class people. Though Christianity proclaims that there is no room for casteism, the Dalit Christians are still treated as untouchables within the church system when it comes to practice. The conditions of Dalits do not change even after changing their religion. Yogisha and Nagendra Kumar write:

> Discrimination against Dalits rampant within the Church is still a grave concern and that has been brought by a recently released report by the Tamil Nadu Untouchability Eradication Front (TNUEF). It describes how these Dalit Christians get lesser roles to play in church and get treated in inhuman manner by other Christians. (Yogisha and Kumar 2020: 150)

Bama recollects how her experiences in the church and at school during her formative years left her bewildered in both her mind and soul. As a child, Bama had an inquisitive nature that prompted her to question everything that came her way in the name of truth. She never readily accepted the knowledge provided by the church. She could discern fraudulent practices that pervaded everyday life in the name of God. Bama experienced inhuman discrimination and oppression in all spheres of life. Neither educational nor religious institutions are free from the evil of power politics. Whether it is an institution or knowledge structure, everything is oriented towards maintaining the power hierarchy within a social body.

If seen closely, it is mainly the imaginary knowledge provided about one group that helps maintain the power hierarchy within a social body. So, the ability becomes one of the means of power and control. The more influential group foregrounds some imaginary weaknesses of the weaker group to weaken their position further and strengthen their own. As opined by M. Foucault, power sustains itself through knowledge projected as the only truth. Foucault says:

> Knowledge linked to power, not only assumes the authority of "the truth" but has the power to make itself true. All knowledge, once applied in the real world, has effects, and in that sense at least, "becomes true." Knowledge, once used to regulate the conduct of others, entails constraint, regulation and the disciplining of practice. Thus, there is no power relation without the correlative constitution of a field of knowledge, nor any knowledge that does not presuppose and constitute at the same time, power relations. (Foucault 1977: 27)

The knowledge about Dalits that they are profane, untouchable, and insignificant people sustains the power relations within Indian society. The body becomes the site for the exercise of power. In the view of the Foucauldian discourse, a body is "a surface inscribed with culturally and historically specific practices and subject to political and economic forces" (King 2004: 30). "Truths" told about the Dalit community through generations led them not only to accept their inferior position in society but also to participate in their own subjectification and subjugation. Bama was puzzled seeing the behaviour of her parents, who exhibited extreme servility before the upper-caste people. They voluntarily participated in their own subjection by willingly conforming to the hierarchical norms. Bama informs:

> Because Dalits have been enslaved for generation upon generation, and been told again and again of their degradation, they have come to believe that they are degraded, lacking honour and self-worth, untouchable; they have reached a stage where they themselves, voluntarily, hold themselves apart.... This is what even little babies are told, how they are instructed. (Bama 2012: 28)

Bama as a child used to play games with the other children in which some of them played untouchables, and the others became upper-caste people. They would also play gender-oriented games. In such games, a boy would act as a patriarch, and a girl pretended to be a passive and helpless wife receiving blows from her husband regularly. Bama writes:

> Even when we played "mothers and fathers," we always had to serve the mud "rice" to the boys first. They used to pull us by the hair and hit us says, "what sort of food is this, di, without salt or anything!" In those days, we used to accept those pretence blows, and think it was all fun. Nowadays, for many of the girls those have become real blows and their entire lives are hell. (Bama 2012: 31)

A Dalit woman undergoes the mental trauma of segregation in society based on caste and suffers physical violence at the hands of the male members of her family, which is reflected in the games the children played. This shows how casteism and gender discrimination have seeped so deeply into their system that even the innocent children's innocent games do not remain untouched. Bama reveals in her fictional work, *Sangati*, how Dalit women are often said to be haunted by spirits. Such knowledge about Dalit women, according to Bama, is nothing but to push them towards more intense forms of marginalisation, "otherness", and rejection in society. Bama looks at such concocted stories about Dalit women from the psychological angle: "[O]ver worked and exploited in the family these women give vent to their mental agony in their possessed state" (Kumar and Sabeetha 2017: 94).

One's social position in society decides one's identity. Identity, which is thought to be fixed, is, in reality, fluid and flexible. Since birth, the fixities and rigidities that inform an individual's life leave no room for change and alteration. Bama experienced the problem of untouchability from an early age. Her young mind failed to understand the meaning of "Paraya". She always wondered, "[w]hat did it mean when they called us 'Paraya'. Had the name become that obscene?" (Bama 2012: 16). Like others, Bama tried to know her identity by placing herself within the network of language. She was caught in the maze of the linguistically defined identity of a person or a community. The term "Paraya" is not used as a different identity from Naicker, but it is used to ascertain the negative attributes attached to the Paraya community.

According to Ferdinand de Saussure, "language constitutes our world; it doesn't just record it or label it. Meaning is always attributed to the object or idea by the human mind, and constructed by and expressed through language: it is not already contained within the thing" (quoted in Barry 2006: 43). If seen under the Saussurean linguistic theory, the term "Paraya" means utterly hostile when it is paired with another word "Necker". Our perception of the world, since Aristotle's time, has been governed by the laws of logic that have divided "the world into strictly demarcated entities" (Habib 2005: 668). "[A]ccording to Aristotle's laws, [...] either one is a man, or one is woman; a person is either black or white, either master or slave" (Habib 2005: 668). Such normative dualism is thought to be based entirely on natural distinctions. However, when seen through postmodern perspectives, they are socio-cultural constructs and mere imaginary structures that largely govern one's identity, sexuality, subjectivity, and the intricate implications of the social spectrum. Any identity is not an essential identity. It is fluid and remains in a state of flux.

Bama breaks away from her subaltern identity and becomes a nonconformist. She comes out of the submissiveness and extreme servility which her community members have been exhibiting for ages. She makes herself believe that she, too, has a right to live with dignity. It is not her caste that will fix her identity and regulate her existence; instead, she relies on her education, abilities, and personality to positively sway her life. Though the educational institutions are not free from such inhuman practices, Bama continues her education, considering it the only weapon that could be used to assert her rights. When she joined college to take up a Bachelor of Education degree, she witnessed the same story there too.

> Yet, because I had the education, because I had the ability, I dared to speak up for myself; I didn't care a toss about caste. Whatever the situation, I held my head high. And I completed whatever I took up, successfully. So, both teachers and students showed me certain affection, respect affection, respect. In this way because of my education alone I managed to survive among those who spoke the language of caste-difference and discrimination. (Bama 2012: 22)

Thus, by using her education and abilities, Bama broke away from the identity given to her by religious and social institutions and adopted a different identity altogether. Bama, like Sharmila Rege, followed what was advised by B. R. Ambedkar: "My final words of advice to you are Educate, Agitate and Organize; have faith in yourself. With justice on our side, I do not see how we can lose our battle" (Keer 2005: 351). Walking on the path shown by Dr. Ambedkar, many women scholars like Rege and Bama have desperately worked towards educating Dalit women. They firmly believed that it is only through education that a suppressed community can elevate itself. These women set the mark by educating themselves, no matter what they faced, as the educational system itself is not free from power politics. They never gave up. They educated themselves and dexterously worked towards educating other Dalit women. It is, thus, liberation through the power of education that they professed through their acts and works.

Bama, in most of her works, portrays every Dalit woman's journey from suppression to resurrection. Bama herself, as she reveals in *Karukku*, does not adjust to the old caste system and patriarchal setup. She instead moves towards self-assertion and liberation. Most of her female protagonists are the prototype of Bama herself. They, in turn, represent all the Dalit women who have undergone almost similar oppression and suppression. Bama, through her writings, shows them a path towards self-respect and dignity. Education becomes one of the powerful tools that can bring change in society. Anshu Sailpar writes, "As a feminist writer Bama protests against all forms of oppression and relying on the strength and resilience of Dalit women, makes an appeal for change and self-empowerment through education and collective action" (Sailpar 2015: 477). They take up steps towards their right to live with dignity and respect. Thus, the book is an essential contribution towards the liberation of every soul that has suffered marginalisation in one form or the other. *Karukku* is about asserting selfhood, refusing to live at the margins, and facing the world. The title "Karukku" gives insight into the author's role in showing a path towards emancipation. Dual meaning is embedded in the term Karukku—a Tamil word for "palmyra leaves, that, with their serrated edges on both sides, are like a double-edged sword" (Holmstrom 2001: n. p.). A part of the word *karu* means 'embryo or seed', which suggests freshness and newness. The term has two levels of symbolic meanings that give twin objectives to the author. The sharp edges of the leaves, which often injured Bama when she used to go into the woods, suggest the intense and painful wounds she received from society in the name of caste and gender. The same term also symbolically denotes new energy to liberate, from the shackles of discriminatory practices, the members of her community and other communities worldwide. Bama, through this pivotal work, does not only relate her painful experiences as a Dalit, but she also becomes a voice of assertion and liberation for all the marginalised sections of society:

> Karukku stands as a means of strength to the multitudes whose identities have been destroyed and denied…. [I]t has reminded its readers not only that Truth alone is victorious, but that only the Truth is the Truth. Karukku has enabled many to raise their voices and proclaim, 'My language, my culture, my life is praiseworthy, it is excellent. (Bama 2012: x)

The oppresses people refuse to live with the identity that is constituted by caste, class, and gender; they instead assert themselves with a different identity. They have a complete view of life as they have understood all the patterns of social constructs living outside mainstream life. They have the status of "outsider-within"—a term coined by P. H. Collins (1986): "'Outsider-within' status holder occupies a special space that their difference makes; they become different people, 'the other', 'marginalised'. It shapes the perspective of the experience, which locates a unique standpoint…. Their difference makes them conscious of the patterns or social constructions that may be beyond the comprehension or sight of sociological insiders" (Sharma and Kumar 2020: 24). Bama, through her own experiences, represents first what it is to live at the most outer layer of the hierarchical organisation of society and then presents a fresh Dalit feminist perspective: refusing to identify with the mainstream life, on the one hand, and asserting her identity as a Dalit woman empowered by education and awakened self-respect, on the other. The work is optimistic in its orientation. It stands true to what Sharanhumar Limbale writes that "Dalit literature is life-affirming literature" (Limbale 2010: 105). Through this pivotal work, the author emerges as a source of truth. She becomes a voice of assertion and affirmation. Thus, in short, the story of Bama's life can be summarised as a journey from suppression to resurrection.

Bibliography

Ambewadikar, J. "Writing Caste/Writing Gender: Perspective of Sharmila Rege". *Journal of Social Science*, no. 22 (June–July 2016): 2-3.

Bama, F. *Karukku*. 2nd Edition. Translated by Lakshmi Holmstrom. Oxford: Oxford University Press, 2012.

Barry, P. *Beginning Theory: An Introduction to Literary and Cultural Theory*. Chennai: T. R. Publications, 2006.

Collins, P. H. "Learning from the Outsider Within: The Sociological Significance of Black Feminist Thought." *Social Problems* 33, no. 6 (1986).

De Beauvoir, S. *The Second Sex*. New York: Vintage Books, 1989.

Foucault, M. *Discipline and Punish*. London: Tavistock, 1977.

Habib, M. A. R. *A History of Literary Criticism: From Plato to the Present*. Oxford: Blackwell Publishing, 2005.

Holmstrom, L. "Introduction to *Karukku*: Excerpted from the Book." 23 April 2001. Accessed 4 June 2020. https://www.outlookindia.com/website/story/introduction-to-karukku/211413

Keer, D. D. *Ambedkar: Life and Mission*. Mumbai: Popular Prakashan Pvt. Lmt., 2005. 351.

King, A. "The Prisoner of Gender: Foucault and the Disciplining of the Female Body". *Journal of International Women's Studies* 5, no. 2 (2004): 29–39.

Kumar, A. Vignesh, and R. S. Sabeetha. "Bama's *Sangati* as a Unique Dalit Feminist Narration from Subjugation to Celeberation". *International Journal of Interdisciplinary Research in Arts and Humanities* (IJIRAH) 2, no. 1 (2017): 92–94.

Limbale, S. *Towards an Aesthetic of Dalit Literature*. New Delhi: Oxford University Press, 2010.

Rege, S. *Writing Caste/Writing Gender: Reading Dalit Women's Testimonies*. New Delhi: Zuban, 2006.

Sailpar, A. "Matrix of Dalit Feminism in Bama Fustina's *Karukku* and *Sangati*: Events". *International Journal of Applied Research*. 1, no. 9 (2015): 477.

Shameemunisa. "Unheard Voices: A Comparative Study of Two Dalit Women's Autobiographies." *Luminaire, a Refereed Journal of the Department of Languages Department of Language*s 4, no. 1 (2014): 101.

Sharma, B., and A. Kumar. "Learning from 'the Outsider Within': The Sociological Significance of Dalit Women's Life Narratives". *Journal of International Women's Studies* 21, no. 6 (August 2020): 24.

Wankhede, M. S. "A Study of Bama's *Karukku* in the Light of Subalterneity". *Lietrary Herald: A International Refereed English e-Journal* 2, no. 4 (March 2017): 141–142.

Yogisha, and N. Kumar. "Stepping out of the 'Difference': Discerning the Dalit Female Stand point in Bama's *Sangati*". *Contemporary Voice of Dalit* 12, no. 2 (2020): 149–164.

Chapter 11

Reinterpreting to Retrieve Lost Women's Voices: Gendered Subalternities in Mahasweta Devi's "Bayen" and Raja Rao's "Javni"

Kusumika Sarkar
Aligarh Muslim University, Uttar Pradesh, India

Abstract

This chapter will closely read the short stories "Bayen" and "Javni" written by Mahasweta Devi and Raja Rao, respectively, to extract the lost voices of the women protagonists of these stories. In "Bayen", the protagonist is presented as a demon or a witch, whereas in "Javni", the protagonist is shown to be simple-minded or a fool by some and as a witch and evil spirit by others. While Bayen eventually is recognised by the state as a hero, Javni is elevated to be a saint or even a goddess. However, what is not presented clearly or rather is left in between the lines waiting for rediscovery and retrieval are the stories of two Dalit women doubly oppressed on account of their gender and caste. The members of the higher castes oppress both women, but rather their oppression is amplified by the actions of their community or family. Therefore, the agencies that subalternise these women include precisely those that should have been at the forefront, ensuring their dignity and autonomy. Through the lives of Chandidasi and Javni, this chapter aims to study the social and material conditions of Dalits and the reasons that propagate the pain and violence inflicted on the women of these communities. As the protagonists of both stories are women, this chapter intends to investigate why the intersection of caste and gender becomes so crucial in understanding the predicaments of Dalit women. This chapter will also unravel how the two women, despite all odds, assert their identities and free will to generate a life free of humiliation, even though the rewards and recognitions awarded to them at the end of the short stories miss the mark completely.

Keywords: intersectionality, doubly oppressed, Dalit women, saint, witch

***

In an article by Seema Yasmin on 11 January 2018, the author cites an incident in Gujarat where the villagers punished three women for being 'dakan' (witches) in Gujarati. As if only physical punishment was not enough to satisfy the cruelty of the villagers, these women also had to transfer their property rights and land ownership to their relatives. In patriarchal and misogynist social structures, women are often considered easy scapegoats who can be blamed for all the illnesses, sufferings, and deaths around them. This witch-hunt most of the time comes from the woman's own family or community since they are entitled to the immediate material gain that such practices provide. This practice makes the already vulnerable and downtrodden group so weak that they can hardly even think about raising their voices in protest.

The incident mentioned above is one among many that emphasises why Dalit women's socio-economic and political conditions call for a movement that is different from mainstream Indian feminism and specifically focused on addressing the issues of Dalit women. Dalit feminism questions the homogeneity between the categories of caste and gender and points out the intersectionality between these two categories that establish Dalit women's experience as different from Dalit men's experience or the experience of upper-caste women. Both the texts under study here reflect the extreme adversities and oppression that the women characters are subjected to due to their status in society as Dalits and as women. Recognising the "dual patriarchies", that is, Brahminical and Dalit, Anindita Pan has pointed out that the oppression of Dalit women "is not one dimensional" (Pan 2021: 33). This chapter will closely read the short stories "Bayen" and "Javni", written by Mahasweta Devi and Raja Rao, respectively, to extract the lost voices of the women protagonists.

As Dalit women, both Chandidasi Gangadasi and Javni respectively are doubly oppressed on account of their gender and caste. Members of the higher castes oppress both women, but rather their oppression is amplified by the actions of their own community and family. Therefore, the agencies that subalternise these women include precisely those that should have been at the forefront, ensuring their dignity and autonomy. Through the lives of Chandidasi and Javni, this chapter aims to study the social and material conditions of Dalits and the reasons that propagate pain and violence on the women of their own communities. As the protagonists of both stories are women, this chapter intends to investigate why the intersection of caste and gender becomes so important in understanding the predicaments of Dalit women. This chapter will also unravel how the two women, despite all odds, assert their identities and free will to generate a life free of humiliation, even though the rewards and recognitions awarded to them at the end of the short stories miss their mark entirely.

In Mahasweta Devi's "Bayen", which appeared as a short story in 1971, the plot moves forward when there is a conflict between Chandidasi's idea of being irreligious and inhuman and society's idea of being heartless. The word "bayen" in Bengali means "witch." As a mother and as a member of the Gangadasi community, not taking care of the dead children's tombs is irreligious and inhuman for Chandidasi. At the same time, society interprets it differently and treats her innate humanity with cruel inhumanity. Javni's passive acceptance of her inhumane conditions, on the other hand, disturbs the first-person narrator, an educated and liberal, Ramappa. The omniscient narrator in "Bayen" gives Chandidasi some space to express her emotions. While in "Javni", Javni's voice is completely lost under the voice of the first-person narrator, Ramappa, subalternising Javni further, as the power of narration lies with somebody else. In "Bayen", the author makes it clear in the very beginning that a bayen is a witch that cannot be killed as killing a bayen can result in the death of one's children. After turning into Chandibayen from Chandidasi, she lives the life of a pariah near the railway tracks. The railway tracks suggest the juxtaposition of modern technology with superstition, therefore, highlighting the contrast. This connection between modern technology and superstition continues till the end when Chandibayen sacrifices her life to stop the havoc that the abuse of technology can cause. This sacrifice silences the superstitious minds of her village, at least for some time when they acknowledge Chandibayen as one of them.

Superstition works in strange ways. According to popular belief, as a bayen, Chandidasi is powerful enough to suck the blood out of anyone she wants to just by casting a glance, but she is kind and generous enough not to do so with those people who even refuse to treat her as a human being. A bayen has to warn people when she walks out so that everybody else can move out of her sight. As a "bayen should not eat too much" (Devi 2004: 2), a man from the Dom community leaves a week's ration for the bayen near a tree. The ration includes half a kilogram of rice, a handful of pulses, salt, oil, and some other food. Sometimes, the dogs steal it, and the bayen has nothing to eat for the entire week. Nobody sells anything to a bayen. So a bayen cannot buy anything even if she manages to get money from somewhere. People throw mud and stones at the bayen. She is even blamed for being a bayen by the same community who forcefully tagged her as a bayen, in a society where women are valued only if they give birth to a son or are beautiful. A woman such as Chandi, who is sensitive towards even the dead is bound to be treated like a pariah. As a descendant of Kalu Dom and as a woman who belongs to the community of Gangadasi, Chandidasi Gangadasi has to bury dead children. After her father's death, since there is no male member in her family, she tries to carry forward her family's legacy by sincerely performing her duty to bury dead children below five years and guard their graves. It is only when Chandidasi becomes a mother herself that she starts feeling the death of children so profoundly that her pain for the dead children and her dedication to saving their corpses from the jackals grows fiercely inside her. She becomes unable to carry out the job assigned to her family by God himself.

However, neither the villagers nor her husband Malindar Gangaputta is ready to let her leave her work. When her sister-in-law's daughter Tukni dies of smallpox, the entire blame comes upon Chandi. However, many children are dying at that time as people prefer to pray for their cure to Goddess Sheetala, who controls epidemics, rather than vaccinate their children. Chandidasi also prays to Goddess Sheetala for Tukni's well-being. Irrespective of that, when Tukni dies, she is blamed for her death. The villagers express their doubts about Chandidasi's emotions and extra dedication for the dead children. An angry Chandidasi immediately leaves her work and silences everybody by saying, "I'll let you cowards guard the graves. I have wanted to leave for a long time. The Gangaputta will get a government job soon. I need not continue with this rotten work anymore" (Devi 2004: 9). Society never likes an independent woman with a voice of dissent. Being a woman from the Dalit community, the intersection of caste and gender makes Chandidasi's position vulnerable. People of the Dom community start keeping an eye on her. Leaving her forefather's job makes Chandidasi afraid of God's punishment as guarding the dead is the duty assigned to her family by God. When jokingly Malindar calls her a bayen, the possibility of going away from her husband and family makes her feel so helpless that she wants to run away somewhere else with her husband Malindar and son Bhagirath. As the author says, "[T]here is nothing a society cannot do" (Devi 2004: 10) and it successfully labels Chandidasi's sensitivity, her dedication towards the job of her forefathers, and her love as well as care for the dead children as the characteristics of a bayen. This again establishes society's inability to accept someone different, especially if that person is a woman doing a man's job in a manly world.

Society's beliefs become deeply rooted in Chandibayen's mind, too, and she stops trusting her inner goodness. This internalisation of societal beliefs and practices turns Chandibayen into a victim that never questions. She does not look directly at her son Bhagirath or her husband Malindar because of her fear of harming them. She never desires that her son know who she truly is. Malindar believes that she cannot hurt her own son. When Malindar reveals Chandibayen's true identity to Bhagirath, he cannot stop himself from going and meeting the bayen alone as a son. As Chandibayen completely mistrusts herself now, she becomes protective about her son and feels angry at Malindar

Reinterpreting to Retrieve Lost Women's Voices 105

that he cannot care for his own son and allows him to come to meet the bayen alone. This feeling of anger that has almost been forgotten is suddenly rekindled in Chandibayen for protecting her son. In her rage, she goes to look for Malindar. While walking along the railway tracks, she finds that a group of people are piling up bamboos and sticks on the railway tracks, intending to loot the five-up Lalgola passenger train about to arrive with its Wednesday mailbag. For the first time, the bayen's appearance stops some unjust action from happening, although she finally has to sacrifice her life to stop the mischief the looters have done. The bayen's arrival makes the group run away in fear, but they run away without removing the bamboos and sticks they have piled on the railway tracks. Chandibayen tries to invoke her supernatural powers to gather the dark demons to help her stop the train and save the lives of many innocent people. But she feels as helpless as she has always been. So she starts running along the railway tracks towards the train, shouting at it to stop. Just as her voice never reaches society, similarly, it remains unable to pierce through the loud noise of the train and get anyone till the train silences her voice completely. Surprisingly, her death again transforms her from Chandibayen to Chandidasi Gangadasi when the Railway Department announces a medal for her sacrifice. Now the Doms accept her as one of them in front of the officer-in-charge. The heartlessness of the community leaves Bhagirath sobbing. As he liberates his late mother's name from the identity of a bayen, the community as a whole hide behind a "suffocating and unbearable" (Devi 2004: 14) silence.

In Raja Rao's "Javni", the protagonist Javni is past 40 and belongs to the washermen community. Like Javni's bare forehead carries the sign of widowhood, her superstitious mind represents the Indian villages. Her disregard for her self-respect leaves Ramappa, an educated, liberal young man, completely shaken. Javni considers Ramappa as God. This comes from Javni's total ignorance about the class, caste, or even gender hierarchy in her society. The necessity of acknowledging the intersection between caste and gender becomes evident when we see the relationship Sita shares with Javni. Despite being a woman and having a cordial relationship with Javni, Sita also participates in oppressing Javni. As a maidservant to Sita, Javni always calls Sita "mother", although Javni herself is older. The way Sita addresses and talks to Javni in a patronising tone makes the class and caste hierarchy very evident. Sita tells Ramappa how she considers Javni almost like an "elder sister or a mother" (Rao 2005: 173). Still, Sita's manner and treatment of Javni never justify her love and affection for Javni as a mother. Despite Ramappa's protest, Sita leaves Javni's food at the byre as Javni is from the lower caste, and she cannot sit and eat with them. Javni, also is not ready to come and have her food in the hall even after Ramappa requests her many times. She prefers to eat in the byre among the cows surrounded by darkness. Javni responds to Ramappa's question about why she does not light a lamp while eating by saying that the oil is too expensive, while for Ramappa the oil price is nothing. This again highlights the class difference that forces her to live a life of disgrace and humiliation.

As a woman, Javni's life was secure as long as her husband was alive. However, after he dies of a snakebite, Javni's misfortune begins. She is thrown out of her house by her sisters-in-law. Having no other place to go, she comes to her brother Bhima knowing that Bhima has always hated her. Also, misfortune does not leave Javni as her sister-in-law thinks Javni can bewitch her child, and Bhima thinks Javni carries misfortune wherever she sets foot. After much pleading by Javni, Bhima agrees to give her a little hut near the garden door. Javni is blamed for all the disasters in her own life and the lives of other people around her. The treatment Javni receives from everybody around her after the death of her husband points out the multi-dimensional nature of the oppression that Dalit women encounter due to the intersection of caste and gender. Despite being called a "witch and an evil spirit" (Rao 2005: 181) by others, Javni never loses faith in Goddess Talakamma. She feels thankful to the goddess for her blessings. Javni's acceptance of the caste system becomes evident when she says to Ramappa that the Brahmins are the "choosen ones" (Rao 2005: 183) and adds further that "the sacred books are yours. The Vedas are yours. You are all, you are all, you are the twice-born. We are your servants, Ramappa. Your slaves" (Rao 2005: 183). Javni's internalisation of class and caste hierarchy makes her indifferent towards her inhuman condition. Towards the end of the story, when Sita leaves Malkad with her brother Ramappa and her husband, Javni keeps following their bullock cart as far as she can. Suddenly after crossing the river, when Ramappa looks at the other side of the river, Javni appears almost like a divine or a supernatural figure to Ramappa.

In "Javni", Javni mentions the suicide of the potter's wife Rangi and the death of children, which echoes the death of children among the Dom community in "Bayen". Only Malindar can sign his name in the Dom community and has acquired a government job by it. Again, In Javni's family, none of Javni's brothers-in-law have stable source of earning. The illiteracy, poverty, and unemployment among these Dalit groups like the Dom and Washerman community become pretty evident from both the stories. To vent their frustration created by the inequality in society, the men of these communities often target their own people and especially women, to assert their power and gain whatever little material profit that practices like a witch-hunt can give them.

Both Chandidasi Gangadasi and Javni carry the epithets of ideal Indian women with virtues like infinite patience, complete selflessness, and an intense desire to sacrifice if the need arises. It becomes deeply rooted in the mind of both Chandidasi Gangadasi and Javni that what has been done cannot be undone, and "this is how society is, this is how it works" (Devi 2004: 13). Both of them never had the agency to question what society does. Chandidasi tries to ask things initially by leaving the work her forefathers were assigned to do for generations, but the fear of ignoring the duty God entrusted to her family makes Chandidasi paranoid about it, and she remains unable to return to her normal life. Superstition works in the same way in Javni's mind as well. She tries to be happy even with the very little that Goddess Talakamma has given her. Although her life is full of suffering and humiliation, Javni never tries to resist the humiliation she is subjected to because of the lack of agency. Neither their religion nor their gender provides them with any agency that they can use to voice their protest against their wretched conditions. By sacrificing her life, Chandidasi Gangadasi becomes a state hero. In contrast, by sacrificing all her desire for respect and love in society and by internalising societal beliefs and practices, Javni rises to the status of a goddess to Ramappa.

What is acknowledged by the state and then by Ramappa in Chandidasi and Javni is the self-sacrifice of both these women. It is their sacrifice, internalisation of oppressive societal beliefs and practices, and passive acceptance of the discomfort imposed equally by upper-caste people and the people of their own communities, which ironically helps them secure their survival. The fear of being irreligious makes Chandidasi the "other", and she imbibes that otherness as part of her identity until she realises that Chandidasi and Chandibayen are equally powerless. Only after her death does the legal justice system intervene to give her the identity of Chandidasi Gangadasi back to her. In Javni's case, the same fear of God, religion, and society makes Javni passively accept her position as the "other." Being called a "witch" by everybody, including her own family members who throw her out of the house, Javni is denied every right over a life of dignity and hard work, along with losing all her rights over the property of both her husband's side as well as her paternal side. Ramappa's attempt at making Javni one with nature and conferring divinity upon her further complicates the matter by taking Javni's oppression away from the radar of the legal justice system. Although Sita finds Javni like a mother, her treatment of Javni highlights the necessity of addressing the intersectionality of caste and gender or the multidimensionality of Dalit women's experiences.

Similarly, the way the Dalit community looks at the bayen's intention of carrying out her forefather's occupation despite being a woman establishes Dalit women's experiences as different from the experiences of Dalit men or upper-caste women. The actions, statements, and even silences have to be interpreted to retrieve the lost stories of these women. Chandidasi tries to create her identity by basing it on her family profession rather than through her husband. Her desire to carry forward the duty God has assigned to her family reveals her yearning for having an identity that society denies her so vehemently. Her strategy for gaining the identity denied to her for her entire life happens by securing martyrdom. Her martyrdom can be read along the lines that for reclaiming her identity, her act becomes a superior act of knowledge, and also it becomes proof of her purity. Her death symbolically resists and overturns the entire social machinery that did not give her any space for resistance. This makes her an active subaltern who, despite her silence, completely changes the way she is perceived. In the second case, Javni denies herself an identity and material wealth, questions and resists the social structure, and creates oppression.

Bibliography

Devi, M. "Bayen". Translated by Mahua Bhattacharya. In *Separate Journeys: Short Stories by Contemporary Indian Women*, edited by Geeta Dharmarajan and Mary Ellis Gibson, 1–14. South Carolina: University of South Carolina Press, 2004.

Pan, A. *Mapping Dalit Feminism: Towards an Intersectional Standpoint.* New Delhi: Sage Publication India Pvt. Ltd, 2021.

Rao, R. "Javni". *In Twelve Modern Short Stories*, edited by Name Surname,166–185. Oxford: Oxford University Press, 2005.

Yasmin, S. "Witch Hunts Today: Abuse of Women, Superstition and Murder Collide in India." *Scientific American* (2018). Accessed 23 May 2020. https://www.scientificamerican.com/article/witch-hunts-today-abuse-of-women-superstition-and-murder-collide-in-india/

PART III
Caste and Resistance

Chapter 12

Casteism and Colonial Discourse: A Projection of Marginality in Bama's *Karukku*

Abdus Sattar
Galsi Mahavidyalaya, Purba Bardhaman, West Bengal, India

Abstract

India is a multicultural and multilingual country based on various castes, classes, creeds, languages, and religions. In a caste-based society like India, one caste is dominated by the other. The upper-caste discriminated against and marginalized the Dalits in every sphere of their life, be it social, cultural, economic, and even political. In the British regime, people were colonized politically, but now they are colonized in the name of birth and denied their fundamental rights and amenities. The Dalit people accept their inferior status because they believe that they are imperfect and born to serve the upper-caste through generations. This hegemonic ideology has been naturally implanted in the psyche of the Dalits. Bama's *Karukku* written by a Dalit woman writer, delineates the problems of casteism and projects the marginality confronted by the Dalits. The present chapter will highlight how the upper-caste brutally sidelined and tortured the Dalits in our caste-based society. Here the article also quests to find the means to eliminate such casteism.

Keywords: Casteism, Dalits, hegemony ideology, lower-caste, marginality, upper-caste

* * *

In the twenty-first century, all countries enjoy political independence and freedom from the British regime, but they fail to ensure and enjoy absolute freedom. The Britishers left India in 1947 that heralded the end of the colonial administration of the occidental people. After the colonial rule, people are still being colonized and suppressed by neo-colonial mechanisms stemming from their internal culture and politics. In terms of gender, power does not come from the outside but inside the state. Like the occidental people, some people who have enjoyed this superior position have succeeded in ingraining hegemonic ideologies in the psyche of needy people. They are dexterously made to believe that they are inferior and born to serve the upper-caste people. These hegemonic ideologies barricade one group of people from the mainstream, ultimately breaking the world into fragments. Narrow domestic walls have broken up the current world. For the vested interests of one group of people, the lower-caste people or the marginalized people have to go through immense suffering that ultimately ends on the trajectory of the self and one's identity.

The Indian Constitution ensures and guarantees equality and liberty to all the citizens of India, irrespective of caste, creed, and gender. The Indian Constitution provides rights to all its citizens; they can freely access public places and can also use wells, tanks, bathing *ghats* (rivers), roads, etc., without any hesitation. In our multicultural and multilingual land, we can find unity in diversity, but the demography of India tells a different story; a specific community, called Dalits, is considered as untouchables/outcasts and deprived of their fundamental rights. In some parts of India, people are primarily measured based on caste, class, religion, sex, and language, and one community is easily separated from other communities. In the introduction of *Karukku*, L. Holmström defines 'Dalits' as those "who are oppressed: all hill peoples, neo-Buddhists, labourers, destitute farmers, women and all those who have been exploited politically, economically or in the name of religion" (Holmström 2012: xviii). They perform the most menial jobs in the most abject situations in society. They are often ousted entirely from society and left to do menial jobs. In her article "Dalit Literature", Bama has extensively discussed and written about Dalit literature. According to her, Dalit literature is:

> Liberation literature like Black Literature, Feminist Literature and Communist- Socialist Literature ... there are traces of the agony and ecstasy of the dalits, the direct and emotional outbursts, the collective identity, the mockery and caricature of the immediate oppressors, the supernatural powers of oracle and the mythical heroism: these are the several elements for the reconstruction of a conscious Dalit literature. (Bama 1999: 97–98)

S. K. Limbale, in his seminal book on Dalits, *Towards an Aesthetics of Dalit Literature*, lays down an inclusive explanation of Dalit consciousness:

> It is a belief in rebellion against the caste recognising the human being at its focus. Ambedkarite thought is the inspiration for this Consciousness.

> Dalit Consciousness makes slave conscious of their slavery. Dalit Consciousness is an important seed for Dalit literature. It is separated and distinct from the consciousness of other writers. Dalit literature is demarcated as unique because of this Consciousness. (Limbale 2004: 32)

Casteism, a social evil, is very common and peculiar to Indian society. Here, certain castes are given high status, and others are marginalized and given low status. Partha Chatterjee argues that caste is the "reproduction of the human species through procreation within endogamous caste groups which ensures the permanence of ascribed marks of caste purity and pollution" (Chatterjee 1989: 203). Casteism refers to the contempt of one caste by the other or the dominion of one caste to gain personal advantages. Such a framework of casteism goes back to the arrival of the Aryans in India, while different communities in India, before their arrival, had different origins, such as Dravidian.

It is the upper-caste community that defines what it means to be Dalits. The upper-caste community considers the Dalits as untouchables and attributes some heinous jobs such as scavengers, servants, farmers, etc., with their professions. The Dalits are regarded as untouchable and polluted for being socially compatible with the lower caste. Mahatma Gandhi, a social reformist, had tried to uplift the socio-economic and political status of the Dalits by providing them various opportunities in the mainstream.

The Indian people got political freedom in 1947, yet many communities are oppressed and suppressed under the colonial mechanism. All Indian people are united by their national identity but divided on the ground of caste and religion. In the colonial era and even after the independence, most people adhere to their traditional social status, but after the 1990s, the trajectory of social status takes a deconstructive stance. Many people took up new professions by leaving their traditional ones. People residing in towns are less affected by the caste system than those living in a village. Even though the Indian Constitution forbids discernment on the ground of caste, it is still visible locally.

Marginality is an ideology of social, political, and economic domination based on beliefs that some designated castes are inferiors, either biologically, culturally, intellectually, or professionally. In the varna system, Dalits stand in the last stance among four basic categories. The lower caste people are coerced to bear all sorts of humiliation until their death. In *Karukku*, Bama unveils all kinds of humiliation and discrimination experienced by the Dalits in various institutions like educational institutions, families, and even in church. It is a subaltern testimonial autobiography that analyses the effect of casteism on Dalits. Bama delves deep into the life of the Dalit people and shows that the

Dalits are the most oppressed and discriminated people in India. In every sphere of life, such as in society, religious places, and even in educational institutions, they are discriminated against and marginalized. Their world is narrow in comparison to the other sections of people in society.

The Dalits are denied their history and identity because of their marginalized position in society. By writing about herself and her caste, Bama asserts her identity and presents "the voice of a deviant sub-alternity committed to writing its own history" (Guha 1997: 12). Bama thinks about the unity of the Dalits and believes that it will be easier for the upper castes to subjugate them if the Dalit people roam here and there and live dispersedly. She expresses her deep concern for the scuffle and dissonance among the dalits. She believes that it will degrade their social status and will be threatening towards their uplift.

Karukku is not just a story that deals with the author's individual experiences alone but seeks to expose all injustices and ill-treatment of thousands of Dalit children in the name of a class, caste, and religion and their harrowing experiences. Dalit children experience severe abuse and torment for their low social status and position. Bama observes that in Indian society, several Dalit people have internalized the inferiority naturally and not by coercion imposed on them by the upper classes. It happened not in a single day but through many generations. They have been enslaved and suppressed for generation upon generation and it has been told repeatedly that they are inferior and degraded, lacking respect and self-worth. At one stage, they start to believe voluntarily their inferiority and untouchability. It leads to that way where the Dalits find no way for freedom and redemption. The societal set-up is solely responsible for Dalits' lower social status and position because it never allows them to grow out of their mould and dismantle the cursed dress of the Dalits.

On the one hand, Bama's *Karukku*, a two-edged sword, defies the tyrants who enslave, oppress, suppress, and disempowered the Dalits in the name of class, caste, and religion. On the other hand, the book seeks to establish a new society based on love, justice, and equality. It does not resort to violence to gain freedom and social status but emphasizes the significance of ethics and unanimity besides education that will eventually provide their lost social status.

Bama, who always believed in love and equality, had a fervent wish to create a new society, a better society. *Karukku* highlights some problems confronted by Dalits, who are considered impure and polluted/Untouchable and given a shallow position in society. In *Karukku*, society is divided into many communities such as the Naicker community and the Nadar, Koravar, Chakkiliyar, Kusavar, and Paraya settlement based on their social status and professions. There is a trenchant division in society, and each community has a distinctive profession. The Dalits confront the marginalization they face in the religious institutions. The Untouchables were neither allowed to enter the temples nor to become priests in the temples. Bama, at first, felt that perhaps the religious institution is free from marginalization and discrimination. So, she left all her professions one by one and became a nun. She also experienced explicit discrimination; she saw specific religious orders for Harijan women and separate charges for the upper-caste women. "I lamented inwardly that there was no place that was free of caste. And so at last I became a nun and was sent to a convent elsewhere" (Bama 2012: 25).

The Dalits are also economically marginalized in society, suffering from many economic problems. The Untouchables are prohibited from choosing occupations as per their choice despite having the required ability and skills. They are generally the agricultural labourers or the servants of upper-class people. They are not given any respect because of their low economic status. A small boy from an upper community even calls out by name to an aged Dalit woman. The Dalits experience discrimination and marginalization in many public areas. The upper-caste people keep themselves to their part of the village, and the Paraya stay in their part. The Paraya community never goes to where the upper-caste communities live except when they are required to work there. The Naicker people never come to their position. There is a school meant only for the upper-caste children in Naicker street: "The post office, the Panchayat board, the milk-depot, the big shops the church, the schools—all these [stand] in their streets" (Bama 2012: 7). In an educational institution, the Dalits face contempt and are marginalized.

The Warden insults the Dalit children in the school when they return to the school after the holidays. The Warden-Sister insults them by saying they become healthy like potatoes in the school but when they come back from home after holidays in the school they look just skin and bone. The moment is very embarrassing for all the Dalit children because they too pay fees for food and everything like everyone, yet they have to listen to all these things. In college, the upper-caste children do not like the Dalit children. Once, when a lecturer asks the Harijan students to stand up, two students stand up, identifying them as Harijans, the other students look at them with contempt eyes. That incident strikes Bama most and makes her believe that she will not get rid of caste divisions easily whatever she studies and wherever she studies. At her place of work, she is looked down upon for her lower caste. In the convent, she is shocked to witness the conditions of Dalit children. The convent is not free from caste divisions. The Dalit students in school are forced to do menial and mean jobs.

> In the school, people of my community were looking after all the jobs like sweeping the premises, swabbing and washing the classrooms, and

cleaning out the lavatories. And in the convent, as well, they spoke very insulting about low caste people. They spoke as if they didn't even consider low-caste people as human beings. (Bama 2012: 25)

In this text, Bama has depicted many social evils and problems confronted by the Dalits. But everything that she has highlighted is not full of murky and gloomy mechanisms. Amidst the winter of despair, Bama finds a spring of hope. The Dalits generally do not get any reverence and dignity in society, but she finds one way through which the Dalits can get reverence and dignity. Bama finds that education means giving the Paraya community relief from the curse of casteism and marginality. So, she repeatedly highlights the importance of education for the Dalit children.

After receiving an education, she and her brother Annan get respect and dignity from people. Once, Annan goes to a library and signs out his books. At the time of signing out, he adds his title, Master of Arts, and after seeing the title, the attendant brings him a tool and addresses him as 'Sir'—

Yet, because I [have] the education, because I [have] the ability, I [dare] to speak up for myself; I [don't] care a toss about caste. Whatever the situation, I [hold] my head high. And I [complete] whatever I [take] up, successfully. So, both teachers and students [show] me a certain affection, respect. In this way, because of my education alone I [manage] to survive among those who [speak] the language of caste-difference and discrimination. (Bama 2012: 22)

In the introduction of *Orientalism*, Edward Said explicitly exhibits the colonial discourse of the occidental people by defining Orientalism "as a Western-style for dominating, restructuring, and having authority over the Orient" (Said 1979: 3). It is in their temperament to rule the Asian people by their perpetual effort of making them realize that they are inferior. They consider the oriental people as uncivilized, barbaric, and uncultured, and they have to make them civilized and cultured. For this colonial hegemonic framework, the oriental people always suffer from an inferiority complex. Jules Harmand, the French diplomat, supports the ideologies underlying colonialism and said:

It is necessary, then, to accept as a principle and point of departure the fact that there is a hierarchy of races and civilizations, and that we belong to the superior race and civilization, still recognizing that, while superiority confers rights, it imposes strict obligations in return. The basic legitimation of conquest over native peoples is the conviction of our superiority, not merely our mechanical, economic, and military superiority, but our moral superiority. Our dignity rests on that quality, and it underlies our right to direct the rest of the humanity. (qtd. in Said 1993: 17)

A similar kind of colonial attitude lies in the temperament of the upper-caste people. The upper-caste people think that they are superior and consider the lower-caste people as polluted and untouchable. The cause of this superiority complex and social hierarchy stems from creating four Varnas from Brahma that is imbued in people's minds. In the mind of the upper-caste people, four varnas are created according to their social status from the various parts of Brahma. The Brahmins are created from the upper part of Brahma, i.e., head; the Kshatriyas from the middle part, i.e., hands; the Vaishyas from the lower-middle part, i.e., thighs; and the Shudras the lower-part, i.e., feet. In society, a conspicuous distinction is discernible between the colonies of the upper-caste people and the Dalits. The upper-caste people never go their side. In every institution—educational, religious, societal, and cultural—Dalits are deprived of their low social rank.

This is an autobiography that throws light only on the writer's encounter with society and various institutions. Bama writes only about Dalit experiences, leaving out all the elements not attached to the life of Dalit people. She talks about the social mobility of Dalits through the means of education. She does not discuss any political involvement of the Dalits for social mobility though it is an inextricable part of social mobility. This may be the limitation of her autobiography that fails to encompass the whole gamut of the Indian spirit.

To conclude, a caste system is filled with inequality and injustice. Casteism is a man-made evil process perpetrated in society to perpetuate colonial hegemony. The Dalit people have to undergo all sorts of humiliation and discrimination in the caste-based society constructed by those who hold the superior position. However, they are human beings deprived of all sorts of rights and prone to marginalization in every sphere of life. By the hegemonic ideologies, it is instilled in their mind that they are inferior and God has created them only to serve the upper-caste community. Bama did not end the novel by providing only the murky aspects of Dalit's life but showed them the path of enlightenment and salvation. She said that the Dalit people could come out from their cursing life and get reverence only through education.

Bibliography

Bama, F. S. *Karukku*, translated by Lakshmi Holmström. New Delhi: Oxford University Press, 2012.

———. "Dalit Literature." Translated by M. Vijayalakshmi. *Indian Literature* XLIII, no. 5 (1999): 97–98.

Chatterjee, P. "Caste and Subaltern Consciousness". In Subaltern *Studies VI: Writings on South Asian History and Society*, edited by Ranajit Guha, 16–209. New Delhi: Oxford University Press, 1989.

Guha, R. *A Subaltern Studies Reader, 1986–1995*. Minneapolis: University of Minnesota Press, 1997.

Holmstrom, L. "Introduction to *Karukku*." Translated by Lakshmi Holmström. New Delhi: Oxford University Press, 2012.

Limbale, S. M. *Towards an Aesthetics of Dalit Literature: History Controversies and Considerations*. Translated by Alok Mukherjee. New Delhi: Orient Longman, 2004.

Said, E. *Orientalism*. New York: Vintage Books, 1979.

Chapter 13

Bhimayana
as a Biographical Stance on Resistance

Anisha Ghosh
University of Kalyani, West Bengal, India

Abstract

The pictorial biography *Bhimayana* (2011) was published by Navayana with art by the Gond artists Durgabai Vyam, and Subhash Vyam and a story written by Srividya Natarajan and S. Anand is based on Babasaheb Dr. B. R. Ambedkar's life. Ambedkar was born in a Mahar family that was considered to be an "untouchable" caste. Despite being a highly educated Dalit, he was the victim of the Indian caste system since childhood and experienced numerous humiliation and denial of fundamental human rights. He has described various accounts of such disrespectful and humiliating behaviour in his diary published as *Waiting for a Visa* (1993). *Bhimayana* is "an imaginative visual treatment of Ambedkar's *Waiting for a Visa*" (Natarajan et al. 2011: 104). Thus, the chapter will enable the readers to situate the importance of Ambedkar within the Dalit movement in India and study the significance of *Bhimayana*'s narrative style concerning Gond art.

Keywords: caste, Dalit, Dalit movement, Gond art, untouchable

* * *

Bhimayana (2011), published by Navayana with art by the Gond artists D. Vyam and S. Vyam and written by S. Natarajan and S. Anand, is the pictorial biography of B. R. Ambedkar. Ambedkar was born in a Mahar family that was considered an "untouchable" caste. Despite being highly educated, he was a victim of the Indian caste system and faced discrimination since childhood because of his Mahar (Dalit) origins and had numerous experiences of humiliation and denial of basic human rights. He described various accounts of such disrespectful and humiliating behaviour in his diary published under the name *Waiting for a Visa* (1993). The aesthetics and narration of *Bhimayana* [challenge] the domains of devastating national histories of India, blurring the difference between a contorted image building process and a real life journey of an impressive figure in the history of the nation. Not only has the visuality made the processes of comprehension easier for the readers, the art which draws on the pathos from the present day world, incidents which take place degrading Dalits interweave to bring out succinct contextual issues relevant for the readers. (Banerjee 2017: 168)

Ambedkar's struggles and writings are considered very inspiring for contemporary struggles endeavoured by the Dalits and Adivasis (tribals) in India. He vehemently criticised the partition created by Hindu society and its oppression of the Dalits. He advocated for the annihilation of the caste system, which is inherently anti-democratic and atrocious. He correctly realised that nothing could emancipate the outcastes or the untouchables except the destruction of the caste system. Ambedkar's goal was to liberate the untouchables from bondage and to raise them to their rightful status. The socio-economic and political stigmatisation that caste practices have inflected on the lower castes and tribals allowed for the emergence of a solid socio-political movement in the form of numerous Dalit and Adivasis struggles all over India. J. Dewey, J. S. Mill, and T. Washington were the social reformers that greatly influenced Ambedkar by their doctrine of liberalism, which helped him to develop a social justice model widely vilified by nationalists such as M. Gandhi. Ambedkar bravely encountered the dominant Brahminical hegemonic forces, and herein lies the significance of the title of the pictorial text, *Bhimayana*:

> *Bhimayana*", gains relevance—that is, in providing a counter-epic to the dominant Brahmanical, nationalist epic of the *Ramayana*; it subverts the commonsensical nationalist narrative of what constitutes an epic. Further, the selection of tribal artists to pictorially narrate the story of Ambedkar in many ways can also be seen as keeping in line with Ambedkar's politics that aimed at freeing the lower castes and tribals from the hegemony of the native elites. (Oza 2011: 353)

Bhimayana turns the pernicious social issue of caste into the medium of the graphic novel, which offers a visual and verbal experience. The chapter describes the incidents that happened to Ambedkar and his struggles to eradicate untouchability and further employs a symbolic visual narrative that has always been a part of Gond art. Gond art is primarily a tribal art tradition practiced by the Pardhan Gonds, a clan belonging to the larger Gond tribal community from Madhya Pradesh in central India. Durgabai and Subhash Vyam, the illustrators of *Bhimayana*, belong to this clan. At the very end of

Bhimayana, S. Anand in his essay "A Digna for Bhim" notes that Ambedkar's struggle against the tyranny of the caste system could not be presented through "the tyranny of conventional panels, without compromising on the [Gond artists'] credo of not forcing people into boxes" (Natarajan et al. 2011:102). What Anand suggests is that the 'tyranny' of the conventional comic book format (panels) would replicate, in an art form, the tyranny of the social system. The artists tried to reflect a move towards openness and caste-less equality in the social domain. The identical faces of the Dalits listening to Ambedkar and the similar faces representing the orthodox Brahmins signify their lack of uniqueness, and in *Bhimayana*, disavowing uniqueness is a political move because it merges Ambedkar's experience with that of Dalits today. The visual narrations created by Durgabai Vyam and Subhash Vyam challenge:

> the conventional way of storytelling in a sequential format like that of a graphic text along with challenging the way in which image-word texts are generally read…. *Bhimayana* have shared a different strategy of storytelling which defies marking this text into categories such as "comic book" or "graphic novel." (Oza 2011: 352)

The book is also very relevant as it is grounded in present-day journalism, where Ambedkar's biography is connected with the events of present-day caste prejudices. *Bhimayana* talks of "social trauma, and opens up the cultural realm, through a popular format, to issues of human rights" (Nayar 2011: 13). The visual-verbal juxtaposition of newspaper reports on anti-Dalit violence in the first few pages of the book, Ambedkar's autobiographical text and official letters, and extracts from the *Constitution of India* constantly forces the readers to move from a personal life story to a larger socio-historical reality. Vasvi Oza, regarding the movement of the narration, says:

> Such gradual movement of the narration into the life of Ambedkar allows the reader to establish a connection between the narration (past) and his/her own present. In between, these narrators keep coming back and discuss about the relevance of Ambedkar's struggles and his ideas. References to recent news articles regarding the atrocities on the marginalized people keep appearing in between the story narration which again allows the reader not to disregard the ideas of Ambedkar as that of the past and to acknowledge that the struggle initiated by Ambedkar is still going on in today's time. (Oza 2011: 353)

The narration of *Bhimayana* starts with a dialogue between an upper-caste man and a Dalit woman. They discuss how, even today, the marginalised people (untouchables) are being mistreated and humiliated every day. The upper-caste man severely criticises the reservation system, which gets the woman started. She starts narrating the story of Ambedkar, but the man does not know about Ambedkar. She highlights the series of struggles led by Ambedkar against the oppressive caste system. The urban youth immediately identifies "Ambedkar" as somebody who is represented by statues around the country. This reference to already existing and, therefore, recognisable visual images is crucial for

> *Bhimayana*'s cultural work is to generate what Sumathi Ramaswamy calls the "interocular" field. The interocular is the field where the visual intersects with other images from other media, thereby reconfiguring the familiar… the statues of Ambedkar and *Bhimayana*'s visual representation of the early life of Ambedkar, the symbolic representation of massacres and suffering—Ambedkar's as well as other instances such as Khairlanji—open up a whole new visual field: of caste-based atrocity that impinges upon us…. The interocularity of *Bhimayana* abandons the traditional mode of sequential art in favour of the traditional form of Gond arts…. Retrieving Gond art for the purpose of narrating Ambedkar's story in the very contemporary graphic novel format has the effect of situating one of the oldest forms of oppression—based on caste—in a new medium and genre…. The power of the interocular field generated by *Bhimayana* lies … in its hybridized *and* demotic register of representation… to make caste-based oppression and its history (hyper)visible by steering clear of standard modes of documenting oppression. (Nayar 2011: 14–15)

The titles of the chapters— "Water", "Shelter", and "Travel"—indicate the basic needs for human life, and these are the things that Ambedkar sought throughout his life. There is also another chapter titled "The Art of *Bhimayana*". Ambedkar experiences the world through violence and becomes very aware of his identity. He struggles for basic needs, and his struggle is basically for equality. The first chapter, "Water", set in 1901, is about the humiliation faced by Ambedkar when he was ten years old. It highlights how he is humiliated by a teacher at school; he is denied water because of being untouchable. It is believed that the water would get contaminated if people like Ambedkar from the lower castes had access to it. Throughout the chapter, other excerpts show the dominance of the caste system, which is still prevalent in today's India.

The second chapter, "Shelter", is about the return of Ambedkar to Baroda from Columbia after completing his studies. The educated Ambedkar thought that he had risen above the social status (lower-caste identity) drawn by society, but a Brahmin co-passenger proves him wrong during his journey on a train. After that, he struggles and tries hard to break such social myths. The also book highlights how people from other communities forbid him. The Parsis cast him off at their inn, a Muslim insults him, and a Christian friend prevents him. It is clear to him that no community is ready to accept the Dalits as equal to them. He finally finds his shelter and solace in Gautam Buddha and takes the route to Buddhism till the end of his life.

The third chapter, "Travel", is about Ambedkar's reminiscence of his travel to Bombay. All the *tongawallas* (tonga drivers) refuse to give him a ride because he belongs to the Mahar community. This same incident teaches him that the roots of casteism still prevail. The upper-caste man of the framed narrative cannot resist himself from respecting Ambedkar. The story ends with important incidents such as the confrontation with Gandhi over separate electorates for Dalits, mass conversion to Buddhism, and drafting the Constitution for independent India. "The personal narrative folding into (but not blurring) the social-historical in a popular format creates a new story-space where we begin to see a history of violations…" (Nayar 2011: 16).

Chapter Four, "The Art of *Bhimayana*", which introduces the Gond artists and writers, is narrated with the voices of S. Vyam and D. Vyam. They unveil their community background and tradition. They further unveil their guru Jangarh Singh Shyam's influence and how they are gradually involved with the modern Pardhan Gond art movement established by him. Durgabai Vyam also describes the plight of Ambedkar in Baroda during one of their visits to Navayana when the landlady "abused us and wouldn't let us go in. She said we looked like yokels. That hurt us" (Natarajan et al. 2011: 99). *Bhimayana* tries to connect the past with the present scenario and rationalises today's circumstances by using the incidents from the past. While framing *Bhimayana*, one of the story writers, Srividya Natarajan "stuck to Ambedkar's versions of the episodes in letter and spirit but also created new characters and scenarios" (Natarajan et al. 2011: 103).

Thousands of years ago, different Hindu religious texts had promoted and rationalised untouchability relating to the previous birth and rebirth deeds. Untouchables became outcastes who were unworthy of being within the caste system as they were believed to have committed crimes and accumulated heinous sins in their previous births. The four-level Hindu caste structure, headed by Brahmins and followed by Kshatriyas, Vaishyas, and Sudras, described the untouchables as impure who are less human should not be touched. This hierarchical structure was based upon exclusion and inequality, which would not function without multiple castes that could be defined against each other in ritual purity. From this perspective, the untouchables became the target of the entire caste system as it was their apparent impurity against which the other castes were defined and ranked. The untouchables were kept permanently in an impure or unclean state, allowing the upper castes to maintain their purity. Jyotirao Phule, a nineteenth-century social reformer, was the first person to refer to untouchables as "Dalits" (broken people), but they were the depressed Class for Ambedkar. Dalits, whom upper-caste Hindus assigned menial tasks, lived in extreme poverty and suffered grave economic inequality and social discrimination. They were prohibited from attending the same temples and detained from drinking water from the same wells. They were subjected to continual harassment at the hands of the upper-caste Hindus.

Throughout his life, Ambedkar campaigned for a just society. He struck a pose against the caste system from the 1920s when he launched an anti-caste newspaper. Ambedkar redefined untouchability as socio-economic deprivation. He always wanted the untouchable castes to be conscious of and involved in political matters, fight for their rights, and not rely on upper-caste Hindus' kindness and good intentions. He realised that the annihilation of the four-level Hindu caste structure is the only way to liberate the untouchables because the lower castes would not unite to overthrow the Brahmins as they were concerned with defending their own privilege in comparison to the degraded untouchables. Ambedkar's call to "EDUCATE, ORGANIZE and AGITATE" (Natarajan et al. 2011: 89) should be noted.

> *Bhimayana* opens up the cultural realm to human rights discourses. The cultural is the space where human rights are staged for *common* consumption. It is the domain where an *implicit* discursive operation of human rights—equal rights, human dignity, protection against torture—can be discerned in narratives of violations, abuse and rights-denial. (Nayar 2011: 16)

In 1923, the Bombay Legislative Council pronounced a decree where it allowed the untouchables to use all public water bodies. Still, this decree was universally disobeyed by the local Hindus, led by the Brahmins, who clung viciously to their traditional privileges. Gradually, Ambedkar became a leading voice and, in 1927, he peacefully led 3,000 Dalits to Mahad. In this town Mahad, they drank a few sips of water from the Chavadar Tank that was so far reserved for caste Hindus only despite being public property. The caste Hindus of Mahad not only drew water from the tank themselves but freely permitted people of any religion to draw water. Only the Dalits were not allowed: "[T]he upper-caste prevented them from drinking the water because the touch of the untouchables would not only pollute, but it would also evaporate or vanish the eater" (Natarajan et al. 2011: 48). Ambedkar wanted to assert that the untouchables "are human beings like others" (Natarajan et al. 2011: 48) by setting up the norm of equality, thereby raising awareness about the civil rights of the untouchables. This event is known as the First Mahad Satyagraha of 1927 that the Dalit movement calls the "Declaration of Independence". The Mahad Satyagraha was one of the most organised efforts under the leadership of Ambedkar to challenge the regressive customs of caste Hindus. Ambedkar compared the potential of the First Mahad Satyagraha of 1927 to the 1789 French National Assembly:

> The French National Assembly sent the King and Queen of France to the guillotine; persecuted and massacred the aristocrats; and drove the survivors into exile. Whether this social revolution will work peacefully or violently will depend wholly on the conduct of the caste Hindus. People forget that if the rulers of France had not been treacherous to the Assembly, if the upper classes had not resisted it, it would have had no need to use violence in the work of the revolution. We say to our opponents too... Put away the orthodox scriptures. Follow justice. (Natarajan et al. 2011: 49)

When the Dalits drew water from the tank, the Brahmins spread the rumour that the untouchables would enter the Veereshwar temple next, leading to riots. Orthodox Hindus attacked the delegates of the 'Depressed Classes Conference.' Twenty Dalits were wounded in the attack. However, Ambedkar asked his followers to observe restraint and not to strike back.

In June 1927, the (colonial) District Magistrate sentenced five orthodox Hindus to four months of rigorous imprisonment. Regarding this, Ambedkar explains that justice would have been denied if the chief officers in the district had been Hindus. Under Brahmin Peswa's rule, he would have been trapled to death by an elephant (Natarajan et al., 2011). But the deep-rooted casteism led the Brahmins to decide that they should 'purify' the 'polluted' Chavadar Tank. So they poured into Tank hundred and eight pots filled with milk, ghee, cow-dung, cow-piss, and curds, with a soundtrack of Vedic chanting. In response to this, on 25 December 1927, Ambedkar led 10,000 protesters in the Second Mahad Satyagraha. Ambedkar with his followers ceremonially burnt a copy of the *Manusmriti*, a Brahminical Hindu text upholding the caste ideology. Ambedkar told that "this was like Indian 'Swadeshi' nationalists burning foreign cloth to challenge colonial exploitation" (Natarajan et al. 2011: 53). Ambedkar intended to mobilise the untouchables through these movements to recognise that only violence characterised their existence.

Ambedkar's position as a Dalit political representative dragged him into controversy with the nationalist elites as they called his demands divisive. Gandhi was more concerned with India's freedom from British rule than with the transformation of Hindu society. When Ambedkar was trying to convince the British government for separate electorates for the untouchable, Gandhi stepped in and forced the British to reconsider granting untouchables separate electorates, as a result of which the government ultimately quit the idea of independent electorates. In a letter to the Minorities Committee of the Indian Round Table in September 1931, Ambedkar also mentioned specific conditions on which the Depressed Classes would consent to place themselves under a majority rule in a self-governing India. These were: equal citizenship, free enjoyment of the equal right, protection against discrimination, adequate representation in legislatures, adequate representation in services, sufficient representation in cabinet, and redress against prejudicial action.

In 1947, Ambedkar became independent India's first Minister of Law and Justice. On 29 August 1947, Ambedkar, appointed Chairman of the Constitution Drafting Committee, was subsequently appointed by the Assembly to write the new Constitution of India because of his political ability and legal acumen. Ambedkar had the most effective and decisive role in making the draft Constitution, which the Constituent Assembly adopted in 1949. He later drafted the Hindu Code Bill to codify, better to say, reform Hindu personal law. The bill sought to preserve gender equality in terms of property rights and marriage. For Ambedkar, it was the country's most crucial reform, but the Constituent Assembly debated it for months and ended up rejecting not only Ambedkar's draft but also a second more watered-down version of it. Ambedkar finally had to resign. He raised questions regarding democracy and the prevalence of social inequality in India to the very end of his life:

> Indian society is a gradation of castes forming an ascending scale of reverence and a descending scale of contempt.
> Political tyranny is nothing compared to social tyranny. Turn in any direction you like; caste is the monster that crosses your path.
> (Natarajan et al. 2011: 92)

Ambedkar had been thinking for many years of publicly rejecting Hinduism: "It was not my fault I was born an untouchable. But I am determined I will not die a Hindu" (Natarajan et al. 2011: 92). He found Buddhism an ethically sound religion: "Buddhism is based on reason. There is an element of flexibility in it not found in other religions." (Natarajan et al. 2011: 92) He wrote a dense and closely argued texts, *The Buddha and His Dhamma*, a mnemonic opus. In October 1956, a few months before he died, he publicly embraced Buddhism, and more than half a million followers converted with him. This is known as the largest conversion in human history.

Aptly, *Bhimayana* talks about Ambedkar and narrates the marginalisation and oppression of Dalits in Ambedkar's time. It is based on his speeches and his 20-page autobiographical text *Waiting for a Visa*, which consists of

Ambedkar's reminiscences and experiences, shows his political influence through the accounts of life-changing events. *Bhimayana* with its "antique" art, subversion of form, and the visual vocabulary of atrocity and social inequality, it offers a different voice—the cultural legibility and legitimacy—to the language of oppression and rights (Nayar 2011: 19).

We need to come forward to debunk the hegemonic myth of casteism, which is still prevalent in independent India. We should realise that no one is born unequal. So, everyone in society has the right to enjoy every right provided by our Constitution. We cannot discriminate against anyone based on caste, creed, and religion. We should have a friendly attitude towards each other if we want the overall development of our country.

Bibliography

Ambedkar, B. R. *"Waiting for a Visa"*. New Delhi: Dr. Ambedkar Foundation, 2014.

———. *The Buddha and His Dhamma: A Critical Edition*. New Delhi: Oxford University Press, 2011.

Banerjee, S. "An Analysis of the Bhimayana: Experiences of Untouchability – A Departure from the History Book Heroism of India." *South-Asian Journal of Multidisciplinary Studies* 4 (2017): 165–172.

Natarajan, S., et. al. *Bhimayana*. New Delhi: Navayana, 2011.

Nayar, P. K. "Towards a Postcolonial Critical Literacy: *Bhimayana* and the Indian Graphic Novel." *Studies in South Asian Film and Media* 3 (2011): 3–21.

Oza, V. "Questions of Reading and Readership of Pictorial Texts: The Case of *Bhimayana*, a Pictorial Biography of Dr. Ambedkar." *Journal of Writing in Creative Practice* 4 (2011): 351–365.

The Constitution of India (As on 1st April, 2019). Government of India, Ministry of Law and Justice. Legislative Department, 2019.

Chapter 14

Orthodoxy in Rituals Creating the Burden of Tradition and Existential Crisis: A Critical Reading of U. R. Anantha Murthy's *Samskara*

Ismail Sarkar
University of Kalyani, West Bengal, India

Abstract

Anantha Murthy's *Samskara* (1965) is an eye-opening novel in Indian literature in general and Kannada literature in particular. Through the central event of the death of a non-Brahminical Brahmin, Naranappa, and his subsequent ritualistic death rite, that is, *samskara*, the novel questions the traditional ways of Brahminhood in the Hindu religion. Hypocrisy, dilemma, gluttony, and the pseudo-ascetic life of the people of Agrahara in Durvasapura have been vehemently criticised in a metaphorical way. All the people of Agrahara and their guru, "the Crest Jewel of Vedic-Learning", Praneshacharya, are incredibly conscious of the traditional rituals found in the "Law Books," but they are unknowingly and blindly guided by the orthodoxies that plague their minds and of Agrahara as well. Due to this state of mind, they cannot live a free life, and, subsequently, a tradition becomes a burden, and they begin to suffer from an existential and identity crisis. This chapter explores how this orthodoxy in rituals creates the responsibility of tradition and leads them to suffer an existential crisis.

Keywords: burden of tradition, existential crisis, orthodoxy in rituals, non-Brahminical Brahmin

* * *

Introduction

U. R. Anantha Murthy asks his readers to solve the problems originating from contradictory thoughts and actions in ceremonial life. In the Hindu religion, an individual has multiple options to choose the path towards salvation depending on one's caste. The only demand that one has to meet on this path is *dharma* or the right conduct. If one can fulfill one's *dharma*, then one comes closer to liberating himself and thus attains *moksha*, that is, salvation. For a Brahmin, this means living life according to the four life stages. But the question which the novel raises is: Are these Brahmins of Agrahara truly pious, refined, civilised, and enlightened enough? The book *Samskara* stimulates a new ideal, highlighting the social intimidation and mental difference of casteism generated in the minds of its followers, predominantly in the minds of Brahmins, while exhibiting few characters as unattended and free-spirited, and "the shifting of Praneshacharya to pragmatic realism from orthodox ritualism is interesting … [for the] process of samskara or purification" (Wani 2017: 793).

The story opens with the death of Naranappa. He was a Brahmin by birth but does not follow the Brahmin rules but instead engages in several immoral practices. He eats non-vegetarian food, catches fishes from the temple pond, keeps company with Muslims, drinks alcohol, throws the sacred stone — 'saligrama' — into the pond, and had illicit relations with the low-caste whore, Chandri. Unfortunately, he dies of a fever. Chandri brings the news of his death to Durvasapura and asks Praneshacharya, the great ascetic, the crest jewel of vedic learning, how to perform the last rite, the *samskara*. The word *samskara* has several meanings. The different meanings of the word are listed in the epigraph. For instance, forming well or thoroughly, making perfect, perfecting, finishing, refining, refined, accomplishment. It could also mean, forming in the mind, conception, idea, notion; the power of memory, faculty of recollection, realizing of past perception. The word 'Samskara' also means- making pure, any rite or ceremony, funeral obsequies. These are possible meanings of the term. In all these senses of the term, the title of the novel is reflective and to the point, and as Maheshwari states: "Samskara means religious purificatory rites and ceremonies for sanctifying the body, mind and intellect of an individual so that he may become a full-fledged number of the community" (Maheshwari 1969: 16).

Samskara, according to A. K. Ramanujan, is "an allegory rich in realistic detail" (qtd in Murthy 2015: viii) and about "a decaying Brahmin colony in the south Indian village of Karnataka" (qtd. in Murthy 2015: viii). Here, we will discuss the ideas of "decaying" and "Brahmins". Who will perform the last rites for the dead Naranappa is the question that plunges Agrahara into a great dilemma. As a result, the hypocritical character of the people of Agrahara comes out vehemently. Even Praneshacharya cannot find the answer, neither from the Maruty temple nor his traditional knowledge of "Law Books"; nothing has given him the solution for Naranappa's cremation. As Aithal notes: "[The] ... study of the history of any culture shows that the conservatism and orthodoxy have a negative side to them. They are themselves often instrumental in bringing about the decay and death of every culture they seek or uphold and preserve" (Aithal 1981: 83). This chapter aims at focusing on how the decaying orthodoxy has destroyed lives and society as well.

Orthodoxy in the Rituals of Agrahara

V. S. Naipaul, in his book *India: A Wounded Civilization*, has described Murthy's portrayal of Hindu society as a picture of "a barbaric civilization, where the books, the laws, are buttressed by magic, and where a too elaborate social organization is unquickened by intellect (except to the self in its climb to salvation)" (Naipaul 1977: 109). Words such as "orthodoxy", "ritual", "tradition", "existence", and "identity" deserve careful attention. Almost all these words, which are sometimes associated with devotion and religion, are connotative and carry layers of meanings. Our particular focus is on the Hindu religion practiced by the Brahmins in particular. The "issues of caste prejudice and untouchability have indeed been dealt with great sensibility and passion before him [Murthy], but he brought an element of contemporaneity, direct engagement, and confrontation" (Prabhakara 2014: 27).

Now, here come the issues of castes and untouchability. What is caste? What is untouchability? How do they operate, and why do they divide? These are fundamental questions that the modern Naranappa often used to ask indirectly, but he never received a suitable answer from those voluptuous, showy Brahmins of Agrahara. As a result, he immediately defies Brahminhood. The caste system, which is generally a social hierarchy, divides society, especially Hindu society, into two categories: the upper castes and the lower castes. This is extremely painful and demeaning for those who live in Agrahara, and this pain indirectly leads Naranappa to reject the Brahminhood. "This social division is permanent, and is backed by a number of Hindu religious scriptures collectively known as Dharma Shastras" (Kumar 2019: 2). Surprisingly, Praneshacharya performs every day the rituals from the Dharma Shastras and even when the question of the last rites of the dead Naranappa arises, Praneshacharya says that he will look into Manu's *Manusmriti*, a sacred religious book and other texts and see if there is any solution of this dilemma. Now, suppose we try to find out where this dilemma comes from. In that case, we have to go back to the basics of orthodoxy, which in general imposes the burden of tradition and subsequently leads people like Praneshacharya to a crisis of existence and a search for identity.

Orthodoxy is very prevalent in the lives of the people of Durvasapura. Each aspect of their lives reflects their traditional beliefs and the narrowness of their minds. They always fear being polluted by the touch of the non-Brahmins, the low-caste people. The narrator says, if the Acharya talks to chandri he would be polluted; he would have to take a bath again before his meal. He also thinks that how can a morsel go down the gullet in front of a woman who is waiting in the yard. The sense of pollution creates an invisible wall between the low-caste people and the upper-caste Brahmins. B. R. Ambedkar was critical of this sense of pollution, or, more specifically, this idea of impurity. Ambedkar coined the term "The Broken Men" to describe the forefathers of these low-caste people who are forced to live humiliating lives under the caste system. In Ambedkar's formulation, caste is a system of "grade inequality in which castes are arranged to an ascending scale of reverence and descending scale of contempt" (qtd. in Chakravarti 2018: 7). The upper-caste Brahmins used to consider themselves as pure and the lower castes as impure based on the "purity of blood and nature of work. The notion of 'pure high' and the 'pure low' was expressed ideologically in rituals" (Chakravarti 2018: 10).

We see in the novel that Chandri has arrived to inform the people of the death of Naranappa, which creates a dilemma in their minds regarding the person who will perform his last rites. Till the end of the novel, no one gets the answer to it because of their orthodoxy and traditional beliefs. Even the great scholar, Praneshacharya, cannot get any ray of hope from the Maruty temple. As they are very blind to traditions, the dead body of Naranappa becomes a threat to their existence. It seems that the people of Agrahara are suffering from a double-edged problem. Praneshacharya is in puzzle and thinks of the way out. He also remembers that according to ancient custom, until and unless a dead body is cremated, there can neither be any religious performance nor any mundane activity be done. And as Narenappa is not excommunicated so no one except a Brahmin can cremate his body.

It is incredibly disheartening that the Brahmins of Agrahara have reduced themselves into a set of meaningless rituals that are hollow and good for nothing. The Brahmins of Durvasapura do their regular work in robotic ways, devoid of genuineness and sincerity. They are now bankrupt physically and spiritually. It seems that the Brahmins are the most sacred people and live in a healthy, hygienic atmosphere. Still, their orthodoxy makes them live in dilapidated houses infested with rats and cockroaches. We see that "they are mostly ugly, with emaciated bodies, sunken eyes, hollow cheeks, and swollen bellies. Their women are all the more disgusting with their short tightly plaited hair, flat chest, or hanging breasts, and mouth emitting sour odour of sari" (Aithal 1981: 84). The physical condition of the Brahmins is very similar to the stinking rotten atmosphere of Agrahara. The narrator says that Agrahara is rotting because of the dead body of Naranappa. And now Naranappa is no more Brahmin nor a low cast, he is bow only dead body emitting foul smell. This rotten stinking dead body is symbolic, as it mirrors the terrible state of minds of those Brahmins who are guided blindly by rituals. The people of Durvasapura blindly adhere to the age-old decaying customs, rituals, and dogmatic beliefs, and due to their blindness, they fail to face reality. In his chapter entitled "A Defence of Vision" in the *India: A Wounded Civilization*, "V. S. Naipaul treats Praneshacharya as a representative of India unable to perceive reality because of his sterile self-absorption" (Aithal 1981: 86). On the contrary, "Naranappa's hedonism contributes a deliberate and systematic attack upon Brahmin orthodoxy, even to the extent of his being one-point agenda" (Pillai 2014: 105).

Naranappa wants a life free from rituals and orthodoxy and believes in the Charvaka concept of the luxury of life. He says that "borrow, if you must, but drink ghee" (Murthy 2015: 21), and he also wants to destroy the Brahmanism. We know "according to the orthodox prescript, a Brahmin is deemed to be possessed of *atmaguna* or the eight virtues of the self/soul" (Pillai 2014: 108). This is very hierarchical because due to this putative concentration, Brahmin people secure high-class positions and demand the homage of lower-caste people. Naranappa acts like a rebel to uproot the orthodoxy from the core of the Agrahara. He challenges Praneshacharya. Even his rebellious attitude wants to win over Praneshacharya, and he says. He wants to destroy it because the orthodoxy increases the burden upon them.

The people of the Agrahara lead a life full of ritualistic concern, but if we go deep inside their minds, we will see many folds of their characters. It seems that they are very ascetic, devoid of any greed or earthly pleasure, but the case is not so. A materialistic maze has engulfed them from within. They are incredibly greedy. Initially, no Brahmins of Durvasapura, even the close relatives of Naranappa, stepped forward to cremate the dead body. As time passes, their greedy nature becomes apparent. Chandri does something which shocks the traditional base of Brahmanism. She loosened her four-strand gold chain along with bracelets, bangles and eventually placed them before Praneshacharya and asked him to perform the last rite inexchange of these gold. This incident/act of Chandri enkindles the latent greed and lustful nature of the Brahmins present there. They instantly calculate that the heap of gold is worth at least two thousand rupees. And here we see Brahmins bowed their heads. Because two thoughts were overlapping in their mind. On the one hand, they thought that the lust for gold may destroy their purity of Brahminhood, on the other hand, they fear that someone among them will achieve those gold by keeping their brahminhood safe.

Thus there is great dilemma they are passing with.

This is what lies in their minds. Their moderate nature is very apparent and showy. Now the question comes: is their Brahminhood able to cleanse these sins of their minds? The answer is no. So whatever they do is because they adhered to traditional rituals full of orthodoxy and blindness. The most important example of their orthodox bent of mind is their latent desire for sexual pleasure. All the Brahmins of the Agrahara are desire sex, but they hide this natural urge because of their orthodox principles of celibacy. Even Praneshacharya avoids cohabitation with his wife Bhagirathi, and to "get ripe and ready" (Murthy 2015: 9), he has married an invalid woman. But what is most interesting is that all directly or indirectly succumb to their pleasure principles. Durgabhatta, for instance, an ascetic Brahmin, praises Chandri as exactly found in Vatsyanyana's manual of love, and as if she is sexually very much adept having hot tight breast with the capacity of sucking the male dry. So much is the thinking of a Brahmin ascetic, a blind follower of rituals but deep inside, like all the others — a sexually starved man. Astonishingly, sexual starvation drives a man like Praneshacharya who will find a new identity after getting the touch/taste of Chandri's bodily pleasure. He intentionally wants a life of celibacy, yet the situation leads him to desire the joy of the flesh: "touching full breasts, which he had never touched before, Praneshacharya felt faint" (Murthy 2015: 63). Can it be possible that a man who devotes his whole life memorising those mantras suddenly get stuck in his throat only after a touch of human flesh? Yes, here lies the power of the reality of the present over the old traditional orthodoxy. But Praneshacharya's surrendering to sexual desire has its positive sides too, because it will lead him to find a new self, a new identity. Still, to get that identity, he, for the time being, is caught in the maze of existential crisis, and the next part of this chapter will deal with the critical aspects of this crisis.

Existence in Crisis

Existentialism as a broad philosophical concept has gained its recognition because of writers such as Kierkegaard and Sartre. The two main keywords of this philosophy are "Existence" and "Essence." Irrationalities and uncertainties very predominantly work in the life of an existential character, very often leading him to an absurd and complex world. Nothing here is permanent and transparent, and instead, everything is vague, hazy, and utterly confusing. The character always tries to detach himself from his own self and occupy another's self.

Ramanujan very beautifully said that "all the battles of tradition and defiance, asceticism and sensuality, meaning and meaninglessness of rituals, dharma and law, desire(kama) and salvation (Moksha) have become internal to Praneshacharya" (Murthy, 2015: 141). When all the external things become internal to Praneshacharya, the confrontation between his former ascetic self and the present changes his state of mind. "Existentialism foregrounds the perplexing condition of the modern subject .... Who is forced to contend with the meaninglessness of life" (Buchanan 2010: 159). Here, Praneshacharya is in a way contending with the meaninglessness of his former self. It is seen that an existential form of identity emerges from static nonexistence ossified in rituals and dogma. Meenakshi Mukharjee says, "[T]he author's attempt to exploit the tension between two world views" (Mukherjee 1999: 166). Then "the difficult and uneasy process of transition between the fixed and settled order of life and the still inchoate strings of self" (Mukherjee 1999: 167) becomes more plausible in the dilemma and dualities of Praneshacharya's life. Praneshacharya is very ambiguous and his physical desires urge him to find Chandri, and at the same time, he feels that if he finds and enjoys chandri he would be responsible for his own act if sin. We see Praneshacharya confess his inability to give them (his disciples) an answer to the question of the funeral rites, and thus he is helpless. Now he is struck in the wheel of Karma because on the one hand, he fails to seek solace in the Sanskrit texts on the other can not reject them and thus the duplicity becomes more plausible to him. And he is unresolved. Praneshacharya's present condition is like Trishanku and thus, in a way, suspended between two worlds. He now realised that the root of all his anxiety lies at his sleep with chandri.

It is pathetic that "in his search for truth Praneshacharya experienced the touch of a woman unexpectedly which pulled him away from his camphor-scented pious world" (Misra et al. 1982: 108). Praneshacharya is now unable to find the way and hangs between the two worlds. He is in constant fear. He cannot come out of his former self and says, "[W]hy this fear in me when I've shed all things? I lost my original fearlessness. How, why?" (Murthy 2015: 96). He keeps on questioning and says that he can not return to Agrahara because of two reasons. One is the fear of not being able to live in full respect and the other is the anxiety that comes from his telling lies. We see that Praneshacharya is trying very hard to find his identity but somewhere, somehow in the process, he loses his path and says that he rushed into the conflict and dualities and thus gets suspended between truths like Trishanku.

Praneshacharya is somehow lost in the world of confusion and dualities, and he understands that there is no mental peace in the world of "Law Books", and. The conflict is growing in his mind, and this growing conflict is manifested in the cock-fight. He feels that there were eyes all around and watching him fiercely. He was in panic. He was, as if, unknowingly dropped into the world of demon and is fearful.

He thinks that he is not himself because he sometimes doubts to himself that "am I to be a ghost or a man, hovering in indecision?" (Murthy 2015: 120), and consequently, he becomes a lost soul Finally, he realises that he needs to shed his traditional orthodoxy and says that unless he sheds Brahminism he can not stand aside liberated from all those sorts of dualities and if he sheds all these, he will fall into the tigerish world of cockfights and eventually he will be burnt like a worm. He meditates the way how to escape this state of neither-here-nor-there, this ghastliness. Thus we see that Praneshacharya is in a state of confusion. Drabble believes that "existentialists tend, for example, to emphasize the unique and particular in human experience; they place the individual at the centre" (Drabble 2000: 342). Therefore, we can say that Praneshacharya is in a sea of doubt, searching for his identity—his existence is in crisis.

Conclusion

Finally, we see that the people of Durvasapura are blind followers of these barren stereotypes, which bear no fruit or add no meaning to the high ideals of existence. Dogma, tradition, rituals, and orthodoxies are seen in their behaviour and are deeply rooted in their livelihood. They always fear being out of these rituals, and subsequently, this fear of losing tradition indirectly becomes a heavyweight which chokes their free will. As a result, reason, rationalities, and common sense are alien to them. The burden of tradition, in a way, becomes so heavy and complex that they lead them to nowhere except frustration. On the other hand, preoccupied with the notions of orthodox prescripts, Praneshacharya "wanders through forests and lonely roads…journeys through a non-verbal world…liminal like the unhoused dead 'betwixt and between'" (Murthy 2015: 142). In search of something, he is constantly mutating and changing from an acknowledged Brahmin. It is found that "sloughing off his responsibility and authority marks the birth of a new consciousness in Praneshacharya. Thereafter, he undertakes a journey of self-discovery that sees him careering from one position to the next in an attempt to arrive at some kind of equilibrium" (Pillai 2014: 101). But unfortunately, he is unable to find that something and cannot arrive at some equilibrium. As a result, he is in a great crisis, and this crisis poses so many questions regarding the validity and usefulness of his so-called blind principles of "Law Books" and rituals.

Bibliography

Aithal. S. K. "Of Culture and Cadaver: Anantha Murthy's *Samskara*". *Journal of South Asian Literature. Asian Studies Centre* (Michigan University) 16, no. 2 (1981): 83–86.

Buchanan, I. *A Dictionary of Critical Theory.* Oxford: Oxford University Press, 2010.

Chakravarti, U, ed. *Gendering Caste through a Feminist Lens.* New Delhi: Sage Publication, 2018.

Drabble, M. *The Oxford Companion to English Literature.* New York: Oxford University Press, 2000.

Kumar, R., ed. *Dalit Literature and Criticism.* Hyderabad: Orient Blackswan, 2019.

Maheshwari, H. *The Philosophy of Swami Rama Tirtha.* Agra: Shivlal Agarwal and Company, 1969.

Misra, N, et al. "*Samskara*: Three Critics on Anantha Murthy's Novel Indian Literature." *Sahitya Akademi* 25, no. 5 (1982): 108.

Mukherjee, M. *Realism and Reality: The Novel and Society in India.* New Delhi: Oxford University Press, 1999.

Murthy, U. R. A. *Samskara,* translated by A. K. Ramanujan. Navi Mumbai: Oxford University Press, 2015.

Naipal, V. S. *India: A Wounded Civilization.* New Delhi: Penguin Books, 1977.

Pillai, S. "Back to the Future: Tracking the Moral Imperative in, of, and through *Samskara.*" *College Literature* 41, No. 2 (Spring 2014): 97–119.

Prabhakara. M. S. "U. R. Ananthamurthy: Writer, Iconoclast, Public Intellectual". *Economic and Political Weekly* 49, no. 36 (2014): 27.

Wani, M. A. "Superiority and Social Injustice in U.R. Anantha Murthy's Samskara." *International Journal of Creative Research Thoughts (IJCRT)* 5, no. 4 (November 2017): 793.

Chapter 15

Bhimayana: A Graphic Projection of History and Plight of Dalits in India

Eeshan Ali
Dukhulal Nibaran Chandra College

Motahar Hossain
Aliah University, West Bengal, India

Imtiaj Alam
Aliah University, West Bengal, India

Abstract

The plight and suffering of Dalits in India can be traced back from time immemorial. Therefore, it would be correct to say that along with the people of India, and even history has been quite ignorant towards the Dalits. Dalits are not just socially marginalised, but are also tortured by upper-caste people. India is a land of multidimensional characters with multi-faced identities and, therefore, Indian society is divided into many shades in terms of identity, culture, tradition, beliefs, and language. *Bhimayana*, the graphic biography of B. R. Ambedkar, exquisitely projects the history of the plight and struggle of Dalits in India. This graphic novel provides a voice to the voiceless people who are never heard on their own land. They are socially, politically, and economically subjugated and exploited in every age. The novel is a beautiful amalgamation between the past and the present situation of Dalit lives. This work of art is a witness to the harsh reality of Dalit lives through the life of B. R. Ambedkar. This chapter will deal with all the issues mentioned above elaborately and investigate the various methods through which Dalit people are internally colonized.

Keywords: Dalit, historiography, internally colonised, subjugated and exploited, upper caste

Introduction

The term 'Dalit' refers to the people of marginalised classes who have been oppressed for ages. In general, the term Dalit is used for the people who have been deemed untouchable by the upper-caste people in India. In short, we can say that they are denied the flow of daily normal cultural acceptance. Dalits have been marginalised and ostracised from normative standards in the form of abrogation. But it is also exemplary that Dalits reject the idea of standard living or accepting the new mode of life in the discourse of modernisation only to keep their nativity. However, they are excluded from the four Varna systems (the division of castes in Hinduism). Dalits are considered to be a *panchama* (fifth) Varna or outsiders. Recently, the term 'Dalit' has been used for political propaganda. Politicians use them merely as voters. They promise massive changes at the time of elections and say that the plight of Dalits is our plight, yet forget everything once the elections are over. Dalits are buried in a caste shroud. They are the victims of social discrimination. It is to be noted that Dalits came into existence when Brahminical (upper-caste people in Hinduism) supremacy tried to impose the order of rank upon them. It is also said that the Dalits did not exist in the Vedic period, but it is pronounced that they were the first ones living in undiscovered India. The term Dalit came into prominence when Brahminical Hinduism befriended them by saying that they were born from the foot of Vishnu. From Valmiki to Ravidas, a fourteenth-century mystic poet, to B. R. Ambedkar, the plight and condition of the Dalits remained the same, and they are still being deprived of their rights for just being Dalits. The upper castes also fought for their tyrannical hierarchy to dominate the "Adivasis" (tribal people). The word 'Adivasi' etymologically has two morphemes: 'adi' means ancient and 'vasi' means inhabitant. In the nineteenth century, a great reformist, Ambedkar, was born who fought for the rights of the Dalit people. The life and history of Dalits were very pathetic before 1945, and it still is.

Of late, a horrible incident happened to a Dalit girl in Uttar Pradesh, India, in 2020; four upper-caste men gang-raped a Dalit-girl and tortured her mercilessly in Hathras district of Uttar Pradesh. The girl later died in the hospital, and the victim's body was cremated at midnight without the family's consent. This clearly shows that Dalits have been inhibited, beaten, and denied justice since their birth. It is unimaginable that such things are happening even in 'Naya Bharat' (New India). The English proverb — *the best thing about time is it changes* — does not help Dalits to get a better place, and the scenario of untouchability is still visible.

Bhimayana, the graphic biography of Dr. B. R Ambedkar truthfully projects the history and struggles of Dalits in India. Ambedkar, the flag bearer and godfather of the Dalit community, worked as a reformist, was born into a Dalit family in the Indian State of Madhya Pradesh. He was humiliated all the time at school by his class-fellows, but he was resolute and continued going to school. He knew that he could not alleviate his tribe without proper education. He went abroad for further studies to raise his voice against the oppression by the upper castes, but after returning from abroad, he was vilified and repressed. He attempted to bring his community out of the shadows. No one was there to consort with him in his movement for Dalit rights. He then established himself as a leader of the Dalits only to promote their rights.

The Touchable of the Untouchables

The graphic novel *Bhimayana* seems to be just a tale about Ambedkar, who hailed from the Dalit community. Still, if we read the text through a Marxist lens, we will find the precarious situation of the Dalits. It shows how Ambedkar was treated in school, where he was forced to sit alone in the corner of a classroom not to touch anyone. The peon says, "Step back now! And when you leave, take your gunny-sack with you—the sweeper won't touch it, and the place won't get cleaned" (Natarajan et al. 2011: 21). The class distinction was very apparent in the school. His class fellows summoned him to play with them, but he refused to play as he was from the Dalit community. He was also not allowed to drink the water from the tube well. The upper-caste people could drink water from the tube-well as they were supreme.

In a feudal society, the upper class controls the dominant discourse and articulates their ideology on the lower class or the proletariat. This concept of ideology, that is, the shared beliefs and values held unquestioningly by culture, has been boldly projected in *Bhimayana*. In the case of Mira aunty, this concept of "ideology" is well equipped. After returning from the school, Bhim complains about untouchability; however, Mira aunty comforts Bhim by saying, "Stop Complaining. You are lucky..." (Natarajan et al. 2011: 24). In effect, the upper class develops the idea of oppression, and the lower class becomes a victim of the superstructure. The bourgeoisie or the upper caste works hard to impose the effectiveness of their ideology upon the lower castes. In such a system, the lower castes believe in the hierarchy of society. Mira aunty also tries to console Ambedkar to accept the fact that they are from a lower class. The lower caste has been deprived of their essential needs. The barbers do not touch them to cut their hair. The class distinction is very dangerous, and it is visible in the way the Dalits are treated in their own land.

Through the voice of Mira aunty, we witness the concept of hegemony. Hegemony in a particular society acts in two ways; one, the upper class or bourgeois exploits the lower class or the proletariat by winning their consent. The other way is to use the proletariat forcefully by turning the modes and causes of exploitation into legal acts. In the case of *Bhimayana*, the very concept of hegemony acts in these two ways. When Ambedkar went to meet his father with his brothers to Masur, they were refused by the bullock cart driver from the station. They had been abused and alienated from the people in Masur. The class relation and social conflict and the discourse of social transformation resulting from the division of labor within capitalist society. Thus, the family of Ambedkar, which symbolically represents the whole Dalit community, becomes the victim of interpellation. They have given their consent to the ideology to be ruled by the upper-class people without being aware of it. It makes them believe that they are independent and possess free will. However, this is not the case.

Refusal to be a Refugee in a Home

The Dalits are treated as second-class citizens in India, while homelessness is always a nightmare to them. The internal clash between the upper class and the lower class has been portrayed through the representation of Ambedkar's life. After completing his higher studies, Ambedkar returned to India and vowed to work under the Baroda State's authority as the state authority sponsored him. When he reached Baroda to pay back his gratitude, he was denied access to the hotel, which, simply put, represents the dehumanising structure of class relations. The novel deals with the structure of a society where Ambedkar symbolises the proletariat and the hotel symbolises the bourgeoisie. Ambedkar disguised himself as a Parsi so that he could stay at the hotel…. But his transformation of identity could not help him stay there. The villagers discovered his identity and they vowed to take revenge by beating him to death. One of the villagers says, "You filthy scoundrel! You have polluted the Parsi inn!" (Natarajan et al. 2011: 68). Ambedkar described the incident and implored them, and at last, the villagers set him free. The affair represents that the upper classes marginalise the proletariat.

The scenario of untouchability can be interpreted in the model of Louis Althusser's Ideological State Apparatus. He states that the State consists of State Power and State Apparatus, where the state power is in the ruling class's hands. Thus, in the case of *Bhimayana*, state power is controlled by the upper-class people. On the other hand, State Apparatus functions on two concepts: Ideological State Apparatus and Repressive State Apparatus. The very tradition of untouchability has been legitimised by upper-class people under the conviction of the ideological state apparatus. Hence, when the State or the upper-class people failed to implement this conviction over Ambedkar, the system takes the help of repressive state apparatus. This apparatus functions by violence and force. Even in twenty-first-century India, the power dynamics roll over in the same manner.

The Trouble of Travel

In *Bhimayana*, Ambedkar bears, which are pathetic and synecdochically, represent the same plight and exclusion of Dalits in mainstream society. Ambedkar with his mates got on the bus to travel, but they agreed that they must conceal their identity on the bus. If anyone of the passengers discovered their identity, they might be thrown out. The manifest and the hidden meaning of the travel are related to the subject matter of class distinction. The constant subjugation of the Dalits reduces them to a mere commodity, which capitalism requires. From a bus to a bullock cart, everywhere, the Dalits were excluded, alienated, and, more importantly, abused. The upper class acts the way they do because they believe they are superior to the Dalits because of their caste system.

False Consciousness

The major problem of third-world countries is how Marxist theory divides the class into two groups or races—the dominant race and the oppressed class. The feudal society significantly impacts the disparity of wealth, education, and social dignity. The cognitive behaviour towards the lower classes is the most discerning matter of the twenty-first century, though it started since humans start living. The class division was always there, and class division is still a striking humanitarian disorder. *Bhimayana*, especially viewed from a Marxist approach, objectively emphasises the domination of the upper class on the lower class. The graphic novel projects the vivid image of the Dalits in a locality, especially in a tribal area of India. *Bhimayana* discusses Ambedkar's struggle against the dominant ideology of caste to get his freedom and rights to be treated well.

He had been made to sit alone in school because of his caste, and he could not drink water from the tap. He was deprived of his rights in school. He could not even play with his mates because of his nativity. We observe that the lower class or Dalits are constantly pushed further. *Bhimayana* presents the dialectic struggle of the Dalits through the visual representation of B. R. Ambedkar. We witness the distinct ruling class and the oppressed class. He suffered tremendously during his school days at a very young age, which enraged him to ask Mira Aunty why he could not drink water from the tube well in school. He asks Mira Aunty, "Mira Aunty, why can't I open a tap and drink water like all the other boys?" (Natarajan et al. 2011: 24). In response, Mira Aunty says, "You know why. Because you're untouchable, boy" (Natarajan et al. 2011: 24). On this aspect, T. Eagleton, in his book *Criticism and Ideology: A Study in Marxist Literary Theory*, states that Marxist criticism "is to show the text as it cannot know itself to manifest those conditions of its making about which is necessarily silent" (1978: 43). *Bhimayana* is fictionalised non-fiction that demonstrates the violent effort of the Dalits to achieve freedom from the attack of the upper castes.

Bhimayana allows us to see the condition of Dalits in India. They are mistreated and seen as untouchables. The Dalits' quest for a meaningful existence in society is visible in the novel. A. Gramsci, in the 1930s, popularised the term 'hegemony', which is quite pertinent to the Dalit community. Hegemony simply means domination by consent. In Terry Eagleton's words, "Gramsci normally uses the word hegemony to mean the ways in which a governing power wins consent to its rule from those it subjugates" (qtd. in Rocco 2020: xv). It is plainly understood that the Dalits keep their fate in the hands of the upper caste. The biography traces that 'character is destiny', resulting in the tragic death of the community.

From the beginning to the end, the concept of "character is destiny" plays a vital role in holding them to their colonised attitude. It was Ambedkar who tried a lot to change the socio-economic condition of the Dalits, but he could not do much for his community. The term hegemony is helpful for describing the success of the upper caste upon the lower-caste people who may outnumber the upper caste in every possible way to occupy the central part of the country. The Dalit people or the lower-caste people themselves give their consent to the bourgeoisie or the upper caste and adapt bourgeois values and beliefs and often couched in terms of social values, stability, and advancement, for example, when Ambedkar made statements to his teacher, "When the bell rings, all the other students go to the tap. By the time they finish, the peon has gone home. And I'm not supposed to touch the tap" (Natarajan et al. 2011: 19). The acceptance of the bourgeois beliefs made them victims of capitalist society. The capitalist enjoys the opportunity to suppress the lower class. It is very simple to note that he becomes the prey of the capitalist. Hegemonic systems have given them immense power to dominate. The adaptability to accept established notions has become a part of the daily lives of the Dalits. The Dalits' difficult task of adapting to modernity meets further challenges from the ambivalent upper-caste people. Ambedkar with his siblings travel to Masur to meet his father but they hide their identity. It simply proves that they are comfortable in hiding their true identity. Consent is achieved coincidentally by the upper-caste people through a prevailing ideology by implying the monumental discourse only to establish the upper caste values and beliefs. The lower caste people want to naturalise the assumptions by saying that "If they say their religion is our religion, then their rights and our must be equal. But is that the case? If not, on what grounds do they say we must remain in Hindu fold in spite of kicks and rebuffs?" (Natarajan et al. 2011: 51).

Conclusion

To change the scenarios of the Dalits, one must think out of the box. The process of decolonisation can be a great help in this regard. Decolonisation is to dismantle the colonial empires in all their forms. The method includes cultural forces that had confined the lower class within a boundary. *Bhimayana* deals with the duality between the upper-caste people and the lower-caste people. The lower-caste people wanted to break the notion of settler colonies, where the upper-caste people were a direct product of cultural expressions. The very idea of Marxism is to dominate the people of the lower strata. In *Bhimayana*, Ambedkar went to meet his father, and he was asked where he is from. He answered that he is from Satara.

Capitalist society does not believe in Creole nationalism where the untouchables can mix their cultures. In India, even in the twenty-first century, the first nationalists are also modernisers whose programme rejects Creole nationalism rather than adopting indigenous culture or mixed culture. In the twentieth century, the lower-class people were treated as untouchables and had no right to speak for their rights, and still, they do not have the right to say what is good for them and could not travel and drink water sit with the upper class. The set norms of capitalism have to be decolonised. However, at times, the news of decolonising a colony is appreciated. If society cares about the Dalit community, it should stop the stamp of the Brahminical attitudes. Maharashtra, one of the states of India, plans to take up the initiative to change the caste-based name of the colonies that can demolish the established idea of the colonies. The colonies such as Maharwada, Mangwada, and Brahmanwada have caste-based names. Several programmes have been taken to change the name of those localities. In *Bhimayana*, Ambedkar is from Satara, and upper-caste people easily deduce the people of that area. A man is a man, and that is his identity to live in the world. We, human beings, think of ourselves as the best organism on earth. Therefore, we must change society's mindset to achieve freedom from the oppression of the bourgeoisie. In *Bhimayana*, we as readers have witnessed that Ambedkar fought for the Dalits and their social, political, and economic changes.

Bibliography

Althusser, L. "Ideology and Ideological State Apparatuses by Louis Althusser 1969–70." *Marxists.org*. Monthly Review Press, 1971. Accessed on 20 June 2027. www.marxists.org/reference/archive/althusser/1970/ideology.htm.

Eagleton, T. *Criticism and Ideology: A Study in Marxist Literary Theory*. London: Lowe & Brydone Printers Limited, 1978.

Natarajan, S., et al. *Bhimayana*. New Delhi: Navayana Publishing Pvt. Ltd, 2011.

Rocco, V. *Photofascism: Photography, Film and Exhibition Culture in 1930s Germany and Italy.* New York: Bloomsbury Visual Arts, 2020.

Further Readings

Abrams, M. H., Geoffrey Galt Harpham. *A Glossary of Literary Terms*. 11th ed. Delhi: Cengage Learning, 2015.

Achebe, C. *Home and Exile*. Oxford: Oxford University Press, 2000.

Al-Sudeary, M. "Rethinking Muslim Woman's Agency in Modern Literature." *International Journal of Humanities and Social Science* 2, no. 21 (November 2012).

Al-wazedi, U. S. N. N. "Motherlands of the Mind: A Study of the Women Characters of Attia Hosain's *Sunlight on a Broken Column* and Salman Rushdie's *Midnight's Children*." Masters Theses, Eastern Illinois University, 2003.

Ambedkar, B. R. *The Untouchables: Who Were They and Why They Became Untouchbales*. Bombay: The Education Department, Government of Maharashtra, 1990.

Ashcroft, B., G. Griffiths and H. Tiffin. *Key Concept in Post-Colonial Studies*. London and New York: Routledge, 1998.

Bandyopadhyay, S. "Subaltern Voices: A Note on Women in Mahasweta Devi's *Five Plays*". *Kakatiya Journal of English Studies* 1 (December 1995): 79–87.

Bressler, C. E. *Literary Criticism: An Introduction to Theory and Practice*. 4th ed. New Jersey: Pearson, 2007.

Chandra, U. "Rethinking Subaltern Resistance". *Journal of Contemporary Asia* 45, no. 4 (2015): 563–573.

Chakravarti, U. "Conceptualizing Brahmanical Patriarchy in Early India: Gender, Caste, Class, and State." *Economic and Political Weekly* 28, no. 14 (April 3, 1993): 579–585. URL: http://www.jstor.org/stable/4399556

Chattopadhyay, G. *Awakening in Bengal in Early Nineteenth Century*. Calcutta: Progressive Publishers. 1965.

Chaudhuri, D. "The House in South Asian Muslim Women's Early Anglophone Life-Writing and Novels". Graduate Dissertations and Theses, 2016.

Chaudhuri, R. *A History of Indian Poetry in English*. New York: Cambridge University Press, 2016.

Cuddon, J. A. *The Penguin Dictionary of Literary Terms and Literary Theory*. Fifth Edition. New Delhi: Penguin Books, 2015.

Darwin, C. *On the Origin of Species by Means of Natural Selection, or the Preservation of Favoured Races in the Struggle for Life*. London: John Murray, 1859.

Dean, A. E. *Peace of Mind: Daily Meditations for Easing Stress*. New York: Bantam Books, 1995.

Jyothi, A. A. V. *Marginalisation in The Fiction of Kavery Nambisan*. Astha Publishers and Distributors, 2020.

McCutcheon, D. "Must Indian poetry in English always follow England?" Edited by M. K. Naik et al. *Critical Essays on Indian Writing in English*. Dharwad: Karnatak University, 1968.

Murad, M. "Under the Radar: *Sultana's Dream*". 17 October 2014. Accessed 11 June 2019. http://www.tor.com/2014/10/17/undertheradarsultanasdream/

Nayar, P. K. *An Introduction to Cultural Studies*. 2nd ed. New Delhi: Viva Books, 2019.

———. *Contemporary Literary and Cultural Theory: From Structuralism to Ecocriticism*. Noida: Pearson India Education Services Pvt. Ltd, 2009.

Needham, A. D. "Multiple Forms of (National) Belonging: Attia Hosain's 'Sunlight on a Broken Column.'" *Modern Fiction Studies* 39, No. 1 (1993).

Said, E. *Culture and Imperialism*. New York: Vintage Books, 1993.

"Woman Jumps into Husband's Funeral Pyre." *The Times of India*. Raipur. 13 October 2008.

Index

A

A Fine Balance (1995), xxxiii
"A Pathway to Diversity? Human Rights, Citizenship and Politics of Transgender" (2009), 6
A Room of One's Own, 34
A Sheaf Gleaned in French Fields (1876), xxxiv
A. Appadurai, 53
A. Beteille, xvii
A. Gramsci, 144
A. Hosain, 15
A. K. Ramanujan, 130
"Abarodhbasini", 75
Adivasis, 120, 140
Age of the Sutras, xxiv
Age of the Upanishads, xxiv
Agrahara, 130
alim (all-knowing), 45
Anita Desai, xxxiv
Anna Karenina (1875), 66
"Ardhangini", xxiv
"Ardhangini" ("The Female Half"), 75
Article 14, xxvi
Article 15, xxvi
Article 16, xxvi
Article 21 (A), xxvii
Arundhati Roy, xxxiii, 10
Arvind Sharma, xviii
Aryans, xxii, xxiv
Ashiyana, 17, 19
Ashiyana (home), 16
atmaguna, 133
"*Aysh*" (Enjoyment), 43

B

B. Crossouard et al., 43
B. R. Ambedkar, xxx, xxxii, 97, 119, 140
badtameezi (impoliteness), 9
Bakhtin's *carnival*, xxxii
Bama, 92, 94, 97, 112, 114, 116, 117
"Bayen", xl, 103
Bhimayana, xl, 120, 121, 126, 140, 141, 143, 144, 145
Bhimayana (2011), 119
Bildungsroman, 18
Blunt, xxii
Bodies that Matter, 42
'body', 42, 47
Bombay Legislative Council, 124
Bombay Talkie (1994), xxxvi
"Borka" ("The Cloak"), 75
Brahminical hegemonic forces, 120
Brahmins, xix, xx, 106, 123, 132
Breast Stories, 54
Buggery Act of 1533, 8

C

C. Gupta, 25, 27
C. Lazzaro-Weis', 18
C. Narendran, xxxvi
"Can the Subaltern Speak?", xxiii, 26, 29, 83
casta, xvii
Caste, Society and Politics in India from the Eighteenth Century to the Modern Age, xxii
casteism, xvii, 113, 117
Chandler, xix

"character is destiny", 144
child marriage, xxvi
Classical Hindu Thought: An Introduction, xviii
Commodities among Themselves, 57
Coolie (1936), xxxi
Creole nationalism, 145
Criticism and Ideology: A Study in Marxist Literary Theory, 143
Cry, the Peacock (1963), xxxiv

D

D. Vyam, 119
Dalit children, 115, 116
Dalit Christian, 93
Dalit community, 95, 107, 140, 141, 144
Dalit feminism, 92, 102
"Dalit Literature", 99, 112
Dalit woman writer, 92
Dalit women, 96, 97, 98, 102, 106
Dalits, xxi, 95, 112, 113, 114, 115, 120, 124, 125, 140, 142, 143, 144
Dark Holds No Terror (1990), xxxiv
Das Capital (Vol. 1), 53
'Depressed Classes Conference', 125
dharma, 130
Dharma Shastras, 131
"Dharma-Sutras", xxiv
Difficult Daughters (1998), xxxv, xxxvi
Discipline and Punish: The Birth of the Prison, 36, 39
Dom community, 106
Dr. M. Murmu, xxix
Drabble, 136
Dravidians, xxii
Duniya (world), 5
"*dwijas*", xxi

E

E. C. M. Senart, xxii
E. Said, 14
early Vedic period, xxiii
Economic dependence, 45
Edward Said, 116
'Employment Non-Discrimination Act' (ENDA), 10
'empty signifier', xix
'endogamous ties', 58
Entwicklungsroman, 19
Erizehungsroman, 19
Existentialism, 134

F

female bildungsroman, 19
Female Infanticide Act, 1829, xxvi
Female Sexuality in the Early Medieval Islamic World, 46
Feminism and Fairy Tales, 39
'floating signifier', xix

G

G. C. Spivak, xxiii, 26, 29, 83
G. D. Berreman, xvii
G. Deshpande, xxxvi
G. Greer, 44
G. S. Ghurye, xvii
Gandhian Nationalism, 24
Gender and the Politics of History (1988), 14
'gender performativity', 50
'Gender Recognition Act' (2004), 10
Gender Trouble, 38
Gender Trouble: Feminism and the Subversion of Identity, 43
Ghost in the Tamarind: A Novel (2017), xxxiii

"*Ghum*" (Disappearance), 43
"God Gives, Man Robs", 75
Gond art, 119, 120

H

H. K. Bhabha, 16
Harijan community, xx
"Harp of India", 84
Hegemony, 141
'Hermaphrodite', 7
hidden apartheid, xxi, xxx
hijras (eunuchs), 5, 6, 10
Hindu Widow Remarriage Act, 1856, xxvi
Hinduism: Beliefs and Practices, xviii
"Home" ("Griha"), 75
Homo Hierarchicus: The Caste System and Its Implications, xvii

I

I. C. Vidyasagar, xxvi
I. Chughtai, 52, 58
I. Gandhi, xxviii
I. Kant, 53
Ideological State Apparatus, 142
Idol Love (1999), xxxvi
Imagined India, xviii
In Custody (1984), 15
India: A Wounded Civilization, 131, 133
Inside the Haveli (1977), xxxvi, 17
Interpreter of Maladies (1999), xxxv
izzat (honour or prestige), 17

J

J. Butler, 38, 41
J. Derrida, xix

J. Dewey, 120
J. Fowler, xviii
J. Genet, 44
J. Lahiri, xxxv
J. S. Mill, 120
J. W. Scott, 14
Jasmine (1989), xxxvi
'jati', xvii
Jauhar, Jowhar, or Juhar, xxvi
"Javni", xl, 103, 105, 106

K

K. Marx, 53
K. Millett, 44
K. Nambisan, 62
Kabir Singh, 69
Kanthapura (1938), xxxii
Karukku, xxxix, xl, 93, 94, 98, 112, 113, 114
Karukku (2000), 92
Kecia Ali, 49
khwab (dream), 5
Khwabgah, 9
Khwabgah (the House of Dreams), 5
Kierkegaard, 134
Kshatriyas, xx, 117, 123
Kumarsambhava, xxv

L

L. Dumont, xvii, xix
L. Holmström, 112
later Medieval Period, xxv
later Vedic period, xxiii, xxv
'lesbian continuum', 50
Literacy Rate Census of India (2011), xxvii
Lord W. Bentinck, xxvi
Luce Irigaray, 57

M

M. Asaduddin, 24
M. Foucault, 36, 95
M. Kapur, xxxv
M. Nussbaum, 53
M. Prasad, xxx
M. Weber, xvii
Madras on Rainy Days, xxxviii, 41, 43
Mahar (Dalit), 119
Mahasweta Devi, xxxiv
Mahatma Gandhi, 120
Mango-Coloured Fish, xxxviii, 66, 68, 69, 70
Mango-Coloured Fish (1998), 62
manjoori (approval), 5
Manu, xxv
Manu Joseph, xxxii
Manu's *Manusmriti*, xix, xxiv, 36
mardana, 76, 78
mardana (manly), 17
Marxist criticism, 143
Masooma, xxxviii, 52, 54
Midnight's Children (1981), 15
"Miss Padma", 31
Mother of 1084 (1998), xxxiv
Mrichchhakatikam, xxv
Mrs. V. L. Pandit, xxviii
"*Mungni*" (Engagement), 43
Munshi Premchand, xxxvii
"*Myka*" (Mother's place), 43

N

Naicker community, 114
Nampally House (1991), xxxvi
"Nari Sristi" ("Creation of Women"), 75
National Commission for Scheduled Castes and Scheduled Tribes 2000, xxviii
"New Woman", xxxvi
nikaah (marriage), 43

O

"On the Abolition of Sattee", 85
On Wings of Butterflies (2002), 67
Orientalism, 116
Orientalism: Western Conceptions of the Orient (1978), 14
Orientalist mimicry, 84
Orthodoxy, 132
"outsider-within", 98

P

P. D. S. Patil, xxviii
P. H. Collins, 98
P. K. Nayar, xxx
P. Myrne, 46
"Padmarag" ("Essence of the Lotus"), 75
Panchama, xx, xxi
panchama (fifth), 140
'Panopticism', 39
Paraya community, 96, 115
Paraya women, 93
Partha Chatterjee, 15
"Pipasa" ("thirst"), 75
"Portrayal of Women in Premchand's Stories: A Critique", 25
post-Vedic period, xxv
Praneshacharya, 133, 135
Premchand, 24, 25, 27, 29, 31
Premchand: Stories on Women, 24, 27
Premchand: The Complete Short Stories: Vol. III, 27
purdah, xxvi

Q

Queer Theory, Gender Theory: An Instant Primer (2004), 6

R

R. A. Wilchins, 6
R. C. Majumdar, 86
R. E. Karen, 39
R. Inden, xviii
R. K. Narayan, 14
R. Manjoo, xxviii
R. R. M. Roy, xxvi
R. S. Hossain, 73
randi (whore), 45
raneshacharya, 131
Raymond, 5
Reina Lewis, 17
Remember the House (1956), xxxvi
Repressive State Apparatus, 142
Rethinking Orientalism (2004), 17
Rich Like Us (1986), xxxvi
Roots and Shadows (1983), xxxiv

S

S. Anand, 119
S. Bayly, xxii
S. D. Saraswati, xxvi
S. de Beauvoir, 14, 35, 44
S. Hines, 7
S. K. Limbale, 112
S. Namjoshi, xxxvi
S. Natarajan, 119
S. Ortner, 41
S. Vyam, 119
Sally Hines, 6
Samina Ali, 41
Samskara, xxxii, xl, 130
Sartre, 134
sati, 85
Section 377 of the Indian Penal Code (IPC), 8
Serious Men (2010), xxxii
Seven Steps Around the Fire (2013), 4
Sexual Ethics and Islam, 49
"*Shaitan*" (The Devil), 43
sharam (shame), 17
sharif (exalted), 52
sharif admi (honest man), 57
Shashi Deshpande, xxxiv
Shudras, xx, xxv, 117
Single Woman (1991), xxxvi
Sir E. Blunt, xxii
Sir W. Jones, xix
Sir William Jones, xxiv
Socialite Evenings (1989), xxxvi
State Apparatus, 142
State Power, 142
Stonewall riots (1969), 6
Stories on Caste, 27
"Stri-jatir Abanati" ("Woman's Downfall"), 75
Stuart Hall, xix
Sudras, 123
Sultana's Dream (1908), 75
Sultana's Dream, xxxix, 77, 80
Sunlight on a Broken Column, xxxvii, 18
Sunlight on a Broken Column (1961), 15
Surya Monro, 6
Susan Stryker, 4
Swayamvara, xxiv

T

T. Eagleton, 143
T. Sanger, 7
T. Washington, 120
Tamil Dalit, 93
"Temple", 30

"Thakur's Well", 30
thakurain (land-lady), 28
"The Annihilation of Caste" (1936), xxxii
"The Art of *Bhimayana*", 122, 123
The Bengal Sati Regulation XVII, 1829, xxvi
"The Broken Men", 132
The Buddha and His Dhamma, 126
The Commission of Sati (Prevention) Rules, 1988, xxvi
"The Condemned", 29
The Constitution of India, xxvi
The Dowry Prohibition Act (1961), xxvii
The Edible Woman (1969), 54
The Equal Remuneration Act (1976), xxvii
"The Fakeer of Jungheera", xxxix, 87
The Fakeer of Jungheera" (1828), 84
The Female Eunuch, 44
The Female Infanticide Prevention Act (1870), xxvii
The God of Small Things, xxxvii, 33, 36
The God of Small Things (1997), xxxiii
"The Goddess from Heaven", 27
The Gypsy Goddess (2014), xxxii
The Handmaid's Tale, 54
The Handmaid's Tale (1985), 54
The Hills of Angheri (2005), 68
The History of Bengal, 86
The History of Mr. Polly (1910), 62
The History of Sexuality, 37
The Home and the World (1916), 17
The Indian Constitution, 112

The Inheritance of Loss (2006), xxxiv
The Inner World: A Psychoanalytic Study of Hindu Childhood and Society, 25
The Location of Culture (1994), 16
the *Mahabharata*, xxv, 7
The Medieval Age, xxv
The Ministry of Utmost Happiness, xxxvii, 4
The Mistress of Spices (1997), xxxvi
The Namesake (2003), xxxvi
The Nation and Its Fragments (1993), 15
The Prohibition of Child Marriage Act (2006), xxvii
The Queen of Jhansi, xxxiv
The Queen of Jhansi (2000), xxxiv
the *Ramayana*, xxv, 7
the Rig Veda, xxiii
The Sati (Prevention) Act, 1987, xxvi
The Second Sex, 35, 92
The Second Sex (1949), 14
The Thousand Faces of Night (1992), xxxvi
"The Transgender Persons (Protection of Rights) Act, 2019", 4, 10
The Transsexual Empire (1980), 5
The Truth (Almost)About Bharat (1991), 68
the Vedic period, xxiii
The Virgin Syndrome (1997), xxxvi
The Weave of My Life: A Dalit Woman's Memoir (2008), xxxiii
The White Tiger (2008), xxxii
This Sex Which Is Not One, 54
"To India - My Native Land", 84
To Whom She Will (1955), xxxvi
tongawallas (tonga drivers), 123

Towards an Aesthetics of Dalit Literature, 112
Transgender History: The Roots of Today's Revolution (2017), 4
Transgender Identities: Towards a Social Analysis of Gender Diversity, 7
Troubling Muslim Youth Identities: Nation, Religion, Gender, 43
"Tulia", 27
Two Virgins (1973), xxxvi

U

U. R. Ananthamurthy, 14
Undoing Gender, 48
Untouchable, xxxi
Untouchable (1935), xxxi
Untouchables, 123

V

V. S. Naipaul, 131, 133
Vaishyas, xx, 123

varna, xviii
"Varna and Jati", xviii

W

W. Bentinck, 85
W. Carey, xxvi
Waiting for a Visa (1993), 119
When I Hit You: Or, A Portrait of the Writer as a Young Wife (2017), xxxiii
Writing Caste/Writing Gender: Reading Dalit Women's Testimonies, 92

Y

Young Bengal Movement, 84

Z

zamindar, 28
zamindar (landlord), 73
zenana, 17, 20, 52, 76

www.ingramcontent.com/pod-product-compliance
Lightning Source LLC
Chambersburg PA
CBHW052119300426
44116CB00010B/1718